The HOUSEHOLD Of The GRAIL

Other Aquarian titles by the same author:

A Celtic Reader

An Arthurian Reader

Gawain: Knight of the Goddess

Hallowquest (*with Caitlín Matthews*)

The Aquarian Guide to British and Irish Mythology (*with Caitlín Matthews*)

The Aquarian Guide to Legendary London (*with Chesca Potter*)

The Arthurian Tarot (*with Caitlín Matthews*)

The Grail-Seeker's Companion (*with Marian Green*)

The HOUSEHOLD Of The GRAIL

Edited by
John Matthews

THE AQUARIAN PRESS

First published 1990

British Library Cataloguing in Publication Data

The household of the Grail.
1. European literatures. Grail legends, history
I. Matthews, John
809.9337

ISBN 0-85030-883-6

The Aquarian Press is part of the Thorsons Publishing Group, Wellingborough, Northamptonshire, NN8 2RQ, England.

Printed in Great Britain by Hartnolls Limited, Bodmin, Cornwall

Typeset by Burns & Smith Ltd., Derby

1 3 5 7 9 10 8 6 4 2

CONTENTS

Dedication

To the Company of the Grail
And to the memory of Charles Williams, luminary of the
Household

INTRODUCTION

The story of the Grail is the product of many things. Influences from Classical Mystery School teaching, Celtic Druidic lore, medieval romance and legend, and oriental mysticism have all left their mark on the great body of material concerning the marvellous vessel and its actions both in the world and out of it.[1]

None of these things would be known to us today if it were not for the writers and story-tellers who helped fashion our understanding as well as our knowledge. Many remain unknown—the earliest authors, dealt with in Caitlín Matthews's essay, are a nameless legion whose legacy has been taken up, shaped and reshaped by countless people ever since.

With the Middle Ages came the first written texts: those of the great courtly poet Chrétien de Troyes, and Robert de Boron, of whom we know little more than his name and the works he left behind, which revolutionized the course of Grail history. Others, notably Sir Thomas Malory, broadened the stream of material with a degree of literary craftsmanship which have made their works live on.

In more recent times writers and practitioners from many fields of expertise have deepened the river-beds of the story to include the ideas of psychology (C.G. Jung), perennial philosophy (René Guénon and Julius Evola), magic (Dion Fortune), poetry (Charles Williams), and myth (Joseph Campbell). The way was opened for them by such inspired scholars as Jessie Weston.

This collection is thus not intended to be read as a chronological account of the development of the Grail in literature (although as many signposts as possible are given to the way the various strands interact). It concentrates on just a few high spots, the works of outstanding individuals—known and unknown—who helped transform our understanding of the Grail. There are therefore many gaps, though the work of some writers flows naturally into that of others. Greg Stafford, in his discussion of Malory, could hardly fail to mention the Vulgate Cycle (attributed by some scholars to the shadowy Walter Map). In the same way, Julius Evola evokes comparison with his teacher René Guénon.

Each of these people have added, in their own way, to our understanding and realization of the Grail. Together they form a Household of the Grail, the lineal descendants of the Grail Family written about by Robert de Boron and others. They carry forward into our own time the vitality of the tradition which places the Grail at the centre of Western culture and thought. There is nothing dry or dead about their words; they are filled with a light which comes of the vessel itself.

John Matthews
London, 1989

Note

1 See *At The Table of the Grail*, ed. John Matthews (London: Arkana, 1987).

THE LAY OF THE WATERS

Whence did those waters flow?
From the first mother, whose course was the route of the migrating family—
The Lady Don, the Dneiper, the Danube
whose cross-tracked, sinuous and embracing tributaries
veined the skin of Europe.
She whose paps are thrust through the soil of Kerry,
whose plenteous milk bestowed fertility upon Ireland.
She, mother of the tribe of Danu,
whose wisdom shines brightly in the starry courts—
Llys Don, where her children still behold her.
Is it she whose nurture brought us the cauldron of many lives,
the cauldron of plenty?
She who likes best to give her children their favourite food?
The cauldron of wisdom, circled by the salmon,
is only for the most worthy.
She whose cup is poured for the King
who will maintain her royal rule.

It was in the hands of her daughter
that the cauldron became cup.
And the hero, seeing her, lost all recollection of his quest,
forgot to ask the question that his tribal elders primed him for.
Upon the bare hillside, in another country,
he awoke and found reproof:
'Why did you never speak when the spear dripped blood,
when the head in the dish was silent,
when the sword dropped lifeless from your hand,
when the brimming dish was full of blood?
Why?' cried the Black Maiden.

'Did you not know you have pierced your mother's heart with sorrow?
Can you not see the widow weeping and the orphan seeking shelter from
  oppression?'
Flailed by questions, he runs into the broad wilderness—
a madman, a wildman, a woodman,
inhabiting silences, familiar with beasts.
Until a day of sudden snow
when the louring clouds have spent
their burden on the hill's shoulder,
when the wild duck plummets at the falcon's stoop:
blood in the snow where the raven tarries at its supper.
And, from his silent enclosure, the wildman wonders seeing the red, the
  white, the black.
'I long,' he said, 'for one whose cheek is pale as snow,
whose lip is as red as is the blood upon the snow,
whose hair is black as is the raven's plumage.'
Entranced, he waits the revelation of the lady of his heart.
And though a crass hunter shakes his arm, spits in his wide-open face,
he does not stir, save to absently unhinge the fellow's arm
like a bear intent upon a hive of honey.
Not until the skilful warrior places his inner vision to the same image
does he know himself again.
'Brother, are you thinking on the lady of your heart?'
And such a sigh as from the first ice breaking in the primal thaw
rends his wild and solitary inscape void.
'Return, be at peace and seek her,' says the wise warrior.
'Join our quest, teach us your knowledge.'
The hero rises, comes and, on the snowy margin of the lake,
consigns his ragged mantle of hair, accepting man's attire.
Her image fills his emptiness, the maiden with the heart of gold,
framed in a threefold mystery of snow, blood and feathers.

The Red, the White, the Black
have ever edged her mantle
and her threefold cup is poured
as men require it.
The White is poured for nurturing the hero—
Heavy milk from her own breast—
she who is foster-mother and maker.
The Red is poured for the making of kings,
the distillation of her own blood,
she who is queen of the rich earth.
The Black is poured for the endtime,
when the hero must forget the world—
eyes waking to the inner realm

where the mistress of magic shall bring healing to all hurts.

Mother river, course of life,
deep are your secrets.
Do the bright mysteries
sing within your waters?
Their sparkle shall
  not cease to dazzle
  the gazing seeker.
Not 'til the last drop
  of moisture evaporates.
And the barren earth
  expires in the sun's fierce embrace.

        Caitlín Matthews

Part One:

THE ORIGINATORS

1

THE VOICES OF THE WELLS
Celtic Oral Themes in Grail Literature
by
Caitlín Matthews

The Blessing of the Wandering Voice

In the dark green forests of the north-west seaboard of Europe, somewhere between the worlds of Imperial and Holy Rome, a story was forged. It was blent of precious ores hoarded since the world was begun, hammered into shape by the tongues of tribal and wandering story-tellers and delivered into the hands of Continental romancers, who wielded it to great effect. Whenever I open the pages of any medieval Grail romance, I am always hearing the distant hammering of those nameless story-tellers in their forge of song.

Our inability to name or identify specific story-tellers in the evasive network of oral tradition is frustrating though hardly surprising. Though we know little enough about the early European romancers, we do at least have their names and can locate with some accuracy both their patrons and fields of influence. The feudal and regnal systems of medieval Europe give us a known framework into which these early writers fit with reasonable ease. Of the nameless story-tellers who brought the Grail legends in their earliest forms, we are less certain, though not from lack of evidence so much as from our inability to assimilate the nature of the oral tradition itself and the society in which it operated.

Our contemporary vaunting of the written word is partly at fault, for we have been educated to believe that books represent the prime instrument of civilization. Pre-literate peoples are not lacking in enriching culture, historical records or considerable bodies of traditional lore. The memory of an average pre-literate person is several times more developed than that of a literate person. Pre-literate societies inevitably boast a specific class of people specializing in the art of memory, and who frequently combine shamanic skills as part of their training.

The specialist in Celtic countries was the bard or *fili* whose 12-year training empowered him to memorize and tell over 350 stories, each of which might take several nights in the telling. In addition to this mind-stretching oral library, the bard was skilled in complex poetic forms, able at will to compose in any given metre and scansion poems of praise or reproof whose magical effects made him a man to both fear and revere. [1] Celtic society fully supported such bards for very good reasons; they were the living memory of the tribe, of laws, precedents, genealogies and the wisdom of the ancestors. Such men were as far removed from the modern Arts Council supported poet as it is possible to imagine, for the Celtic bard was essential to the ordering of life, being mystically attuned to the processes of the Otherworld by virtue of his training.

Becoming the living memory of his people brought the bard the Otherworld. This was likewise the realm of the gods and other spiritual beings. With such knowledge in his head, the bard was attuned to the workings of the Otherworld whence his poetic and musical powers were likewise thought to derive.

The mystical *baraka*—the transmission of spiritual blessing—which happens in the presence of such attuned people is something which literary critics rarely deign to speak of. The indefinable translation of being which occurs when one sits in the presence of such artists is of course widely sought after in the field of media and general entertainment where people will pay thousands of pounds to be present at a performance of their favourite opera singer, ballet dancer or actress. The barriers of perception are down and the heart is open to receive the full force of 'art'.

But what is this 'art'? Is it not nearer in nature to the *darshan* experienced in the presence of holy people? This is the real immediacy of the oral tradition, in which complex images and symbolisms are imparted by the combination of voice and body in a way which cannot be identically repeated because it is not merely performance but the shamanic sharing of vision. [2]

We may instance the manner in which spiritual teachings are

imparted in Tibetan Buddhism, whereby even the audition of a spiritual text brings merit to the hearer, and where specific empowering initiations are imparted by a spiritual teacher to a pupil by means of oral exposition.

The oral tradition needs its living memories, the poets and story-tellers, but it also needs listeners in whose minds and hearts the symbols and images of the story are recreated. To this extent, pre-literate societies win out over ours, for the modern literate person is almost entirely symbolically illiterate or symbolically impoverished.

In this manner, bards supported themselves by noble patronage for many generations. But the structure of Celtic society suffered innumerable knocks. In Britain, the Roman colonization, followed by Saxon and Norman invasion, brought the Celtic framework toppling down. In Ireland, bards remained in full activity until the Norman colonization in the twelfth century, after which the long historical round of invasion and cultural repression brought the exponents of the living Celtic memory to virtual vagrancy.[3] However, such great learning, the fruits of memory, did not merely disappear; it was caught up, recognizably harmonious with existent native traditions in Europe, particularly Brittany, and grafted onto the Matter of Britain.

The oral tradition of the Celtic people has been an enduring one. Even up until the last century, traditional *seanchais* were telling folk-stories which still bore the traces of the proto-Grail legend within them.[4] It is now, sadly, a dying tradition. What centuries of oral memory has preserved television and state education have eroded. The struggle of one such traditional Irish story-teller, Sean O Conaill, to retain his memory's store is recorded in *Celtic Heritage*:

Lest he should lose command over the tales he loved, he used to repeat them aloud when he thought no one was near, using the gesticulations and the emphasis, and all the tricks of narration, as if he were once again the centre of a fireside storytelling. His son, Pats, told me that he had seen his father thus engaged, telling his tales to an unresponsive stone wall, while herding the grazing cattle. On returning from market, as he walked slowly up the hills behind his old grey mare, he could be heard declaiming his tales to the back of the cart.[5]

This is a far cry from the kind of rapt attention which Sean O Conaill's forebears enjoyed:

> The fair company gave ear to the Lay of Alys, sweetly sung by a minstrel from Ireland, to the music of his rote. When his story was ended, forthwith he commenced another, and related the Lay of Orpheus; *none being so bold as to disturb the singer, or to let his mind wander from the song.*[6] (My italics.)

This passage comes from Marie de France's *Lay of the Thorn*, written in the mid-twelfth century, probably somewhere in England at the court of Henry II. Apart from the internal evidence that the said minstrel was performing from memory and was thus part of the enduring oral tradition, this story suggests a cultural interface with which we are perhaps unfamiliar.

The Middle Ages are often thought of as hidebound, culturally insular and intellectually naïve. This proves to be far from the case, for though the land-bound peasant was a virtual slave of the land, there was considerable movement of people and ideas from region to region. Clerics, craftsmen and courts were as well-travelled as the average modern tourist, describing a well-trodden route between abbey, cathedral and European city. The expansionist dynasties of medieval Europe, particularly that of the Plantagenets, began to connect regions as far distant as Ireland and Provence, so that it would have been quite possible for an Irish minstrel to be present at an English or even French court and be understood in the *lingua franca* of the time— Anglo—or Norman-French.[7]

The *lai*, so familiar from French romance, has another origin entirely. The word *lay* itself derives from the Irish word for song *laoidh*. When the Irish wish to express that a person has no evidence whatever to support his case, they use the expression *ní laoidh ná litir*—he has 'neither song nor letter'—which may indicate the original force of the spoken word, considered to be of equal value as the written word. Yet the *lai* was almost entirely imported from Ireland into France via Brittany.

There is little doubt that the key Celtic nation in the transmission of the proto-Grail stories was Brittany. Armorica had already started to be colonized by Britons in the troubled times even before the Roman withdrawal from Britain. The troops of Magnus Maximus had already been given grants of land there some years previously. Brittany, or Little Britain, as it became, was one of the chief repositories for stories about King Arthur. The memory of the exiled is generally strong, and so it was with the Bretons who preserved the core of the Matter of Britain so ardently that, after becoming proficient in French, they transmitted Arthurian tales into French romance.

In many ways, the Norman Invasion of 1066 was, for some Bretons, a strange homecoming or kind of reconquest, for many of William of Normandy's knights were Breton and they doubtless brought with them their household, including story-tellers. Once the Norman dynasty was established in Britain, tales of Arthur began to percolate back to Brittany and France.

The name of but one oral story-teller remains: Master Bleheris, variously referred to by the romancers as Blihos, Bliheris, Blihis, Bledhericus or Bledri. Medieval manuscripts are littered with what might be called 'literary coathooks',—supposed learned sources, fabricated 'old books' and legendary story-tellers which give the writer his literary justification. Master Bleheris may well prove to be one such coathook, though there is a sufficiently large amount of evidence to posit otherwise.

The second continuator of Chrétien de Troyes' *Conte del Graal* speaks of his literacy authority as a certain Bleheris 'who was born and reared in Wales...and told it to the Count of Poitiers, who loved the story, and held it more than any other firmly in memory'.[8] Many attempts have been made to date this character by establishing just which Count of Poitiers was intended. It has been proved that the earliest French references to Tristan occur in the works of Cercamon and Bernard de Ventadour, both attached to the court of Poitiers in the 1150s.[9] This evidence may lead us to suppose that Bleheris did visit the court at Poitiers or briefly enjoyed the patronage of the Count and that he had a command of Norman-French.

Gerald of Wales in his *Description of Wales* likewise refers to a 'Bledri, the well-known story-teller, who lived a little before our time'.[10] Since Gerald was writing in 1188, we may conclude that Bleheris or Bledri flourished some time in the early 1100s.

But Master Bleheris turns up again, this time as a protagonist in *L'Élucidation*, an early thirteenth-century prequel to the *Conte del Graal* (though in fact written about 40 years after Chrétien's book). In this illuminating text, wherein we are told an alternative story about the origins of the wasteland, the Round Table Knights fight a group of knights found wandering in the forest, guarding certain maidens. They capture one of the company, Blihos Bliheris, who yields himself to Arthur: 'but right good stories he knew, such as that none could ever be aweary of hearkening to his words'. He relates the history of his company, telling how they are destined to wander the world until the finding of the Courts of Joy.[11]

L'Élucidation begins interestingly:

> Here worshipfully beginneth a Romance of the most delightsome story that may be, to wit, the story of the Grail, the secret whereof may no man tell in prose nor rhyme, for such a thing might the story turn out to be before it were all told that every man might be grieved thereof albeit he had in nowise misdone. Wherefore it is that the wise man leaveth it aside and doth simply pass on beyond, for, and Master Blihis lie not, the secret should no man tell.[12]

Truly this ill-named text, rather than shedding illumination upon the inner meaning of the Grail, merely strives to obscure it even further. While Bleheris' appearance in L'Élucidation is obviously a literary device to lend the authenticity of a proven story-teller, we must ask, what status Bleheris held during the preceding twelfth century to be accorded such a key appearance here. For Blihos tells the Round Table Knights about the adventures which those who seek the Grail may find, and therefore initiates the quest.

Perhaps the answer lies in Blihos' own words:

> (we) all shall journey in common, and the damsels in likewise that wander at large through this country by forest and field behoveth it thus to fare until such time as God shall give them to find the Court from whence shall come the joy whereby the land shall again be made bright.[13]

The knights and damsels in whose company Blihos wanders are the descendants of the Otherworldly Damsels of the Wells who once used to serve all travellers with the food they most desired, in the manner of Irish *beansidhes*, the women of the Faery Host. King Amangons, in an age long before Arthur's, raped one of the damsels and stole her golden cup. His followers likewise raped the other damsels, until they no longer served at the wells. The text tells us that in the land of Britain 'they lost the voices of the wells and the damsels that were therein'.

Although there are other mystical analogues to this text, which I have discussed elsewhere,[14] it would seem that here we discover the true Household of the Grail. The story-tellers such as Blihos are the wandering 'voices of the wells', for they tell the story of the Grail's secret—neither in prose nor verse, as the text says, but in their own lives. They are the true memory of the Grail, these wanderers, telling no-one its secrets but implanting the seeds of the quest in the hearts of their hearers.

This is the function of the oral tradition: that the speaker should impart the story's *baraka*, the spiritual transmission of power, to the hearer who should become empowered by the story. As long as the traditional form is preserved, the *baraka* cannot be diffused, but lies dormant even in the mind of an ignorant story-teller. It needs only one hearer attuned to the story to realize the empowerment of the Grail legends anew for that transmission to become activated.

Bleheris is perhaps one of many such story-tellers who stand between the transition from oral to literary tradition. He is one of the very last story-tellers personally to enthuse his hearers in this way.

There are numerous witnesses to the fact that this *baraka* was passed to auditors of the Matter of Britain during the Middle Ages. Peter of Blois speaks of how *histriones*, by which he means wandering players, moved people to tears by their retellings of Arthur, Tristan and Gawain. St Ailred of Rievaulx, no less, reproaches himself, remembering how, as a novice, he could work himself up into considerable emotion over stories about Arthur, but could hardly shed a tear when reading the scriptures.[15]

The exponents of the oral tradition are, perhaps mercifully, beyond the reach of literary biographers who would psychoanalyse their lives and motives to come to definitive criticisms of their *oeuvre*. In attempting to discover the original or proto-Grail story, we can only be aware of underlying Celtic themes, not of authorly motives. The oral tradition is remarkably conservative, since successful transmission of tradition depends on accurate memory. This is why the transcriptions of Celtic stories from Ireland and Wales in the Middle Ages can be regarded as authentically ancient for, while they may only have been written down in the thirteenth and fourteenth centuries, the story-teller behind the transcriber was in receipt of a lineage of oral transmission which was unbroken. If variations creep in, it is usually at this point; the transcriber has less scruples about tampering with the story than the story-teller.

Thus, even within the complex *entrelacements* of medieval literary Grail texts, we may discern echoes of the forge of song in the images of Grail, quest and hero, in the descriptions of the Otherwordly Grail Castle, Faery opponents and supernatural wonders. How these ancient attributes of oral tradition voyaged to the shores of literary tradition is an interesting speculation.

The Matter of Britain was the chief vessel in which the Grail legends came to French shores. Within its hold, a host of stories, ideas and influences came to shelter, further enriching the Arthurian tradition beyond the wildest dreams of the first tellers.

The Saving Story

Every tradition has its own salvific or saving story. Psychoanalysis has discovered this and works on discovering and applying the indwelling saving story to its clients. Religion consciously operates along the lines of a sacred story to live by. The entire TV soap industry attempts to provide the same service, though with considerably less success. Story-tellers have always known about the sustaining quality of the story, none more so than the guardians of Grail story. The Grail is at once a potent symbol of transformation, a catalyst or touchstone of the emerging cultural blend of the Middle Ages; it is also the mythic corollary of timeless spiritual aspiration.

The fertile waters of the oral tradition are the medium of mystical concepts. 'We see by means of water,' says Wolfram von Eschenbach in Chapter 16 of his *Parzival*.[16] And it is only by crossing the waters which lie between us and the Otherworldly realms of the Grail Castle, by allowing the Grail story to work so upon our hearts that our eyes shed the cleansing tears which bring illumination to our inner sight, that we perceive the Holy Vessel.

We are driven to ask: What kind of spiritual empowerment or validation lies behind the Grail? How was it perceived by those who listened to the stories? Was the Grail originally central to native spirituality? There is clearly more to the story than a collection of Celtic cauldrons, transmogrified into celestial vessels. There is obviously more to the story than a straight parallel of the Christian redemption myth.[17]

The spiritual centre of Celtic society is the earthly paradise of the Otherworld, sometimes depicted as the Blessed Isle of the West, to which people sail never to return. It is a place of perpetual joy, where life wells up eternally. It is a place of empowerment, where the ancestral memories are accessible.

In the ancient Irish story of *Cormac's Adventures in the Otherworld*, Cormac mac Airt is miraculously transported to a marvellous fortress made of bronze beams, with wattles of silver and a thatch of bird's wings.

> Then he saw in the enclosure a shining fountain, with five streams flowing out of it, and the hosts in turn drinking the water. Nine hazels of Buan grew over the well. The purple hazels dropped their nuts into the fountain and sent their husks floating down the streams. Now the sound of the falling of those streams was more melodious than any music that men sing.[18]

He is later told by Manannan, the god of the Otherworld that he has seen the Fountain of Knowledge, and that the five streams are the five senses through which knowledge is obtained. Whoever does not drink the fountain or the streams will never have knowledge. And he says, 'The *folk of many arts* are those who drink them both.' He refers to the *aos daoine*—the gifted people, the poets and visionaries, who interpret the Otherworld to the created world. And it is such folk who are moved to find the Grail and bring its healing waters to the world through the medium of the story.

This story takes us directly into the Celtic Otherworld whose reality is timeless, accessible now as then by means of our imaginal involvement with the things eternal. The Celtic Otherworld is full of beauty, the primal pleasures of the earthly paradise. Here everything is complete, whole and perfect.

This wonderful image of the fountain which flows from the Otherworld into our own imaginal realms shows us the spiritual power of the talismanic symbol to bridge the worlds.

The Grail itself is such a symbol. But in the Celtic world it is one among many. The concept of the Hallows—the holy empowering objects of spiritual and earthly sovereignty—encompasses several such talismans.[19]

The cauldron sought by Arthur in the ninth-century British poem *Preiddeu Annwn* is but one among many Hallows which are found in British and Arthurian tradition.[20] The Thirteen Treasures of Britain, supposedly guarded now by Merlin in his Otherworldly observatory, form part of our native tradition.[21] The Irish preserve a similar tradition of treasures, which are kept in the Crane-Bag of Manannan mac Lir.[22]

The Tuatha de Danaan, the ancient gods of Ireland, brought with them four such symbols from the four mysterious cities from which they derived their strength. Since the Danaans themselves appear as gods within Irish tradition, we must struggle imaginatively to picture the kind of realms from which they bring symbols of even greater power:

the Sword of Nuada from Findias given by Uscias;
the Spear of Lugh from Gorias given by Esras;
the Cauldron of the Dagda from Murias, given by Semias;
the Lia Fail from Falias, given by Morfessa.[23]

Each of these great symbols has its intrinsic virtue: the sword deals certain death to whomever it wounds; the spear brings victory to whomever bears it; the cauldron satisfies all who eat of it; while the Lia Fail screams under a rightful king. Each of these Celtic Hallows has its equivalent in the Grail legends, where the sword is that carried by the Grail-winner. (Galahad pulls such a sword from a floating stone where other knights have failed, in likeness of Arthur's exploit with Excalibur.[24]) The spear's analogue is found in the spear which causes the Dolorous Stroke by which the Fisher king and the Land are simultaneously devastated.[25] The cauldron's bounty is transmuted into the abundant blessing of the Grail itself; while the Lia Fail, the stone of kingly inauguration, becomes the Siège Perilous—the seat at the Round Table which is strictly reserved for the destined Grail-winner and in which Perceval sits in presumptious and untimely haste.[26]

What other analogues of the Grail do we find in Celtic tradition? We cannot detail every cauldron or vessel from British and Irish tradition, for they are too numerous. But we can look at the properties of a few.

The cauldron of Ceridwen was to have brewed a draft of wisdom intended for her son, Afagddu (Darkness). However, Gwion Bach, set to stir the cauldron, accidentally splashed some of the fluid on his fingers and, thrusting them into his mouth, received enlightenment. After a long totemic chase, he was reborn of Ceridwen's womb as Taliesin, the great poet. She cast him on the waters in a basket and he was discovered in a salmon weir.[27]

The image of the salmon is paramount in Celtic tradition. It is a beast of everlastingness and of greatest wisdom, and it figures in many myths as the oldest animal who remembers things from the beginning of time. The salmon which swims in Conla's Well eats the hazel-nuts of knowledge. In another tale it is told how Fionn mac Cumhail helped catch and cook this very salmon for his Druidic master but, as in the story of Taliesin, Fionn alone was the recipient of the wisdom intended for another.[28] Both Taliesin and Fionn are initiates of wisdom who share the omniscience of the salmon.

The cauldron of Bran is, on the other hand, a vessel of rebirth. In the tragic British tale of Branwen, Daughter of Llyr, we read how the cauldron originally came from Ireland and that it had a singular property. Dead warriors who were put into it could be revived. However, they were subsequently unable to speak, for it is only the initiate who sees the Otherworld and can speak of it—but then only in the riddling tongue of poets which only other initiates can comprehend.[29] From Bran's terrible journey to Ireland to rescue his sister, Branwen, only seven return. Bran, mortally wounded, instructs his followers to cut off his head and bury it under the White Mount (the site of the present Tower of London). On route, they sojourn in an Otherworldly hall, forever feasting and enjoying the conversation of Bran, whose head regales his followers so brilliantly that they fail to notice the passage of time until one opens a forbidden door and remembrance or mortality falls upon them. As one who entertained his company for 87 years, Bran the Blessed can perhaps be lauded as the patron of all story-tellers.

The brilliant ninth-century poem Preiddeu Annwn (or The Spoils of Annwn) contains one of the earliest textual references to

Arthur.[30] It incidentally provides us with his association with the prototype of the Grail—the cauldron. The cauldron for which Arthur goes in search in the *Preiddeu Annwn* is owned by Diwrnach. It boils a brew fit only for heroes; it will not boil the meat of a coward. This vessel is related to the Celtic tradition of the hero's portion—the cut of meat reserved for the most worthy warrior of the tribe. Arthur descends into the Underworld of Annwn on his ship Prydwen on an *immram* (wondrous voyage) of the great peril. As on Bran's journey to Ireland, only seven return to speak of their adventures; Taliesin, the great poet, is significantly present on both Arthur's and Bran's journey to make report. Arthur is here shown to be the earliest Grail-winner, a long way in advance of Peredur (Perceval) or Galahad, whose stories are not recorded until the twelfth and fourteenth centuries.

So then, the cauldrons of Celtic tradition have one of the following properties:

they give rebirth;
they bring initiation into wisdom;
they give plenty.

The idea of nourishment, of fertility, whether of land or of spirit, is at the heart of the Grail story.

These three qualities are retained by the Celtic cauldron's Christian analogue, the Grail, but before we pass on, let us note that we stand here at the heart of Celtic spirituality. The Celtic proto-story of the cauldron, like that of the Grail, is about finding wisdom in the uncreated world, in ways that have an effect on the created world itself. The waters of life which well up, whether from Otherworldly springs or magical cauldrons, are only achieved by those who are most worthy—by the gifted people who have made wisdom their study, or by those innocents who already have their steps set upon the path unknowingly. They drink from these vessels and are conveyed to another dimension; they enter into communion with the Otherworld. This is the ultimate Celtic spiritual vision.

This sense of Otherworldly communion is seldom absent from the medieval Grail legends. Faery women, white stags, lonely hermits of great wisdom—all derived from the Celtic Otherworld tradition—throng the medieval stories. If we strip away the Christian accretions which make the Grail the Cup of the Last

Supper and the Grail hero a second Christ, we are left with a hero in search of an Otherworldly treasure which will empower, in different combinations, himself, his king or his land.

If we look at the medieval Christian manifestations of the Grail we find that it has the following properties:

it gives the food most desired;
it restores the Wasteland and the Wounded King;
it empowers its finder with the spiritual gnosis.

These exact qualities are identical to the effects of the Celtic cauldrons, which gave plenteous nourishment, rebirth and wisdom. Like the Celtic vessels, the Christian Grail is only achieved by the most worthy: those who have pursued wisdom with great and urgent simplicity.

Between the earliest of our literary sources (the ninth-century poem about Arthur's raid on Annwn) and the achieved Grail stories of the Middle Ages, there is a significant and quite mysterious gap; for between these two traditions we pass from the pagan Celtic Otherworld to an apocryphal Christian alternative to the gospels. By what means does this transformation come about?

We are so used to looking at the Grail legends from the point of view of a Christian allegory that we are perhaps blinded to the cohesive nature of the oral tradition which incorporated both the old and the new into its vision. The Otherworld still held sway in the imaginations and hearts of many well on into the Christian era. It takes a considerably long time for old tribal and ancestral beliefs to become totally superseded by the new—a fact which St Gregory the Great exhorted his missionaries to Britain to be aware of lest 'by scraping off the rust from the vessel they shatter it'.[31] Although we think of missionaries as zealots eager to purge old beliefs, in practice things were more organically integrated. The old customs of well-dressing, the sacred festivals of pagan deities and the elemental spirits of the land were gradually incorporated into the local usages of Christianity.

The founding of Christianity upon certain elements within the Druidic tradition is one which has been perpetually remarked upon. Certainly the manner in which Christianity was rapidly assimilated suggests that the ground was fertile. However, it is not possible to assimilate fully any new spiritual tradition in one generation; it takes very many for spiritual consciousness to operate with the new symbols, characters and images. The first-century Christian apologist St Clement of Alexandria, in order to acquaint an Hellenic audience with the Christian message, metaphorically described Christ as Odysseus strapped to the mast of the barque of the Church to avoid the cries of Scylla and Charybdis.[32] Likewise, the *Dream of the Rood* speaks of Christ as the young hero who stripped himself to mount the tree, like Odin, a concept familiar to Saxon listeners.[33]

There is no doubt that, at one level, the Grail legends typify the syncretic links between traditions which enabled Britons to accept the gospels more readily though this was not the sole purpose of the Grail tradition. The Grail legends were not at first conceived of as Christian documents or alternative mystical parables. They were told as part of the Matter of Britain—the Arthurian Legends—part of an ongoing and vast cycle of stories which it was a story-teller's duty to recite to his patron. The romancers certainly knew a salvific story when they came across one and certain analogies were obviously drawn. We are looking at the unconscious construction of an apocryphal Christian tradition into which certain native British strands are woven. People were more readily moved by the stories of their king and his heroes undergoing purgative quests amid the ancestral forests of home then they were to hear about the alien ramblings of foreign saints.

We should bear in mind that, though Europe was nominally Christian by the Middle Ages, the consciousness of the people had older mythic archetypes embedded within them, for, in the hearts and minds of the people, it was the old characters who held sway. In this way Arthur passed from military commander—whether as Romano-British *Dux Britanniarum* or as proto-Celtic war-leader— into a semi-deified state, becoming the sleeping Lord, the land's protector for all time. People likewise looked to the sustaining myths and stories of their ancestors; it was a skilful story-teller who knew how to weave the old gods and heroes into saints and martyrs of Christian tradition. This long looking over the shoulder to the eaves of the Otherworld was productive when it came to the retelling of the sacred vessel which heals, and gives life and empowerment to the chosen tribal representative.

From many of the Celtic pagan elements, and from an assured story-telling tradition, the first fires of the literary Grail were kindled. In the finely wrought pages of the medieval texts, some primal features of Celtic tradition emerge, giving tantalizing glimpses of themes and stories once commonly circulating but now voiceless. If we look at some of the medieval Grail texts, we frequently discern the vigorous voice of the Celtic story-teller.

The organic enfolding of Grail literature was primarily dictated by the audience which, during the early Middle Ages, was still largely a pre-literate one, used to hearing oral stories, not literary ones. But the audience was no longer a native one: the travelling story-tellers must have quite consciously adapted some parts of their telling for courtly audiences, just as Chrétien de Troyes continually admits to doing in the retelling of his romances. The raw material which the Grail writers worked from included a British story concerning the hero, Peredur, who achieves fame by his prodigious deeds in the service of King Arthur; he was later woven more intimately into the prevailing Christian tapestry. Peredur (and the proto-heroes before him) is shown to be akin to the Celtic archetype of the *Amadan Mor*, the Great Fool, a character whose quest is still central to the Gaelic folk tradition.[34]

Peredur is the earliest British literary Grail story. It is a story which had been exported from Britain, translated into French and reimported into Britain, where it was retranslated into Welsh and where it may or may not have been interwoven once more with extant oral sources.[35] It follows a similar shape to that of Chrétien's *Conte del Graal*, but *Peredur* betrays a far more pagan origin, and makes no association between the Grail and vessel of the Crucifixion. Indeed, it has been proved that *Peredur* contains elements of a far older tradition, incorporating such Celtic elements as the spear which drips blood, the head in the dish (which serves as the holy vessel in this story) and the hero's search for the empowerment of the Goddess of the Land, Lady Sovereignty.

I have written extensively elsewhere about this powerful figure who stands at the epicentre not only of the Grail legends but also of the Matter of Britain.[36] Within a society which saw a devolution of both women and female archetypes, it is not surprising that the strong female characters of Celtic tradition should have been diluted and diffused into more and more minor characters within the Grail legend. The Grail knights are frequently faced with challenges in which they must defend a defenceless woman or restore her to her rightful place. In these multiplications of wronged virgins, mourning widows and dispossessed wives, we can yet discern the features of the Goddess and her representatives. This mighty figure was one of the great deities of the Celtic peoples who continually looked back to her as the ancestress of their tribe, the preserver of memory and the mother of all people.

The nature of the Celtic clan system is discernible within the subtext of the Grail legends. Both the *Elucidation* and Wolfram's *Parzival* allude to a tradition of Grail guardianship which includes a combative military knighthood or warrior-caste with a complementary priesthesshood of women—a royal and holy family which is comprehended in the medieval pun of San Greal/Sang Real (Holy Grail, Holy Blood). Wolfram's Grail is a Stone which has been brought to earth to remain in the guardianship of a Grail lineage (perhaps an analogue of the inaugural stones of a Celtic kingship?). Behind both texts there is a tradition of a sacerdotal caste or royal clan, figured forth as warrior-heroes and empowering priestesses, in whom the blood of memory flows. These potent figures are the mythic analogues of the story-tellers themselves on whose tongues the immortality of the saving story was assured.

The clan was the prime unit of Celtic solidarity. From its extended familial network would have been drawn the *tanaiste*, the candidate king who was appointed as regent before the demise of the king. Royalty, royal-connection, responsibility for the land and its peoples is a major theme running throughout the Grail legends. Similarly, the numerous empowering women who are guardians of the Grail have their root in the primeval matrilineal frameworks of pre-Christian Europe, where the royal woman was the priestess of her tribe, the intermediary between the people and the gods.[37]

Of course, one of the major factors underlying the Grail legends is the Wounded King, behind whom we can trace the very roots of Celtic kingship. A blemished man might not hold office since the king must physically embody the health and well-being of the land. A wounded king was demoted and his *tanaiste* appointed during the remainder of his life. This factor is plainly borne out in the Grail hero's championship, for though Perceval finds the Grail, and heals the Wounded King, he usually replaces him as the new Grail guardian.

The Wasteland motif is a universal one which has particular prominence in Celtic tradition. The wounds of the Fisher King are really reflections of the enchanted land which is doomed to sterility, through which the healing waters have yet to flow. The Grail hero is called 'the Freer of the Waters', a ritual title which might well have its warrant in Celtic tradition. The hero who goes to the world's end to gain the waters of life is still very much part of Gaelic story-telling.[38]

The Wasteland of the Grail legends is closely paralleled in Celtic tradition by the enchantments of the land. This theme reveals that the land has been overlooked by an Otherworldly agency, as it is within the stories of *Manawyddan, Son of Llyr* and *Lludd and Llefelys*, in the *Mabinogion*.[39] In both instances, Manawyddan and Lludd, as wise rulers, must use their skilful wisdom to overcome or subvert these powers. Within *Peredur*, we see the hero battling with several *gormesaid* or plagues—monsters, giants and black wildmen—which he must overcome in order or become a 'Freer of the Waters'.

Peredur shows us also a very Celtic instance of the warrior-woman where Peredur is professionally instructed in the use of arms by the Nine Witches of Gloucester, who act as his foster-mothers in arms. Similarly, Cuchullin is instructed by the warrior-woman Scathach, in the Ulster Cycle.[40]

The Grail romances can also be seen as continuations to the *immrama*— the wondrous voyages to the Otherworld undertaken by Maelduine, Bran mac Febal and St Brendan.[41] All find Otherwordly treasure, wonders and challenges to overcome. The *immram* returns in *The Quest of the Holy Grail* of the Vulgate Cycle where Galahad, Bors and Perceval take the Ship of Solomon to the Otherworldly city of Sarras, there to participate in the mysteries of the Grail.[42] Similarly, in *Perlesvaus*, Perceval goes to a mysterious island, the Island of Ageless Elders, where a band of elderly but youthful sages sit in converse as ancient as that of Bran the Blessed and his company in the timeless bliss of the Otherworld.[43]

In the course of literary transmission, the home of the original Grail story is often visited by the new romance, and so it proves in the *Didot Perceval*, where it is revealed that the Grail Castle is established in Ireland:

The Fisher King dwells in the island in one of the most beautiful places in the world.[44]

Elements of *Perlesvaus*, perhaps the most Christianized of the Grail texts, reveal a preoccupation with central Celtic themes: with the triple aspect of the Goddess of Sovereignty, the enchantments of the land and the blessed Otherworld.

The further into the Middle Ages we go, the more Christianized the Grail becomes. The writings of Robert de Boron give the Grail its full Christian antecedents with the story of Joseph of Arimathea's guardship of the Grail and his journey to Europe.[45] Until de Boron's *Joseph d'Arimathie*, the Grail story was firmly rooted solely in the Matter of Britain. De Boron's prequel connects the Matter of Britain to a specifically Christian tradition which provides Perceval and later Galahad with saintly ancestors, for Joseph founds a lineage of Grail guardians from whom the Grail-winners spring.

De Boron was quick to pick up on clues from Gnostic and apocryphal scriptural sources concerning Joseph's familiarity with the secrets of Christ. For Joseph is held in prison by Vespasian and fed by the Grail at the same time as receiving guardianship of the vessel and its secrets. And so the story of his coming to Britain and founding a lineage is tacked on to the existing story to form a kind of biblical prequel to the native story. These legends have themselves become inseparable from the ongoing folklore of the Matter of Britain in common consciousness.

When we reach the story of *Perlesvaus*, which is one of the crowning glories of the Grail legends, we find that Perceval has become analogous to Christ himself—a kind of superhero and saviour combined. He is reverently referred to throughout as 'the Good Knight'. This is a long way from his origins as a foolish young Welshman who can mistake knights for angels and catch deer with his bare hands. In this wonderful story the Grail quest becomes a mixture of redemptive pilgrimage and Otherworldly journey. The Matter of Britain has also been incorporated into the myths of Glastonbury in a new way. As the end of *Perlesvaus* relates:

... the Latin text from which this story was set in the vernacular was taken from the Isle of Avalon, from a holy religious house

which stands at the edge of the Land of Adventure: there lie King
Arthur and the queen, by the testimony of the worthy religious
men who dwell there.[46]

Perlesvaus and *The Quest for the Holy Grail* both draw on this
blended tradition of Celtic hero turned Christian saviour. But
these are late texts, and tastes had changed. Perceval, the
original and only Grail-winner, now becomes part of a
composite questing company in which, with Bors, he plays
second fiddle to Galahad. Malory's *Le Morte d'Arthur* and, more
recently, Tennyson's *Idylls of the King* similarly promoted
Galahad as the Grail-winner supreme, so that the earlier
traditions have become overlaid and forgotten. The Celtic
Amadan Mor with his innocent ignorance has been replaced by
a faultless, Christly hero.

So we are left with an incredible strata of material which now
includes native British myth, apocryphal Christian traditions,
and the Arthurian legend. This brew is as potent as anything
found in the cauldron of Ceridwen. Like any good soup the
Grail legends have a basic stock and lots of mixed ingredients.
The result is a salvific or redemptive story which has all the
nourishment of native spirituality combined with the exotic
spice of the Christian legend. The course of the Grail legends
fulfils the criteria outlined in the Passover Haggadah, where the
story of the Exodus from Egypt, the salvic Jewish myth, is
rehearsed for the benefit of the whole company; 'the story must
be given life and meaning'.[47]

The Grail legends form, in effect, a native apocryphal gospel in
which the native hero stands in the place of Christ. He fulfils the
same redemptive role as that of Christ, becoming the One who
Frees the Waters. For the waters of life are understood to be
chained until the Grail is found and manifest again.

The Otherworldly Celtic story transmutes to its Christian
analogue with scarcely an alteration in the original motivation of
the hero who is destined to gain the cauldron. He is still one who
has an aptitude or predisposition for Otherworldly communion.
The cauldron-heroes and Grail-Knights become bridges from
this world to the other, allowing the healing influence of the
empowering vessel to percolate between the worlds, just as the
waters of Conla's Well bring wisdom into our world.

And if we look closely at the composition of the medieval Grail stories, we find that each is concerned with a spiritual obstruction—the waters of life are not reaching the land and its people. By the action of one man and his communion with the Grail, the Wasteland is healed, the Wounded King is made whole and the people once more enjoy spiritual bounty.

The timeless qualities of Grail and cauldron transcend the apparent barriers between Celtic and Christian stories. Both traditions are fundamentally telling the same story, seeking the same spiritual communion. The characters and events may change, but the story never changes. It merely finds new variations, each adapted by the writers, dreamers and visionaries of every generation—the 'gifted people' who hold open doors between the worlds.

It is they who go down to the roots of the world to find the waters of life and bring spiritual nourishment to those who hunger and thirst. That is the task of those Grail-seekers who are also the Walkers-between-the-Worlds.

In the story of 'Branwen Daughter of Llyr', Bran the Blessed, the titanic king of Britain, comes to Ireland to rescue his sister, but his troops cannot pass over the river which obstructs them and which has no bridge. His men come to ask his counsel. He says: 'He who will be chief let him be a bridge.' And he lies down across the river, hurdles are laid over him and his troops pass over his body to the other side.

We have no space to investigate the heroic and sacral manner of Bran's actions but his saying applies to all who go on the quest for the Grail. For they become bridges between the worlds just as Perceval penetrates the dangers of the darkness of Annwn, just as Christ descends into the realms of Sheol in order to overcome death for all time.

For the Grail Knights do not fulfil some pious but personally beneficial action in finding the Grail; they are in the process of becoming channels through which the waters of life may irrigate our world. Having found the Grail, however, they have entered another, holy, dimension. They cannot remain part of the world but are destined to be living bridges to the Otherworld, to Paradise.

Thus, if we look at the evidence of the Grail texts, we find that Galahad, though he seems to die on looking in the Grail in the mystical city of Sarras, is assumed to another state of life. Perceval returns to the world, but remains withdrawn from it as the new Grail guardian, as a kind of Hermit King. In the Celtic stories, Arthur and Bran both enter the Otherworld to find the power of the cauldron. They do not suffer death but remain the undying guardians of the inner realms. Christ dies on the cross but passes to the realms of Sheol to liberate the people of the past; he is resurrected with a promise of life for all ages to come.

The deathless waters flow down through time, ever waiting for new Grail-seekers to find the channels which may open in any generation.

Each generation has its own story-tellers, its band of eager auditors who seek the empowerment of the Grail for their time. Its appearances may differ, but its effect is always the same— spiritual regeneration. It is that most precious of all spiritual treasures, whatever our tradition, our sense of inner belonging. Whatever story causes our blood to quicken, our senses to be revitalized, our hearts or be gladdened *is* our path to the Grail. By aligning with the salvific story we are enabled to embark on our own quest for the waters of life.

The Grail romancers did not lose the secret of the story. They rewove and heightened the tradition, so that the ancient echoes of the 'carpenters of song' sounded once more in melodious harmony:

> And Bron the old placed the vessel in Perceval's keeping between his hands, and from the vessel there came a melody and a secret so precious that it seemed to them that they might be in Paradise with the angels.[48]

And so the story comes full circle, for so does the Celtic Otherworldly well of nine hazels dispense its secrets through the paradisal beauty of its song. From the intertwining of two traditions, the Grail emerges as the most powerful music of the spirit—the overspilling fountain caught by any with open hands for service by any with receptive, loving hearts to remake creation in the likeness of our spiritual home.

We do not know the names of those story-tellers and poets who moved over the face of Europe, promoting the ancient gnosis of the Grail. They are as brilliant as they are nameless. Yet why should we remember the story-teller? It is sufficient that we should remember the story—and what a story, a story whose power was so strong that neither time nor change of faith could condemn it to forgetfulness.

The Grail legends have been remembered because they are not just ancient stories but living myths which feed the spirit. Eternally current, they flow from the nameless sources of the dark forests of Britain and Ireland into the wider confluence of other rivers where the medieval romancers fitted them ready for sea. For the crystal *curragh* of Manannan, erstwhile god of the Blessed Isles, is the same as the Ship of Solomon in which Perceval, Bors and Galahad sail. It bears us to shores and dimensions beyond our beleaguered coastlines to the country of the Grail.

We may be sure that there the original story-tellers sit with those named romancers in the glorious entertainment of the Grail, forever telling and retelling, continuing and amending its never-ending story of wonder.

Notes and References

1 A.&B. Rees, *Celtic Heritage* (London: Thames & Hudson, 1961).
2 F.M. Cornford, *Principium Sapientiae* (Cambridge Univ. Press, 1952, Chap. VI).
3 Daniel Corkery, *The Hidden Ireland* (Dublin: Gill & Macmillan, 1967).
4 J. Curtin *Hero Tales of Ireland* (London: Macmillan, 1894).
5 Rees, p. 211.
6 Marie de France, *Lays*, trans. E. Mason (London: Dent, n.d).
7 The standard of Irish education remained high even after the restrictions and proscriptions upon the language. Irish sailors often spoke Spanish and Arabic in their maritime dealings with the south-western seaboard of Europe and the Mediterranean, while ploughboys and shepherds spoke a Latin and Greek often superior to their English employers in the last century, having been taught by the descendants of the bards in proscribed hedge-schools.

   Though there is a tendency for early Arthurian texts to appear in Latin, presumably so transcribed by the only literate people—the clerics—the preferred language of Arthurian texts in the Middle Ages became the vernacular, simply because the audience spoke it.

8 Chrétien de Troyes, *Arthurian Romances* (London: Dent, 1987).

9 R.S. Loomis *Wales and the Arthurian Tradition* (London: Folcroft Library Editions, 1977, p. 193).

10 Gerald of Wales, *A Journey Through Wales*, trans. L. Thorpe (Harmondsworth: Penguin, 1978, p. 252.)

11 Evans, S., *In Quest of the Holy Grail* (London: Dent, 1898).

12 Ibid., p. 99.

13 Ibid., p. 105.

14 C. Matthews, *Arthur and the Sovereignty of Britain: King and Goddess in the Mabinogion* (London: Arkana, 1989).

15 R.S. Loomis, *Arthurian Tradition and Chrétien de Troyes* (New York: Columbia Univ. Press, 1949, p. 17).

16 Wolfram von Eschenbach, *Parzival*, trans. A. Hatto (Harmondsworth: Penguin, 1988).

17 I use the word 'myth' with respect, denoting 'a powerful salvific story grounded in ancestral memory'.

18 T.P. Cross & C.H. Slover, *Ancient Irish Tales*, (Dublin: Figgis, 1936, pp. 504-5).

19 A fuller exposition of the Hallows can be found in *The Arthurian Tarot: a Hallowquest* (Wellingborough: Aquarian Press, 1990).

20 Loomis (1977), op. cit., p. 131.

21 *Trioedd Ynys Prydein* , ed. R. Bromwich (Cardiff: Univ. of Wales Press, 1961 p. 241).

22 P.B. Ellis *A Dictionary of Irish Mythology* (London: Constable, 1987).

23 Cross, op. cit., p. 11.

24 Sir Thomas Malory, *Le Morte d'Arthur* (New York: University Books, 1961, Book 13, Chap. 3).

25 Ibid., Book 2, Chap. 15.

26 *Didot Perceval*, trans. D. Skeels (Seattle: Univ. of Washington, 1966, p. 13).

27 *The Mabinogion*, trans. Lady C. Guest (London: Ballantyne Press).

28 D. ó hógáin, *Fionn Mac Cumhail* (Dublin: Gill & Macmillan, 1988).

29 *Mabinogion*, op. cit.

30 C. Matthews, *Mabon and the Mysteries of Britain* (London: Arkana, 1987, p. 107ff.).

31 Rule of St Benedict, n.d.

32   *Clement of Alexandria*, trans. G.W. Butterworth (London: Heinemann, 1968, p. 253).

33   C.W. Kennedy, *Early English Christian Poetry* (London: Hollis & Carter, 1952).

34   R.S. Loomis, *The Development of Arthurian Romance* (New York: Norton & Co, 1963).

35   *The Mabinogion*, op. cit.

36   C. Matthews *Arthur and the Sovereignty of Britain*, op. cit.

37   Ibid., p. 14.

38   Ibid., pp. 187-97.

39   *The Mabinogion*, op. cit.

40   Cross, op. cit., p. 162ff.

41   Lady A. Gregory, *The Voyages of St Brendan the Navigator* (Gerrard's Cross: Colin Smythe, 1973).

42   *The Quest of the Holy Grail*, trans. P. Matarasso (Harmondsworth: Penguin, 1969).

43   *The High Book of the Grail* trans. N. Bryant (Cambridge: D.S. Brewer, 1978).

44   *Didot Perceval* op. cit., p. 6

45   Robert de Boron in *Medieval Narratives*, trans. M. Schlauch (New York: Gordian Press, 1969).

46   *High Book of the Grail*, op. cit., p. 265.

47   H. Bronstein, ed., *A Passover Haggadah* (Harmondsworth: Penguin, 1974, p. 32).

48   *Didot Perceval*, op. cit., p. 68.

2

CHRÉTIEN DE TROYES AND THE CAULDRON OF STORY

by
Diana L. Paxson

Chrétien de Troyes wrote his *Contes del Graal* in approximately 1208. It is the first written account of the Grail we possess. Chrétien wrote for a sophisticated audience who liked a good story with plenty of action, some love-interest and perhaps a pinch of religion. In other words, he was writing very much what we would nowadays call a novel. But Chrétien's work is not a novel. It is a poem. And, although it possesses all the qualities listed above, it is *not* typical of its time. Also, it was left unfinished, and thereby began one of the most extraordinary trails devised by the imagination of man.

Four other authors tried to continue where Chrétien had left off, with varying degrees of success. But the way remained open, and it still is.

Diana Paxson looks at the *Contes del Graal* with the eyes of a story-teller in her own right, and finds new things within it. Her essay shows us something we may have forgotten about Chrétien—that he wrote about 'something that must be experienced, not heard'. What Chrétien gives us still is just that—an experience that is not easily forgotten, the first, in all probability, of many, on what may well become an ongoing, personal search.

❧

I want to tell you a story, '... the best tale ever told in any royal court.'[1] That is what Chrétien de Troyes, writing at the end of the twelfth century, called *Le Conte del Graal*, and he had good reason to know.

It is the story of a boy brought up (like most of us) in ignorance of his true heritage who one day sees something wonderful and goes after it. He has many adventures along the way, although none of his deeds turns out quite as he expected, for each achievement only serves to show him that there is more to learn. Finally he encounters something so remarkable that he does not even have the words to ask what it means, and so it is withdrawn from him, and he spends the rest of his life trying to find it again.

This, broadly outlined, is the story of Perceval. It could also be the story of many of the academics who have spent their lives trying to discover the meaning of the Grail. As Jean Frappier, perhaps the leading scholar on Chrétien de Troyes, has said, 'Today *The Story of the Grail* has become an adventure especially for erudite critics anxious to explain the origins of the mysterious and intriguing legend. Their own quest is strewn with enigmas, pitfalls, and temptations ...'[2]

Perhaps, like Perceval, they do not know what questions to ask. Or perhaps the answer is something that must be experienced, not heard. The genius of Chrétien de Troyes lay in his ability to construct a story which would allow his audience to experience the quest along with Perceval. This is the difference between sub-creation and scholarship.

What did Chrétien do? How did he do it? And most important of all, what does that accomplishment mean?

Interestingly enough, these three questions correspond roughly to Chrétien's own analysis of the major elements involved in creating a story. Not only did his Arthurian tales give definitive form to a new genre, the *roman*, he developed a critical language with which to describe it. In the prologue to his *Lancelot* (v.26) Chrétien states that a story must contain both *matière*—'matter' (as in the Matter of Britain), or source material, and *sen*—'sense', a meaning or theme. At the beginning of *Erec et Enide* (v.14) he says that a story requires *bele conjointure*—an effective joining of story elements into a coherent narrative.

If I bring any particular expertise to the consideration of this story, it is because I am a writer of much the same kind of tales, as well as being a long-time seeker of the Grail. As an author I find analysis of the creative process in other writers fascinating. It seems to me that by looking at the *Conte del Graal* from the point of view of a writer; by using Chrétien's own critical concepts as a framework for the examination of his creation, we may all not only arrive at a better (or at least a different) understanding of his achievement but also gain a new insight into its meaning.

Chrétien's *matière* was the Matter of Britain, the complex of motifs and characters which were precipitated around the figure of King Arthur. Although Celtic in origin, the Arthurian mythos included elements from a variety of sources; some of those which are considered most typical (and thereby, by extension, labelled 'Celtic') were introduced in their surviving form by Chrétien de Troyes. By *matière*, I believe that Chrétien means the kind of source material that fills what J.R.R. Tolkien, in his essay 'On Fairy Stories', calls 'the Cauldron of Story'. It should be no surprise that it is the author whose impact on modern Fantasy has been comparable in magnitude to Chrétien's influence on the literature of his own time who has analysed the writer's use of sources in this way.

> The Cauldron of Story has always been boiling, and to it have continually been added new bits, dainty and undainty ...
>
> It seems fairly plain that Arthur, once historical (but perhaps as such not of great importance), was also put into the Pot. There he was boiled for a long time, together with many other older figures and devices, of mythology and Faerie, and even some other stray bones of history ...
>
> But if we speak of Cauldron, we must not wholly forget the Cooks. There are many things in the Cauldron, but the Cooks do not dip in the ladle quite blindly. Their selection is important.[3]

Chrétien de Troyes was an expert Cook. How much of his material he invented may be desputed, but certainly he was the first to combine all of the elements of the Grail legend in such a way as to capture the imagination of his audience and not only to fix the quest for the Grail firmly within the Arthurian canon but to develop it into a major theme of Western literature which could be treated independently.

The question of Chrétien's sources seems to exercise a powerful fascination for the academic mind. It is certainly true that the medieval respect for *auctoritas* was a powerful inducement for a writer to conceal his originality (perhaps for the same reasons that many who wish to convey spiritual teachings today ascibe them to Ascended Masters, Wiccan grandmothers, or Native American shamans). And it is also true, as Tolkien points out, that no matter how far back one traces a tale there has to be an inventor *somewhere*. But it seems to me that we should at least consider believing what the poet himself has to say about the origins of his material.

In the introduction to the *Conte del Graal* (v.67) Chrétien states that his tale came from a book given him by the count (Philip of Blois). In the prologue to *Erec et Enide*, he introduces his story—

... d'Erec, le fil Lac, li contes,
que devant rois et devant contes
depecier ct corronpre suelent
cil qui de conter vivre vuelent.
Des or comançerai l'estoire
qui toz jors mes iert an mimoire
tant con durra crestiantez;
de ce s'est Crestiens vantez.[4]

(... of Erec, son of Lac, the tale which before kings and before counts, those who wish to live by tale-telling have only torn apart and corrupted. Now I will begin the history which I have had in mind, so that it will last as long as Christianity, this is Chrétien's boast.)

Our poet is certainly not over-modest. In his introduction to the *Lancelot* he speaks feelingly of the *peine* and the *entencion* (the hard work and intense concentration) which is his own original contribution to the tale. If he had invented the *matière* of his tales he might even have admitted it. The tale-tellers he refers to seem to have been the Breton *conteurs* which are also mentioned by Marie de France, by Wace, and by Thomas. Among the scholars, the general opinion is that the migration of Breton bards into French courtly circles would have been quite sufficient to have given Chrétien access to a considerable body of traditional material. For a detailed examination of Celtic motifs in the work of Chrétien de Troyes, see the work of Roger Sherman Loomis in *The Grail: From Celtic Myth to Christian Symbol*, and elsewhere.

Scholars discussing Chrétien's sources often ask why, if an earlier version of the Grail story existed, it has not survived. One possibility is that it was not written down. In pre-Christian Ireland, the highly-trained *filidh* who had memorized the ancient poetic repertory and the sophisticated rules that governed its composition scorned the bards who invented and performed their own material. But when the old culture that had supported the *filidh* was destroyed only the bards, and their heirs, the story-tellers, remained. The Breton story-tellers were in even worse case; hedge-poets who struggled to communicate an ancient tradition in a foreign tongue. The results must have been much like '… the absurd English songs composed by some of the Irish peasant bards who knew English only imperfectly'[5] referred to by Kathleen Hoagland in her note on 'Castlehyde' in *100 Years of Irish Poetry*.

There is some evidence that the name of Perceval was already associated with a visit to the Grail Castle. In a poem by Regaut de Barbezieux, written before 1160, we find—

Just as Perceval, when he was alive,
was lost in wonderment at the sight,
so that he could never ask
what purpose the lance and grail served,
so I, likewise, mielhs de Domna,
for I forget all when I gaze on you.[6]

Chrétien certainly knew his hero's name before he wrote the *Conte*. He includes Perceval in his catalogue of Arthur's knights in *Erec et Enide*, and mentions him as a knight of great reknown in *Cligés*. Perhaps the reason that Chrétien's immediate source for his story did not survive was simply that if it *was* written down it was very bad! No wonder if Chrétien, whose effortless skill in French poetry led men to acknowledge him the master throughout the next century, thought he could improve upon his original!

Although the scholars speculating about Chrétien's sources express their interest more elegantly, they are asking essentially the same question that has at one time or another exasperated most writers of my acquaintance: 'Where do you get your ideas?' The question itself arises from a basic misunderstanding of the creative process. Ideas are everywhere; they come from a phrase in something one is reading, a comment made by a friend, sometimes one even seems to pluck them from the air. As in science, the same insights may come simultaneously to two writers who have had no contact at all. The problem is not where to find ideas but rather, sometimes, how to beat them off. The working writer goes through life like a hunter, noting every track or broken branch that indicated the presence of game. But he does not follow every trail. Every writer I know has enough story ideas in mind to last several lifetimes. The problem is to select those that will appeal to one's audience and that one can handle well.

The operative question in looking at a piece of literature should not be where the writer got his ideas but what he did with them once they were acquired. There are very few really new ideas around; the more deeply a story affects the human psyche the more likely it is to have been told before. Even when two writers do get the same idea at the same time, or work from the same source material, their results are very different (compare the story of Arthur as told by T.H. White and Marion Zimmer Bradley!) I believe that combining the elements effectively is what Chrétien means by *bele conjointure*.

Single story elements, like unmated human beings, have no progeny. It is only when they interact with others that a new story begins to grow. Whether or not Chrétien invented his story elements, he did select and interweave them—and therein lies his true originality. He seems to have been the kind of writer who approached his work with the intellect as well as with the emotions. His style is sophisticated; even at his most evocative, his effects are always completely under control. Despite the romantic image of the artist as some kind of wild man writhing in the throes of creation, literary production is often a rather cold-blooded affair. As Tolkien points out:

> Fantasy is a natural human activity. It certainly does not destroy or even insult Reason; and it does not either blunt the appetite for, nor obscure the perception of, scientific verity. On the contrary. The keener and the clearer is the reason, the better fantasy will it make.[7]

The genius of Chrétien was to turn the clear light of French reason upon the misty wonders of Celtic legend. When the critic does so, he is likely to make them disappear, but the artist illuminates them in the light of human experience. We cannot have any sure knowledge of Chrétien's creative process, but I know the kinds of questions that I (being the kind of sub-creator who likes to understand process as well as engage in it) ask myself in planning a new work; Chrétien's comments on his art suggest that he may have been this kind of thinker too.

Chrétien began with a selection of elements derived from the *matière*: the unknown youth who seeks his fortune at the court of a great king; the education of the hero; the damsel in distress; the visit to the fortress in the Otherworld; the wasteland and the wounded king ... I have given these motifs in the order in which the poet used them—in retrospect, it seems inevitable—but his first question must have been how to arrange them most effectively, followed closely by some decision regarding the perspective or narrative point of view.

Most of the young heroes who emerge from the wilderness make mistakes before they are integrated into civilized society, but surely none of them acts with quite so blithe a lack of social sensitivity as Perceval. From the first moments of the story, he is sublimely oblivious to the consequences of his actions and, like Odie in the Garfield cartoons, he leaves a trail of destruction behind him. I cannot think of another writer apart from John Erskine (*Galahad, Enough of his Life to Explain his Reputation*) who dares to suggest that the Grail story might at times be funny. In the immortal words which Anna Russell applied to another epic hero, Perceval is 'very strong, very handsome, very brave ... very stupid!'[8] He is the 'innocent fool', and the action is presented from his naïve point of view. The audience has no choice but to identify with him. It is only after laughing at Perceval's mishaps that the reader begins to realize that, in proceeding through the story along with him, he or she is sharing in the fool's experience.

Perceval is, above all, profoundly unaware. He is at once completely self-centred and completely unselfconscious. He is not an allegory but rather an example of the spiritual state in which most people live their lives. A variant manuscript tradition includes some lines following v.342 in which it becomes clear that at the beginning of the story Perceval does not even know his own name. His encounter with the knights is his first exposure to a larger world; his reactions show that he understands both their responses to his questions and his mother's counsels only in the most superficial way. He leaves her fainting at the gate and gallops away to seek adventure without any suspicion of the impact of his actions.

His encounter with the lady in the tent is only the first of a series of incidents in which his literal-minded interpretation of advice gets him into trouble and, like his abandonment of his mother, it will have serious consequences. Now that the poet has established Perceval's character, his next task is to give the story a broader context. Therefore he brings his bumptious hero to the paragon of all earthly courts, King Arthur's castle at Carduel. However mythic its beginnings, in the context of the story, the court represents the civilized world, an idealized version of the royal courts that Chrétien knew. Against this glittering background, Perceval stands out in striking comic relief. However, in his next encounter his lack of either empathy or imagination stands him in good stead. His fight with the Red Knight is one of the great humorous scenes in medieval literature, and he is able to defeat his opponent partly because it never occurs to him that he could fail. He is the Fool who stands with one foot poised above the precipice, the *puer aeternus* who transcends mortality.

By this time, the reader assumes that he understands what is going on, and has settled down to enjoy a nice comedy. But one of Chrétien's major strengths is his ability to delineate subtle changes in character, and with the next sequence, Perceval's knightly education by Gornemant, the poet begins to transform him. Structurally, this episode provides some needed exposition of the process by which Perceval becomes the perfect knight. Perceval may be a 'natural', but the poet does not require us to suspend our disbelief beyond reason by having him overcome all opposition with no training at all. The poet, having gotten his audience thoroughly interested in his protagonist during the earlier episodes, can afford to slow down the action long enough to explain how Perceval's prowess acquires enough polish to get him through the rest of the story.

The second essential piece of exposition provided by this episode is Gornemant's fateful advice to Perceval to stop asking so many questions.

'*Oui trop parole, it se mesfait*',
Por che, biax amis, vos chastoi
De trop parler. (vv. 1654–56)

('Who speaks too much does himself an ill deed', therefore, fair friend, keep yourself from talking too much.)

It is at this point, when Gornemant's teaching has begun to make Perceval self-aware, that he realizes for the first time that he should not have left his mother so abruptly. The motive that impels him away from his teacher's castle and eventually leads him to the Grail is the first impulse of concern for another. This, not the showier episode at Arthur's court, is the moment in which Perceval begins to change.

The result of this development becomes apparent in the sequence that follows. Having begun to think of others, Perceval is becoming capable of love. His next stop is the castle of Belrepaire, whose young mistress, Blancheflor, is being besieged by a villainous fellow who wants both the lady and her land. It is at this point that we remember that until now Chrétien was renowned as a teller of love stories. His previous surviving works focus on the romantic problems of hero and heroine, not solely for the sake of entertainment but as a means of exploring the relationship between love and life. Unlike the usual love story, which ends when the hero gets the girl, Chrétien's stories tend to focus on what happens after the wedding. Perceval wins Blancheflor without difficulty, although the marriage is delayed. The purpose of this episode is not to involve our hero in romantic entanglements but to further mature him by teaching him more about love.

Some scholars seem to be fixated on the question of Perceval's chastity. In some of the later Grail romances, the purity of the hero is indeed a major factor—but not, I think, in this one. Chrétien avoids both the churchly preoccupation with fleshly lust as sin and the defiant passion of the poet of courtly love. Whether his couples make love before marriage or wait, what matters is not the durability of their virginity but of their commitment.

By the end of the Belrepaire episode, Perceval is not only determined to do his filial duty to his mother but he has pledged himself to return to Blancheflor. The *Conte del Graal* differs from Chrétien's other romances in that the love story is only a means to further the main plot line. However, it is typical of Chrétien that the incidents that prepare Perceval to encounter the Sacred affirm rather than deny his ties to the world.

Here, I think we must pass from admiration of Chrétien's skills and sources as a writer to a consideration of his *sen*—the meaning of which his story was intended to convey. Without an underlying purpose, a medieval romance, like many contemporary fantasy novels, is only a collection of adventures. In the immortal words of Harold Shea, 'Travelling through Faerie is just one damn encounter after another'.[9] Chrétien rises above his contemporaries because his work is always 'about' the development of character. In each of his *romans* he shows believable people learning how to cope with real human problems, and sometimes something more.

Perhaps the key to what that something more in the *Conte del Graal* might be may be found in the introduction, in which Chrétien praises his patron above all for the virue of *carité*, the Latin *caritas*, which is love (v. 43). However many notable questions Philip of Blois may have had, I think that the poet's choice of this particular virtue for praise serves as an indication of his intention.

As a writer, Chrétien's main concern was with the many faces of love. In *Erec et Enide*, in *Yvain* and in *Cligés*, he showed the stages by which love matures; in *Lancelot*, he portrayed the mysticism of a martyr of love. Having covered human love so exhaustively, it is perhaps not surprising that he should have eventually attempted to tell a story which pointed toward union with the Divine—without rejecting humanity. The twelfth century may have been the only time during the Middle Ages when this was possible. A major concern of the times was the nature and practice of love, both carnal and spiritual. This interest culminated in the doctrine of *fin amor* in the court, and in the cloister it produced the mysticism of Bernard of Clairvaux. In succeeding centuries the clouds darkened, and later quests for the Grail are characterized by a desperation lacking in the serene narrative of Chrétien.

According to the Abbot of Clairvaux, the love of God begins with the soul's love of itself for its own sake, proceeds to the love of God for the self's sake, the love of God for God's sake, and finally the love of the self for God's sake alone. Its goal is the mystical union, which requires an apprenticeship having the stages of humility gained through a consciousness of sin, the development of charity, spiritual vision, and finally union.[10] The story of the Grail is not a Cistercian allegory, but Bernard's theology of love may well have influenced Chrétien's characterization of Perceval, which is not only a subtle piece of psychological analysis but a study of the evolution of spiritual consciousness.

At the beginning of the story Perceval deserts his mother—a

sin against charity. In Bernard's terms, at the beginning of the tale he loves himself for his self's sake. Like a small child, he cannot even imagine that his actions might hurt another. By the time he leaves Blancheflor, he has begun to act altruistically. Without rejecting *Eros*, the poet moves beyond it to explore the meaning of *Caritas*.

What is remarkable is that the sequence of events through which Chrétien conveys his meaning is not Christian in any obvious sense but rather an experience that transcends the conventions of religion as it was commonly understood in his day, and still is in ours. After he has left Belrepaire, Perceval's wanderings lead him to the Castle of the Fisher King and the Grail.

In the *matière* of Celtic legend, Chrétien found a source of archetypal riches which challenged his sophistication and skill. It is when he dips most deeply into this part of the cauldron that he is at his most evocative and profound. The fountain of Barenton in Broceliande where Yvain wakes the storm, the sword-bridge which Lancelot must cross in order to reach Guinevere, and the Procession of the Grail in the Castle of the Fisher King belong to another order of reality than the passages of love and war which are the stock in trade of romance.

Valiantly, the poet tries to civilize his wonders—he is a Mozart, rather than a Wagner, in his orchestration and harmonies. Still, when Perceval comes to the swift flowing river where the *Roi Pecheur* is fishing, a deeper note sounds through the music of Chrétien's sprightly couplets, and we realize that we are moving from the fields we know (however legendary) to the borders of the Otherworld. The shift would have been even more apparent to the *roman's* original audience. To the modern reader, the court of King Arthur and that of the Fisher King are equally fantastic, but the medieval audience would have found the former an idealized version of royal courts, as the glittering lifestyle of the soap operas is a fantasy of the lives of the rich and famous today.

The Fisher King's directions lead Perceval into an even deeper wilderness, and it is at the moment when he is despairing of ever finding his way, that—

Lors vit pres de lui en un val
Le chief d'une tor qui parut. (vv. 3050–51)

(Then he saw near him in a valley the top of a tower which appeared.)

Whether he lives in the twelfth century or the twentieth, the reader who sees the Castle of the Grail manifesting in the wilderness before him recognizes, like Dorothy upon catching her first sight of Oz, that he is not in Kansas any more. If only Perceval had been so perceptive!

He is welcomed into a great square hall more like King Cormac's hall at Tara as traditionally described in Irish literature than any French castle of the time. He is given a marvelous sword, which for him alone is '*voëe et destinee*', (vowed and destined) (v. 3168). And then—

> Uns vallés d'une chambre vint,
> Qui une blanche lance tint
> Empoignie par le mileu,
> Si passa par entre le feu
> Et cels qui el lit se seoient.
> Et tot cil de laiens veoient
> le lance blanche et le fer blanc,
> S'issoit une goute de sanc
> Del fer de la lance en somet,
> Et jusqu'a la main au vallet
> Coloit cele goute vermeille ...
> Atant dui autre vallet vindrent,
> Qui candeliers en lor mains tindrent ...
> Un graal entre ses deus mains
> Une damoisele tenoit ...
> Atot le graal qu'ele tint,
> Une si grans clartez i vint
> Qu'ausi perdirent les chandoiles
> Lor clarté come les estoiles
> Font quant solaus lieve ou la lune.
> Aprés celi en revint une
> Qui tint un tailleoir d'argant.
> Li graaus, qui aloit devant,
> De fin or esmeré estoit;
> Prescïeuses pierres avoit ...
> Tout ensi com passa la lance ...
> Et d'une chambre en autre entrerent.
> Et li vallés les vit passer,
> Ne n'osa mie demander
> Del graal cui l'en en servoit ... (vv. 3191–3244)

(A youth from a chamber came who grasped a white lance by the middle; he passed between the fire and those who were on the couch. And all those who were within saw the white lance and the white steel, from which issued a drop of blood; from the tip of the iron lance down to the hand of the youth rolled this vermillion drop ... Then two other youths came who bore candelabra in their hands ... so great a radiance from it came that the candles lost their light as the stars lose theirs when rises the moon. After her came one who held a platter of silver. The Grail, which had gone before, was of fine, pure gold; precious stones it had ... In this way it passed, like the lance ... and from one room entered another. And the youth [Perceval] saw them pass, *and did not dare to ask who was served by the Grail.*)

This episode is one of the major battlefields of Arthurian scholarship. Roger Sherman Loomis has analyzed the Celtic analogues to its various elements in exhaustive detail. Other scholars have viewed the Grail Procession as a reflection of any one of a number of kinds of Christianity or Judaism, or as the last glimmer of a pagan fertility rite. In later versions of the story the Grail is said to give each one whatever he likes best to eat and drink; even in Chrétien's version, it seems to offer each scholar whatever meaning he or she would most like to find! But as Ursula K. Le Guin points out, 'Any creation, primary or secondary, with any vitality to it, can "really" be a dozen mutually exclusive things at once, before breakfast.'[10]

This polymorphic symbolism is indeed the trademark of Faerie. Perhaps the reason that the story has proved so enduring is that those elements that its author drew from the Cauldron are ancient indeed. The last spicing before Chrétien dipped in his spoon may have been Celtic, but I think that the essence of the Grail episode may well belong to that level which feeds the mythologies of many lands.

We have no reason to doubt that Chrétien de Troyes was a good son of the Church. Certainly the hermit who advises Perceval at the end of the story is orthodox in his counsels. But the Grail procession itself is like no known Christian ceremony. The combination of the Castle, the Procession and the Unasked Question may have come from Count Philip's mysterious book, but it was Chrétien who decided how to present them. In later versions of the story, the Grail is firmly identified as the Chalice of the Last Supper, and appears either as a vision or in a ceremony reminiscent of the Mass—but not so in Chrétien's presentation. Eventually we (with Perceval) will be told that the Grail holds a Christian Mass wafer, but the episode in which it appears has not even a veneer of Christianity. Why should a Christian poet portray this holy thing in such a strange way?

The same question might be asked of some of the great fantasists of modern times. Why did J.J.R. Tolkien, a devout Roman Catholic, invent an entire mythology of Middle Earth with its own pantheon? Why did C.S. Lewis, famed as an apologist for the Anglican communion, set his version of the Christian story in a secondary world inhabited by creatures out of classical and medieval mythology? Why do so many contemporary writers of fantasy, whether they be good Christians or no kind of Christian at all, invent worlds whose mythologies and religions are peopled by old gods with new names, worlds which shimmer with a magic as marvelous as ever illuminated any Breton bard's tale?

C.S. Lewis provides a possible explanation when he discusses his reasons for writing about Narnia. He is careful to point out that in his case it was always the image that came first, bubbling uncontrollably from the depths of the Author's unconscious and demanding to be made into a tale. It was only afterward that the Man in him would apply his critical judgement to decide whether he ought to write the story, and what it might mean. To use a popular model of consciousness, for a successful act of sub-creation both the left and right must work together.

> I thought I saw how stories of this kind could steal past a certain inhibition which had paralysed much of my own religion in childhood. Why did one find it so hard to feel as one was told one ought to feel about God or about the sufferings of Christ? ... But suppose that by casting all these things into an imaginary world, by stripping them of all their stained-glass and Sunday School associations, one could make them for the first time appear in their real potency? Could one not thus steal past those watchful dragons? ... That was the Man's motive, but of course he could have done nothing if the Author had not been on the boil first.[12]

The brilliant, allusive world of the fairy-tale affected Lewis in a way which he perceived as being related to his response to religion. By turning to the world of myth for his matière, as well as for his form, he was able to write a story which could communicate a Truth beyond sectarian theology.

Faerie lies between the worlds, and what is between the worlds transcends the world we know. When we enter the realm of myth and magic we leave behind the internal censor, who demands that things be real, and thus we are enabled to experience a deeper level of Reality. The archetypal motifs which appear in the Grail episode bypass the conscious mind in order to convey a truth which might be rejected if presented objectively, or ignored through apparent familiarity. Is this a Christian truth? Perhaps—or perhaps the Christian story, speaking the language of history, is communicating in another way a Truth that lies beyond all languages. Like Perceval, we may not understand what the Grail is or what it is for, but as the eyes see that blaze of light that outshines all others, the spirit recognizes that something numinous is here.

To write a story which will speak to its audience in this way, the author must walk like a shaman between the worlds, at once transcending consciousness to respond directly to the myth and shaping it with conscious judgement and skill. This is the genius of all great fantasists. Certainly it was an ability possessed in full measure by Chrétien de Troyes.

'What is fantasy?' asks Ursula K. Le Guin, and answers—

... as art, not spontaneous play, its affinity is not with day-dream, but with dream. It is a different approach to reality, an alternative technique for apprehending and coping with existence. It is not antirational, but pararational; not realistic, but surrealistic, super-realistic, a heightening of reality ... It employs archetypes, which, as Jung warned us, are dangerous things ... Fantasy is nearer to poetry, to mysticism, and to insanity than naturalistic fiction is. It is a real wilderness, and those who go there should not feel too safe. And their guides, the writers of fantasy, should take their responsibilities seriously.[13]

Chrétien thrilled to the horns of Elfland, thence came his power, but like Lewis he accepted the responsibility of the Man as well as the inspiration of the Author. When he wrote about romantic love, the honeymoon was only the beginning; his main concern was with the problem of making love work while living in the world. It is not too surprising that when he wrote about an experience whose impact was profoundly mystical that moment of illumination should be only the beginning.

It is symptomatic of Perceval's spiritual state that when he comes to the Grail Castle he is still paralyzed by a literal understanding of his teacher's counsels, and thus is unable to ask the question that would have healed the Fisher King and his land. The problem is not unusual. History is full of individuals who have kept the law of their religion while losing the spirit! But immediately after his unceremonious ejection from the castle. Perceval meets his cousin, who informs him in no uncertain terms just what he did wrong. It is at this moment that he for the first time becomes aware of his own name. Even though he failed the test, he has passed through an initiation. He learns also that his inability to ask about the Grail is the result of the same sin— or condition of character—that caused him to leave his mother to die. In the language of Bernard of Clairvaux, although not quite in the same order, Perceval has achieved vision (albeit momentarily) and consciousness of sin, and is beginning to develop the *caritas* that is the prerequisite to union.

'What is there left for me to seek?' he asks (v. 3622). He must wander for many years before he finds out.

His life has been changed, but he does not know what to do with it. It is only after his wanderings have finally brought him back to the court of Arthur, where he rights some old wrongs, that the Loathly Lady appears to upbraid him and amplify his cousin's explanations. Whether she is the other face of the Grail Maiden or an externalization of his own guilty conscience, her words restore his sense of purpose. He swears that he will neither stay two nights in one place nor refuse any challenge.

Tant que il del graal savra
Cui l'en sert, et qu'il avra
La lance qui saine trovee
Et que la Veritez provee
Li ert dite por qu'ele saine. (vv. 4735-39.)

(Until he knew whom the Grail served, and had found the bleeding lance, and proven the truth of why it bled.)

But though he is pledged to seek the mystery, Perceval is not destined to withdraw from the world. His task is to understand what he has experienced so that he can use that knowledge. His spiritual path is knighthood, and marriage with Blancheflor. Even before he wrote the *Conte*, Chrétien was a heretic in the theology of courtly love; except for the *Lancelot*, his works display a conviction that love is manifested most fully in marriage, or at least in equal commitment. Among Chrétien's successors, the idea that Perceval must marry in order to fulfil his destiny as the sacred king was developed by Wolfram von Eschenbach, while the later tradition of the *Queste del Saint Graal* and Malory replaced Perceval with the virginal Galahad. The German version is probably the most consistent with Chrétien's intentions.

Even when Perceval's wanderings lead him at last to the hermit who proves to be his maternal uncle as well as his mentor, the advice he is given is on how to live a holy life in a secular setting. One of the distinguishing characteristics of the *Conte* is this awareness that the world of the spirit is no distant paradise but a realm that interpenetrates our own, and that the sacred is part of the life of the world.

Perceval has had a glimpse of that radiant splendor which is one of the most commonly reported characteristics of mystical experience; as his uncle informs him, he has seen a thing whose purpose is to mediate union with the Divine. After five years of directionless wandering he is recalled to awareness and is able to perceive the connection between his failure at the Grail Castle and what has happened to him since then. Perceval has forgotten God, been silent before the Grail, and left his mother to die—he has not obeyed the call, he has not recognized the vision, and he has failed in love. He is one of those who—

> For all their effort have not attained the vision ... They have received the authentic light, all their soul has gleamed as they have drawn near; but they come with a load on their shoulders which holds them back from the place of Vision.[14]

One of the primary characteristics of the mystic illumination is the experience of supernal love. Chrétien's mystics, whether their religion be that of divine or earthly passion, must practise their faith in the world. That world is an idealized medieval landscape illuminated by the light of the Otherworld, in which, although the divine archetypes that speak directly to the spirit appear and disappear, *caritas* and piety are continually required.

Throughout the story, it is Perceval's spiritual development that determines his ability to benefit from the gifts he is given, and the stages in his progress are marked by changes in his ability to care about others. As the visions of mystics from many times and faiths point to a single reality, so the quest for illumination is in essence the same. The way to the light is love.

The *Conte del Graal* was left unfinished. Although it includes further adventures of Gawain which are outside the scope of this discussion, the story of Perceval ends with the scene in which he is instructed by his hermit uncle. This truncated conclusion is even more frustrating for a writer than it is for the average reader. The frustration was obviously too much for Chrétien's successors for, in the generation that followed, Gerbert de Montreuil and others produced endless and only marginally successful continuations of the tale. Like Perceval they wander, but without Chrétien's clear vision they found it impossible to bring the story to a conclusion. That task was left to later writers, who returned to the beginning and assigned their own meanings to the tale.

To leave the story unfinished is unsatisfying, but it is perhaps more realistic—to very few is it given to attain more than a glimpse of the Grail. We are like Perceval in our ignorance when we begin, and we follow his path through the wilderness, only gradually coming to understand what it is we are looking for and learning how to recognize what we see. The Grail appears to each seeker in a different guise, and each author who tells the tale must dip into the Cauldron of Story anew.

To ask 'What is the Grail?' leads the scholar astray. The question which must be asked is that of the writer whose artistry draws meaning from his *matière*. 'What is the Grail *for*?'

Notes and References

All French quotations form the *Conte du Graal* in the essay are from the edition of William Roach, (Paris: Librarie Minard, 1959).

1 Chrétien de Troyes, *Perceval, or the Story of the Grail*, trans. Ruth Harwood Cline (Athens, Georgia: Univ. of Georgia Press, 1985 vv. 63–4).
2 Jean Frappier, *Chrétien de Troyes, the Man and his Work*,

trans. Raymond J. Cormier (Athens Ohio: Ohio Univ. Press, 1982, p. 151).

3 J.R.R. Tolkien, 'On Fairy Stories', *The Tolkien Reader* (New York: Ballantine, 1966, pp. 27, 29, 30).

4 Chrétien de Troyes, *Erec et Énide* (Paris: Librairie Honore Champion, 1963, v. 19-26).

5 *100 Years of Irish Poety*, ed. Kathleen Hoagland (New York: Grosset & Dunlap, 1962, p. 254).

6 Quoted in Rita Lejeune, 'The Troubadours', *Arthurian Literature in the Middle Ages*, ed. Roger Sherman Loomis (Oxford University Press, 1959, p. 396-7).

7 J.R.R. Tolkien, *op cit.*, p. 54.

8 Anna Russell, 'The Ring of the Nibelungs (An Analysis)' (*The Anna Russell Album*, Columbia Records, 1972).

9 L. Sprague de Camp and Fletcher Pratt, *The Incomplete Enchanter* (New York: Pyramid Books, 1962, p. 140).

10 Etienne Gilson, *The Mystical Theology of St Bernard*, trans. A.H.C. Downes (London: Sheed and Ward, 1940, pp. 98-9).

11 Ursula K. Le Guin, 'Dreams Must Explain Themselves', *Fantasists on Fantasy*, eds. Robert H. Boyer & Kenneth J. Zahorski (New York: Avon Books, 1984, p. 191).

12 C.S. Lewis, 'Sometimes Fairy Stories May Say Best What's to be Said', *Ibid*, p. 117.

13 Ursula K. Le Guin, 'From Elfland to Poughkeepsie', *Ibid.*, p. 196.

14 Plotinus, *The Enneads*, vi. 9, quoted in Evelyn Underhill, *Mysticism* (New York: Meridian Books, 1955, p. 207).

3
ROBERT DE BORON: ARCHITECT OF TRADITION

by
John Matthews

Of all the medieval authors who added significantly to our conception of the Grail, Robert de Boron is unique. He stands between the earliest, oral traditions and the later literary heritage, drawing upon varied sources to create an individual synthesis which was to shape the future of the Grail ever after. We know little about him, but we can judge from the nature of his existing works that he was devout, serious, and widely read. He was also a very poor stylist, whose clumsy sentences fail to hide the luminous nature of his vision. But above all he saw that the Grail was much more than just a symbol. It had a concrete reality which made those who served it into a family—that very family who form the Household of the Grail.

The Story

In the early part of the thirteenth century there appeared a work sometimes called *Le Roman d'Estoire du Graal*, sometimes *Joseph d'Arimathie*[1] by someone calling himself Messires (or Meistres) Robert de Boron. The story it told was an extraordinary one, part romance, part adventure story, part theological tract. With elements drawn from Celtic myth, Arthurian literature and Christian apocrypha, it changed for ever the matter of the Grail, then just beginning its extraordinary rise in popular consciousness with the *Conte del Graal* of Chrétien de Troyes.[2]

The story may be summarized as follows.

Beginning with a prologue summarizing the history of creation from the Fall to the Crucifixion, the text goes on to describe how the vessel in which Christ celebrated the first Eucharist at the

Last Supper came to be given first to Pilate and then to Joseph of
Arimathea who, during the deposition from the Cross, caught
some of the blood of the Messiah within it. After this Joseph is
imprisoned by the Jews and at this time is visited by the risen
Christ who entrusts him with the 'Secrets of the Saviour'
concerning the Grail and its uses.

Joseph remains in prison for many years, forgotten by the
outside world but sustained by the Grail. The Roman Emperor
Vespasian contracts leprosy and is miraculously cured by the
Veil of Veronica. Determined to find out more about
Christianity, the Emperor journeys to Jerusalem and there
discovers Joseph, still alive, and sets him free. Joseph, together
with his sister Enygeus and her husband Brons or Hebron, and
a small following of Christians leave Judea and journey into
other lands. There they dwell for a long time until some of the
company commit the sin of lechery so that their crops fail and
they all suffer from starvation. Requesting help from the Holy
Spirit, Joseph is commanded to build a table in memory of that
at which Christ celebrated the Last Supper. Brons is then told to
go forth and catch a single fish, which is then laid upon the table
opposite to the Grail. The company are then summoned to eat
and only those who have remained pure and true to their beliefs
are able to sit there, the rest being somehow prevented. All who
sit at the table are fed from the one fish, for which cause Brons
is ever after known as the Rich Fisherman. And all sitting there
'perceived a sweetness which was the completion of the desire of
their hearts'.[3]

One place at the table is left empty, in token of Judas the
betrayer, and when one of the outcast company, a man named
Moyses, tries to sit there he is swallowed up by the earth. The
voice of the Holy Spirit declares that the seat will remain empty
until the grandson of Brons comes to sit in it.

Time passes and Bron fathers 12 sons, all of whom marry
except for one, Alain, who declares his intention of remaining
celibate. By this sign Joseph knows that he is to be the destined
father of the one who will become the Grail's later guardian, and
takes him in and begins to train him in the ways of the Grail.
Eventually the Holy Spirit tells him that it is time for various of
the company to depart for the West, preaching the gospel. The
first to depart is Petrus, who is to journey to 'the Vale of Avalon'
to await the coming of Alain's son. Next Brons departs, having

learned the 'Secrets of the Grail' from Joseph. He journeys to Ireland (according to the *Didot Perceval*), there also to await his grandson. Thus will the meaning of the Trinity be fulfilled.

Joseph remains behind, happily prepared for death. Messire Robert de Boron promises to tell what happened next, where Alain went, what befell him and what son he had and who mothered it, and what also happened to Petrus and Moyses, who was swallowed up. All these things he will recount if he can discover them in a book.

Who was Robert de Boron?

Who was the man who told this strange, mystical tale? Robert de Boron is an elusive figure who has been variously described as a Burgundian, a Swiss and an Anglo Norman, with the status of knight or clerk. He himself tells us little. In a much-quoted passage from *Joseph d'Arimathie* he describes himself as *Meistres Robers dist de Bouron*, (Master Robert of Boron), suggesting that he was a clerk, possibly in holy orders, as indeed the nature of his writings would also bear out. However, in a later part of the same text he appears as *Messires* (Master or Sir) Robert, which is to say a knight. Which of these are we to believe?

Elsewhere in *Joseph* Robert speaks of his authorship and patronage in these terms:

A ce tens que je la [l'estoire dou Graal] retreis,
O mon Seigneur Gautier en peis,
Qui de Mont Belyal estoit,
Unques retreite este n'avait.

When I told [the History of the Grail]
In time of peace to my Lord Gautier,
Who was of Mont Belyal,
It had never been told before. (My trans.)

This Gautier has been identified as Gautier de Montbeliard, Lord of Montfaucon, who went on the Fourth Crusade in 1202 and never returned. Nearby is the village of Boron, which we may presume to be either Robert's birthplace or the place where he settled and where he wrote his cycle of romances about the Grail. It is also generally presumed that Robert was in the service of Gautier and that he wrote his trilogy (or possibly tetralogy)[4]

of poems for him, or at his behest, some time between 1191 and 1210, the year in which Gautier died. The words
'in time of peace' have been taken as a suggestion that the works
were completed *before* Gautier set out on crusade, implying that
Robert completed them in approximately 10 years.

Other clues to Robert's identity are the number of Burgundian
dialect words in the poems, which seem to confirm Boron as his
place of origin. There is also mention in an Essex charter of a
certain Robert de Burun, who is described as granting land in
Hertfordshire, England, to a monastery in Picardy. While this
connection is properly regarded as doubtful[5] it is interesting for
the implied connection with southern England. Robert seems to
have been familiar enough with this part of the country to
identify the place to which Petrus journeys as Avalon, then
widely believed to be identified with the town of Glastonbury in
Somerset. This also incidentally provides a possible *terminus ad
quem* to the dating of the *Joseph*, since the 'discovery' of Arthur's
body at Glastonbury and its subsequent identification with
Avalon took place in 1191.

Apart from the *Joseph*, which is the only one of Robert's poems
to have survived more or less intact, he is known to have written
a *Merlin*,[6] of which only 405 lines now survive, and a *Perceval* of
which nothing more is known. The possibility of a fourth book,
a version of the *Mort Artu*, has been put forward recently[7] and
more than one commentator has suggested that Robert may also
be the author (or immediate source for) the so-called *Didot
Perceval*.[8]

The complexity of manuscript traditions relating to Robert are
outside the field of this present essay. However, certain points
relating to his use of source material need to be examined for the
light they throw on Robert's contribution to the history of the
Grail.

Sources

It is not known whether Robert's presumed patron Gautier
provided the *matière* (matter) of his works, as Count Philip of
Flanders is supposed to have done for Chrétien de Troyes (see
Paxson). But though Robert certainly derived parts of his
material from the writings of the more famous poet of
Champagne, it is clear that he also had access to a very different
set of materials.

His own statement regarding sources comes in vv. 932-6 of *Joseph d'Arimathie*, where he refers to

Se je le grant livre n'avoie
Ou les estroires sunt escrites
Par les granz clers feites et dites.
La sunt li grant secre escrit
Qu'en numme le Graal et dit.

('The great book in which are the histories told by the grand clerks; there the mighty secrets are written which are named and called the Grail.' Trans. Charles Williams)[9]

These words have given much trouble to interpreters, who have been puzzled by the 'mighty secrets' which are the Grail. Richard O'Gorman suggests that a reading of the prose version of the *Joseph* which bears an alternative reading referring to the books as the place wherein 'the secret which is held concerning the sacraments of the Grail'.[10]

This certainly makes more sense at one level, though it must be said that the idea of the Grail being a body of secret tradition is not in itself nonsensical; indeed, it is more often the *content*, or the very *idea* of the vessel which is important rather than the vessel itself.

Nevertheless, this passage does raise a problem. On the one hand Robert states quite equivocally that he is the first person to tell the story of the Grail, and though this may be seen as a piece of typical medieval self-aggrandizement, it is somewhat in conflict with the reference to a *grant livre* or 'great book'.

Richard O'Gorman again comes to our rescue here. Examining the prose redaction he finds that in the famous passage quoted above Robert is probably referring to his own work, newly completed, in the hands of the reader; in the earlier passage he is in all probability referring to a book or books from which he obtained 'his rather conventional Eucharistic symbolism which he transforms into the secrets of the Grail'.[11]

This 'rather conventional symbolism' can be traced to two main sources: the *Gemma Animae* of Honorius of Autun[12] and the *Versus de Mysterio Missae* by Bishop Hildebert of Tours.[13]

In the first we find:

Dicente sacerdote, 'Per omnia saecula saeculorum,' diaconus venit, calicem coram eo sustollit, cum favone partem ejus cooperit in altari reponit et cum corporali cooperit, praeferens Joseph ab Arimathie, qui corpus Christi deposuit, faciem ejus sudario cooperuit, in monumento deposuit, lapide cooperuit ... Hic oblata et calix cum corporali coopitur, quod sindonem mundam significat, in quam Joseph corpus Christi involvebat. Calix hic, sepulcrum; patena, lapidem designat, qui sepulchrum clauserat.

(As the Priest, said, 'For ever and for ever,' a deacon came, and, uplifting the chalice, laid it down upon the altar, covering it with a *corporal*, as Joseph of Arimathea did, when he took down the body of Christ, covering Him with a shroud, and placed the body in his own tomb, and closed it with a stone ... Here the offering and the chalice, with its corporal, signify the shroud in which Joseph wrapped the body of Christ, while the chalice signifies the tomb, and the paten the stone which covered the tomb.) (trans. John Matthews).

The connection with Honorius is interesting since there is a link between this popular theologian and southern Britain, with which Robert may also have had connections. It is possible that he encountered Honorius' writings while on a journey to Britain, perhaps at the behest of his master, but it is unlikely that we can ever know this for certain. The fact that Honorius talks of the 'rite of Joseph of Arimathea' is certainly suggestive, though no other trace of such a rite exists.

Apart from these sources Robert almost certainly drew upon the *Gesta Pilate* and the *Evangelium Nicodemi*[14] as well as, to a lesser extent, such apocryphal works as *Vindicta Salvatoris* and *Curia Sanitatis Tiberii*.[15] In each of these we find details of the part played by Joseph of Arimathea in the events of the Crucifixion, Deposition, and Resurrection, very much as relayed by Robert—though they do not, of course, refer to the Grail or to Joseph's guardianship of it.

The *Acts of Pilate* tells the following story.

After the Crucifixion 'a certain man named Joseph, being a counsellor, of the city of Arimathea, who also himself looked for the Kingdom of God, this man went to Pilate and begged the body of Jesus. And he took it down and wrapped it in a linen cloth and laid it in a hewn sepulchre wherein was never man yet laid.'[16]

The Jews were so angered by these actions that they seized Joseph and imprisoned him in a house with no window and placed guards on the door. But when they returned two days later thay found Joseph gone, and he was later discovered to be safely returned to his home, though the doors remained closed and sealed in the house where he had been imprisoned. Joseph is therefore summoned by the elders and an explanation demanded. He tells how:

> As at midnight I stood and preyed the house wherein ye had shut me up was taken up by the four corners, and I saw as it were a flashing of light in mine eyes, and being filled with fear I fell to the earth. And one took me by the hand and removed me from the place whereon I had fallen; and moisture of water was shed on me from my head unto my feet, and an odour of ointment came about my nostrils. And he wiped my face and kissed me and said unto me: Fear not, Joseph: open thine eyes and see who it is that speeketh with thee. (Ibid.)

The speaker is Christ, who takes Joseph out of the house where he was imprisoned to his own home and then departs. There is no mention here of the 'secrets of the Grail', which we must ascribe to Robert's own hand in lieu of any other source. Other details, Vespasian's miraculous cure and his releasing of Joseph from the tower years rather than days after his imprisonment, derive from the *Vindicta Sanitatis* and the *Curia Sanitatis Tiberii*, already mentioned above.

Celtic Tales

Other influences, however, are to be detected within the matter of Robert's tale, which derive from a very different source. It has long been recognized that a considerable amount of material relating to the Grail derives from Celtic myth—in particular the various stories relating to Cauldrons of Rebirth, which are recognizable prototypes for the later Christian Grail. Caitlín Matthews has already dealt with this material in some detail, and we need only touch here upon one text and one character—*Branwen Ferch Llyr* from the collection of early tales known as *The Mabinogion*,[17] and the figure of Bran the Blessed, the semi-divine king of Britain and the guardian of the sacred land after his death.

Bran has long been recognized as a prototype of the suffering Grail king who appears first in Chrétien and thereafter in most of the texts which follow.[19] Like the Wounded King, Bran suffers from an unhealing wound, remains in suspended life for a number of years, and entertains a company of followers with his bounty. He is also the possessor of a magical cauldron which gives back life to dead warriors placed within it. Add to this the fact that one of the key figures in Robert's poem is called Brons (sometimes Hebron), suggesting a conflation of two figures, the Celtic Bran and one of the guardians of the Ark of the Covenant named Hebron, son of Kolath, in the Biblical Book of Numbers, and we have a fairly conclusive case for the Celtic influence.

If, as has been suggested by several commentators,[19] Robert either wrote or was directly influential in the composition of the prose *Didot Perceval*, this would further support the idea of extensive borrowing from Celtic sources. The *Didot* contains more Celtic themes than any of the texts normally associated with Robert, as a brief summary will show.

The Holy Spirit informs Alain that he must take his son Perceval to the court of King Arthur, and that after winning great honour he will go to Ireland, where he will visit the court of his grandfather, Brons, and cure him of a painful wound. But Alain dies before he can take the youth to court and when Perceval arrives alone he does indeed win honour in the tournament, but then foolishly sits in the Perilous Seat the Siège Perilous, which cracks beneath him and gives forth a great roar and a cloud of black smoke. A great voice announces that because of Perceval's temerity his grandfather will not be cured, nor will the stone seat be joined together again, nor will the 'enchantments' be lifted from Britain—until a knight comes who will ask what the Grail is and whom it serves.

Swearing never to remain more than one night anywhere until he has found the court of the Rich Fisher, Perceval sets out and has a number of adventures, including the overcoming of a proud lady in the Chess-board Castle where a magical set of pieces plays against him, the pursuit and capture of a white stag, a combat at a ford with Urbain (Owain) who is guarded by a flock of black birds who are really women in enchanted form, a vision of two children in a tree, an encounter with a shadowy figure of Merlin, who prophesies his destiny to arrive at the Castle of the Rich Fisher and achieve the quest.

Arriving at last at his destination Perceval sees the king fishing from the boat, watches the Procession of the Grail, but fails to ask the question. Outcast, he is reproached by a sorrowful damsel and then wanders for seven years until he happens on the cell of his hermit uncle and learns what he must do. Now he again approaches the Grail Castle, asks the Question and heals the Wounded King, who then gives the Grail into his keeping after teaching him its secrets. The Siège Perilous then reunites and Merlin announces the end of the quest and retires to have his master Blaise write all this down.

There then follows a section which is really the substance of the *Mort Artu*, following the usual direction of that story, including Arthur's success against the armies of Rome, his hasty return to Britain on learning of Mordred's treachery, the last great battle and Arthur's withdrawal to Avalon.

It will be seen that there are several points of overlap between this story and that of the *Joseph*, though it is not exactly a sequel. Episodes such as the quest for the white stag, Urban and the flock of black birds, the children in the tree, and Merlin's appearance as a shadow, and the character of Blaise and the episode of the Chess-board Castle all derive from Celtic sources.

Elements which specifically tie the *Didot* to those works definitely attributable to Robert are that of the Siège Perilous, which cracks and roars as it does in *Joseph*, and the continuing intervention and instruction received from the voice of the Holy Spirit, which in both texts acts as a kind of invisible counsellor to Joseph and his descendants.

The *Didot* itself lacks colour and characterization such as are found so abundantly in Chrétien. In an attempt to compress the quest for the Grail and the death of Arthur, along with something of the history of Merlin, into a brief space (the *Didot* is only 90 pages long in the modern edition), the author or compiler has lost much. This clumsiness of presentation has also been seen as a possible link with Robert's work, which is generally characterized by its poor quality of language, its often muddled thinking and careless construction. However, as Richard O'Gorman has shown, a comparison of the prose redaction, made only a short time after Robert had completed his work, indicates that the manuscript containing *Joseph*, the beginning of the *Merlin*, and a version of the *Didot Perceval* is itself corrupt, and that the prose redactor had access to a better copy which contained few if any of the clumsy transitions and constructions found in the existing manuscript.

Many of the contradictions found within the *Joseph* are in fact easily explained either by reference to the Prose version or by a careful reading of the original. We have seen already that the apparent discrepancy between the two statements regarding Robert's sources does not really exist. The same goes for the matter of Brons' son Alain, who in one part of the manuscript is described as electing to remain celibate—as in fact stating that he would as soon be flayed alive than marry—while later he sires a son, is easily explained by consideration of the text. There we find that of Brons' 15 children only Alain refuses to marry, and that this sets him apart in such a way that Joseph recognizes him as his father's successor. He is then given into the keeping of Joseph, who undertakes to train him in the ways of the Grail and eventually, when the time is right, to impart the 'Secrets of the Saviour' to him. Once he is in possession of these facts, and has furthermore become the Grail's new guardian, what more natural than that he should father a son to succeed him, *now that the time is right?*

New Architecture

All of this brings us to consider the way in which Robert used his sources. We have seen that he drew upon Christian apocryphal texts, as well as oral tales then circulating in Europe. Apart from these obvious materials there are subtler influences. He is clearly influenced by Chrétien, in that he brings the Grail to Britain, and makes it a provider of sustenance—though in Robert it contains the Holy Blood of the Saviour while Chrétien's Grail is said to hold a wafer and possibly a fish. Both poets refer to the Rich Fisherman, though in Chrétien the reason for the name is that the Wounded King fishes for amusement because he is too infirm to do more, while in Robert's text he acquires the title when he emulates Christ in feeding the Company of the Grail with a single fish. On the other hand Robert does not mention the Lance, which has a central place in Chrétien's narrative.

These points of similarity and variance may simply arise from the different source material available to the two authors. Robert seems to have spent much of his time searching actively for new material. It is clear that he meant to return to the stories of

Petrus, Brons and Moyses 'if he could find them written in a book', an indication that he was not inventing the material at all but following a trail of his own devising after the elusive Grail, thus making him, satisfyingly, a Grail quester himself!

The change in the narrative between the section dealing with the history of the Crucifixion and its aftermath and the latter portion which deals with the adventures of the Grail Family may well mark a point of departure in Robert's work. It is almost as though having reached a certain point, and having heard perhaps of Chrétien's success, Robert strove to unite the two themes by the invention, or elaboration, of additional themes.[20]

One such theme in particular seems to have been Robert's own invention. If so, it was a happy one, which united the earlier and later material in a way which offered much food for elaboration. I refer to the three tables, the first of which is the one at which Christ celebrates the first eucharist, the second constructed at the behest of Joseph of Arimathea *in likeness of the first*, and the third, made at Merlin's command by Uther Pendragon and later conferred upon Arthur as the Round Table of romance, in imitation of the two earlier tables.

By establishing these three physical links between the cosmic events of the Crucifixion and the mythic world of Arthurian Britain, Robert also established a connection which allowed for the Arthurian Grail Quest to develop as it did. It is even possible that it would never have manifested there had not Robert de Boron made this connection. For in so doing he soldered for ever the Matter of Britain with Christian legendry, and enabled the Celtic myths to enter the world of the Grail.

An example of the way in which these intricate matters are worked into the texture of the story is the statement which refers to the meaning of the Blessed Trinity being fulfilled by the three who will hold the Grail—Brons, Alain and Perceval, who must therefore represent the Father, the Son and the Holy Spirit. The third and final emanation of the Godhead is therefore Perceval, who contains the essence of the two earlier guardians. Earlier, three of Joseph's original company go forth from the rest: Petrus to Avaron (Avalon), Alain to the far West (Ireland in the *Didot Perceval*) and Brons also to the West, perhaps somewhere in the south-west of Britain, maybe Cornwall with its strong traditions of Joseph and his family.

Looking again at the sources of Robert's work, and his place in the development of Grail literature, we see just how central is his place in the formation of the literary heritage.

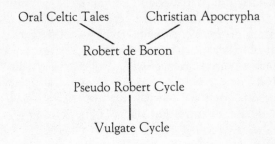

Thus from Robert's work came the so-called Pseudo Robert Cycle,[21] which in turn gave rise to what must rank as the greatest and most evolved of all Arthuriads, the Vulgate Cycle.[22]

From this flowed many other important works of the mythus, including Malory's great interpretation (so called rather than a translation because of its individuality) *Le Morte d'Arthur* (see Greg Stafford's essay). Robert de Boron's version of the Grail text makes him a most valuable and important member of the Household of the Grail; one who expanded the already existing and emerging material in a way that made it wholly new and individual. He it was who stamped it for ever with the seal of Christianity, who shaped its potential for all times, and who provided matter on which many further versions could be based.

Notes and References

1 W.A. Nitze, ed., *Le Roman de l'Estoire dou Graal* (Paris: Champion, 1927). All quotations from this text unless otherwise stated.

2 Chrétien de Troyes, *Arthurian Romances*, trans. D.D.R. Owen (London: Dent, 1987).

3 Trans. Margaret Schlauch in *Medieval Narrative* (New York: Gordian Press, 1969).

4 R. O'Gorman, 'The Prose versions of Robert de Boron's *Joseph d'Arimathie*', *Romance Philology*, 23 (1970), pp. 449-61.

5 Ibid. See also: W.A. Nietz 'Messire Robert de Boron: Enquiry and Summary', *Speculum*, 28 (1953), pp. 279-96.

6 Included in W.A. Nitze (ed), *Le Roman de l'Estoire dou Graal*.

7 O'Gorman.

8 Dell Skeels, *The Romance of Perceval in Prose* (Seattle and London: Univ. of Washington Press, 1966).

9 Charles Williams, *Arthurian Torso*, edited by C.S. Lewis (Oxford Univ. Press, 1948).

10 O'Gorman.

11 Ibid.

12 Helen Adolf, *Visio Pacis: Holy City & Grail* (Pennsylvania State Univ. Press, 1960).

13 Ibid.

14 M.R. James, (ed), *The Apocryphal New Testament* (Oxford Univ. Press, 1924).

15 O'Gorman.

16 M.R. James.

17 *The Mabinogion*, trans. Jeffrey Gantz (Harmondsworth: Penguin, 1976).

18 Helaine Newstead, *Bran the Blessed in Arthurian Romance* (New York: Columbia Univ. Press, 1939).

19 Pierre le Gentil 'The Work of Robert De Boron and the Didot Perceval', in *Arthurian Literature in the Middle Ages*, edited by R.S. Loomis (Oxford Univ. Press, 1959).
    W.A. Nitze, *Speculum* (1953).
    R.S. Loomis, *The Grail: from Celtic Myth to Christian Symbol* (New York: Columbia Univ. Press, 1963).

20 Linda M. Gowans, 'New Perspectives on the Didot Perceval', in *Arthurian Literature VII* (Cambridge: D.S. Brewer, 1987).

21 Fanni Bogdanow, *The Romance of the Grail* (Manchester Univ. Press, 1966).

22 H.O. Sommer, *The Vulgate Version of the Arthurian Romances*, 7 vols. Washington: The Carnegie Institution, 1909-1916.

4

SIR THOMAS MALORY

by
Greg Stafford

Sir Thomas Malory (whichever contender one chooses) lived in an age when Chivalry was almost over. The institution of knighthood would continue for many years; tournaments would be fought on the green meadows of England and France—but Chivalry itself, what Thomas Malory called the 'High Order', could not survive the changing social and moral attitudes of the medieval world. Malory, therefore, entered into a world where nostalgia for the past already existed. His great book, perhaps the greatest single book on the Arthurian legends yet written, is a threnody for those lost times.

His version of the Grail myth, scaled down from the earlier, theologically weighted-down Vulgate Cycle, has a power and clarity rare in medieval authors. As Greg Stafford notes, Malory was not much interested in spiritual matters, but his vision was all-embracing; he had room for the Grail as well as for Arthur, Guinevere and Lancelot.

Greg's highly personal essay constitutes a love story as much as an examination of myth-making. He loves Malory's work and brings a remarkable sense of vision to play upon him. He shows very clearly why Sir Thomas is in the forefront of the Household of the Grail. He forms a living bridge between the originators and the continuators, shaping the earlier materials in a fashion that made them acceptable to both the audiences of Malory's time and those who came long after.

Sir Thomas Malory stands along the long literary trail of the Holy Grail like one of the mysterious guides a questing knight is likely to meet on a lonely road in the midst of a dark forest. He is really the first of the modern Companions of the Grail. He appears, at first, to be only a simple knight who can tell a great story. On closer inspection we seem to find a great gap between the story of the High Order of Chivalry and the man who did such a job of telling it.

Knights were my special way into the story. Back in the days of Dick, Jane and Spot literature, I traded all my indians and cavalry for other kids' knights, and assembled the neighbour-hood's *hugest* knight army. Why I had this pre-literate fascination cannot be answered: it is a mystery. What I can tell you is that it led me to the realm of personal mythology. I think that anyone who has read this far would benefit from making a personal mythology.

To make a myth of your own it is sometimes useful to be irrational first. I suggest, for this essay, that you pretend you have a special perception which most people don't have: arthuring. It is a new use of your sixth sense, beyond seeing, smelling, tasting, touching, and hearing. Arthuring allows you to perceive some things which other people cannot fathom, because they don't have the sense. It also allows you to see some things in a new way.

When I was a kid I read Malory. I was in 5th grade, about 12 years old. Or, to be honest, I tried to read Malory. The language, lack of paragraphing, and sentence structure were too alien for me to understand fully. But in my perusal I was fascinated to discover a whole bunch of stories other than those in Bullfinch, and determined to figure it out somehow.

Like all the senses, your arthuring has to be practiced, used, and trained to get better. When you were an infant your eyes showed only light and dark, and blurry images, like my sense of knights. Then it became real perceptive sight, like my sense of arthur. Later it may become a full-blown case of mythification.

One of the first things your arthuring sense tells you is that there are several basic story themes. You might call them the King Story, Knightly Adventure Story, Love Story, Grail Story, and so on. With further arthuring you will eventually learn that there are the Merlin, Tristram, Arthur, Lancelot, and Grail cycles which contributed to the mythos, and that the Love Story might be, in your arthuring, the True Love of Lancelot and Guinevere and the Illicit Love of Tristram and Iseult.

Sir Thomas knew how to arthurize. He had to in order to rework his source material into his *Works*. In fact, he was a genius at it, and recorded a sense of King Arthur which speaks of us, modern people over 500 years later.

This version is important to us. From it come almost all the images and stories in modern Arthurian understanding. You must leave the mainstream to find a version other than a Malory-derived version. Tennyson's poems were inspired by Malory's text. T.H. White's *Once and Future King*, the single most useful book for introducing people to the legend uses Malory as its starting place. The musical and movie *Camelot* and the movie *Excalibur* both derive from Malory's work.

Malory's work has acted as a bridge between the Middle Ages and the modern age. His works do not depict the medieval attitudes which are found in the literature that he worked from, but instead provide us with a view which we can understand today. Our task, as myth makers, is to integrate the story and adapt it to our needs and understanding.

Part of the process of arthurizing is to let the story tell us what it has to say rather than just reading into it. This is an openly subjective input. It is a simple fact that certain parts of the story make us *feel* funny, or maybe just uncomfortable. Arthurization involves remembering those feelings, and in various ways getting into communication with them. Communication means receiving and giving information, and since most people are unfamiliar with communicating with ideas it is very hard at first. In fact, it is impossible to understand some of the processes, even after it is experienced several times.

I will arthurize first the story of the Holy Grail, and then the legend of Sir Thomas himself, our erstwhile Companion of the Grail. I cannot guarantee that you will understand this stuff. Especially my personal story, which this inevitably is.

But I think that anyone who has now come *this* far has at least a rudimentary sense of arthuring, and can use it to look at my version of the story. Remember how the knights come upon an obstacle and, if they fail, return home and relate it so that someone else can try to go farther. Those who follow up usually take a trail which is similar, but not the same. If you can arthurize my path, find the truth and falsehood and the personal from the universal, maybe you will go a step further than I went, or take a better path.

The Works

We need to look at least briefly at the rest of the works which Sir Thomas penned to gain some perspective on his interpretation of the Grail Quest, which was only one of eight books which he wrote. Although he had to constrain himself to remain within some limit of the stories, Sir Thomas was a vigorous re-interpreter, not an author who supported outdated sentiments.

We will concentrate upon what appears in print, and we will also look at the new material which Sir Thomas added to his sources. These will give us a clear idea of the points which he wished to emphasize. The changes occur mainly in his view of the Good King, the High Order of Knighthood, his views of Love, and his retelling of the Grail quest.

The eight books of Malory's *Works* are:

1 *The Tale of King Arthur*
2 *The Noble Tale of King Arthur and Emperor Lucius*
3 *The Noble Tale of Sir Launcelot du Lake*
4 *The Tale of Sir Gareth*
5 *The Book of Sir Tristram de Lyones*
6 *The Tale of the Sankgreal*
7 *The Book of Sir Launcelot and Queen Guinevere*
8 *The Most Piteous Tale of the Morte Arthur*

The first two books center upon King Arthur. They emphasize the role of the Good King and the benefits to be gained thereby. Tom rewrote his sources to make King Arthur's campaign against the Romans similar to the conquests of King Henry V, a near-legendary warlord who was the last strong king of England and who died when Tom was a young child.

These books introduce the great knights of the later stories: Launcelot, Gawain, Kay, and the rest, but is primarily about the Good King. Arthur is shown to be the fount of authority and leadership. He is not without fault, and he is not a great paragon of kindness. He is, when need be, ruthless and cruel to his enemies. yet he is also the origin of all the traditions which make men good. Arthur is a heroic warrior himself, and his personal activities inspire his knights to good acts and great deeds.

One of the striking features which appears in several of the tales which Malory chose to tell has to do with forgiveness. Most of the great heroes of the legend commit at least one grave error, yet mend their ways and rise to greater heights. King Arthur grievously committed the sin of Herod and destroyed the innocents born on 1 May, hoping thereby to destroy Mordred. Yet Arthur went on to become the ideal ruler, protector of all who were weak and helpless. Sir Gawain, on his first quest, recklessly slew a woman even though she was begging for mercy, yet he went on to become the great defender of all women. Sir Launcelot committed the greatest error of all by breaking trust with King Arthur and committing adultery with the Queen, yet in the end Launcelot found sainthood—he even rose immediately to heaven upon his death.

The next three books elucidate the tales of famous knights, recounting a series of adventures which illustrate the virtues of High Order of Knighthood. They center on Sir Launcelot, Sir Gareth and Sir Tristram. The basic format for adventure is for the knights to go out into the world to encounter whatever adventure they meet. Most affairs are fights against robber barons, outlaws, long-standing family foes, and occasional monsters. Personal virtue as well as martial prowess carry the day. If lovers, they dedicate their work to their lady.

These form the central set of examples for Sir Thomas' highest ideal: the High Order of Chivalry. This practice can change the ordinary knight into a gentleman, and more importantly, make its practitioners 'the sternest knights to their foes'. This is a practical guide to knighthood. Good breeding, gentleness, and loyalty contribute to the knight's battle prowess.

One of the things Malory did was to ground the lofty ideals of earlier works. Chivalry is not an abstract moral code, but a set of practical practices. Sir Thomas expresses an earnestness of belief in knighthood as a fellowship controlled by the heroic example of a strong king. He expresses no apologies or shame in the brutality of the task.

Tom's rewrite changed the emphasis of love in the story too. It was no longer the *fine amor* portrayed in the Vulgate Cycle. *Fine amor* was the formalized passion which indentured a lover to his lady, and ennobled the suffering as part of the process. The situation always struck me as a terrible form of love. It is too much like the dependency relationship, rather than love, which so many of us have discovered ourselves to be trapped in. Tom altered the understanding of what love was so that a knight is ennobled not by suffering, but by constancy. Constancy will provide stability to his life. In any altercation or misfortune, true love can help the lover through.

Sir Launcelot was already the knight in Malory's sources. In his version sympathy is increased for the knight. Through selected editing Tom shows us the type of love that is the highest form of existence. He added some significant passages. My favorite is the one where he compares love to the seasons (Caxton's XX, 1). Love is not some sort of rarified bliss but is a thing of this world. Elsewhere he praises the constant love which is not like love in his day which 'blows now hot, now cold'.

The next book is the one which concerns us here: *The Tale of the Sankgreal*. Details on it are given below.

The last two books depict the downfall of the Arthurian realm. They are grievously pessimistic, and both cold and cynical in their interplay of politics and personality. They portray the failure of great ideals when personal goals are at stake.

Tom rewrote an older French text called the Vulgate Cycle. We need to rewrite his story for ourselves. We can discover the potential range of our deviation from his text by comparing some of the changes which Tom wrought in his original.

Myths hold something which is universal, but they are also inevitably products of their time. They are mirrors for the ideals of the age in which they were created, and are always skewed by the author's point of view. Myth is liquid, contrasted with dogma, which is solid, inflexible, and immobile; it can be reshaped without changing its essence.

Thus we would expect Tom to make some changes to a story written 250 years earlier when Europe was undergoing a great social and cultural renaissance in affairs of church, state, art, and culture. The author of the Vulgate Cycle was a cleric and highly placed courtier for King Henry II, founder of the Plantagenet dynasty. Likewise, we must expect to make some changes to the story for ourselves as well.

The Vulgate Cycle was written in a style called *entrelacement*, or 'interlacing'. In this method a story, say about Sir Launcelot, is begun, but abruptly stopped before its conclusion. Then the plot with Sir Gawain starts and is similarly stopped, and then the Perceval story is begun. Then we return to the Launcelot story for a while, the plot around Sir Bors is started and stopped, Gawain and Launcelot join together for a while, Launcelot goes again and spins off a tale about Sir Lionel, Perceval goes on a bit,

Gawain and Lionel go on for a while together, Launcelot and Galahad go on, then Gawain, then Perceval, then maybe Bors and Lionel, and so on and so on, creating many threads of stories, characters, and settings which weave back and forth to create the vast tapestry of Arthurian adventure.

Such a style was admirably suited for the audiences of the time. The books were made to be read aloud to the largely uneducated members of a court who had long winter hours to be entertained. It is easy for us to hear the wind howling outside a dark, drafty castle, and then to imagine the half-drunk knights listening intently as Sir Gawain goes about the countryside bashing heads and seducing maidens; then turning to joke as the giggling young girls sit up when their favorite Sir Launcelot enters the scene for a while; and then the idealistic younger sons paying close attention when Perceval comes into the picture. All the Round Table knights get some story time, and the story goes on and on over the long winter nights.

Thomas made a modern version of the story. He changed the method of story-telling from the French interlacing by unthreading several of the major, more interesting plot lines and stringing them into narratives. This type of lineal thinking, a natural outgrowth of Western thought, was already rooted in his age. Tom lived at the start of the age of print—his publisher was the first printer to use Gutenberg's invention of movable type in England. The way that he thought: along single story lines rather than tapestried weave, was very modern. The mass-produced books were also very modern. So were the ways that he thought about chivalry, love, the Good King, and the Holy Grail.

The stories preceding the Grail tales establish the boundaries of Arthurian civilization and culture. They provided a realm of ideals which were rarely practiced by the knights of the fifteenth century. Yet they were ideals, and recognized as being superior to plain brutality and bloodshed.

From this background we can peer closer at details of Sir Thomas's Grail Quest.

THE TALE OF THE SANKREAL

The title originally continued ... BRIEFLY DRAWN OUT OF FRENCH, WHICH IS A TRUE TALE CHRONICLED FOR ONE OF THE TRUEST AND ONE OF THE

HOLIEST THAT IS IN THIS WORLD.

Miracles begin the Grail adventure. Prophecies abound: Launcelot is decried as no longer the best of knights; an unknown name appears on the Siège Perilous, one of the Round Table chairs which has destroyed every knight who sat on it. A sword, stuck through a stone and floating on water, appears and cannot be pulled from its place. At the feast a handsome young knight appears, dressed in red clothes and armor, but without sword or shield. The Grail itself makes an appearance, giving each person the food which they most desire. The entire body of knighthood swears to search for the Holy Grail.

The knights depart together, leaving behind an unhappy king and queen. Eventually the knights separate and, though their trails cross and recross, each knight maintains an essentially solitary quest to find the Grail.

During this story everything which has been formerly held dear by the knights of the Round Table is cast down. Moral behaviour in the world of the Grail quest is reversed so that chivalrous acts of honor and martial vigor, the very stuff of the High Order, are condemned. Only spiritual virtues such as humility and chastity open the doors to the Big Adventure. The Grail quest is an anti-romance because of the way it inverts ideals of love, and exalts chastity as the highest of all ideals.

The tales illustrate how different types of knight relate to the spiritual quest. Three knights succeed, and other Round Table favorites illustrate the consequences of leading an ordinary, non-spiritual life.

Most of the questing knights are practical and worldly, and fall prey to their own vices. They practice the gentle ways of court and the violent ways of knighthood, but fail in the realm of the sacred. They naturally bring great harm to their fellows.

Sir Gawain is foremost among these knights. He was the first to swear to seek the Grail, but he is also among the most unfit to compete. Gawain is recognized as being courteous, chivalrous, friendly, and generous, but so imbedded in the mundane world that he cannot recognize the spiritual nature of his quest. Even when he gets explanations, Gawain makes excuses why spirituality will not work for him. Unable to discover any spectacular adventures he returns to Camelot, but only after accidentally killing several other questers, and inadvertently violating the Round Table oath against fighting other members of the fellowship.

Launcelot follows a path different from Gawain. The former Greatest Knight in the World is shown to have considerable moral fortitude, but his sinful liaison with Guinevere prevents him from participating directly in the Grail Mass. The love which was a noble philosophy and practice before is instead a weight which cannot be borne to the presence of the Grail.

All is not lost, and the Malorian attention to forgiveness comes again to the fore. Launcelot is dragged through the marsh of guilt and desire finally to renounce his worldly ways. His path is that of redemption through penance. No humiliation is too great for Launcelot to endure. Subsequently he is allowed to view a Mass of the Grail. Unfortunately, the old man presiding holds aloft the Grail and falters. Launcelot rushes to help him, crosses a line which he was told not to cross, and—pow!—he's out of the Grail quest.

Sir Bors was the least pure of the three successful questers, having once been tricked into a woman's lustful embrace. Bors is a knowledgeable knight whose intellect is continually challenged with moral dilemmas. For instance, on the quest he was once confronted with a choice: should he rescue his blood brother, Lionel, or a fair maiden who was being kidnapped. He chose the latter, and was tricked into thinking his brother was subsequently killed. Shortly after he found his brother alive, but Lionel fell into a fratricidal frenzy because he was so enraged at the decision, and Bors was saved only by the intervention of God.

Percival, who had been the lone hero of all tales preceding the Vulgate Cycle, maintains the simplicity which he exhibited in earlier tales. In fact, it is exaggerated to the point that Percival is stupid. He cannot recognize a miracle when he experiences one, and he shows he cannot even recognize evil when it manifests as the sexually alluring temptress. Percival succeeds through absolute total abandonment to his faith, a virtue which prompts his intuition enough to be saved by apparent accidents.

Sir Galahad is the third successful Grail quester. It is his appearance, in red armor without sword or shield, which initiates the Grail quest. As grandson of the Fisher King he is the fulfiller of many prophecies, and the ways of adventure open before him. He is more than saintly, being Christ-like in his perfection. Like Christ, Galahad is not entirely devoid of humanity. He reveals some of his human traits during meetings with his father and other knights, and over the grievous concern he shows when he kills his first enemies.

However, the allegory is so pertinent that it is impossible to ignore. Intentionally, of course, by the design of the author. In many cases the allegory intensifies the meaning of the story, and makes it more enjoyable. Sir Launcelot, for instance, mirrors the role of Adam as the Perfect Man who has been led astray by that greatest of sins, unchastity. Galahad, the son of Launcelot, is the Second Adam who has come to redeem humanity.

The Vulgate author added many other parts to the Grail story. To the thirteenth-century audience, the Grail quest was entertainment, but also a guide to spiritual life for the members of court. In case the audience might misunderstand a point the author had monks regularly appear to explain what is going on. These wise men are invariably clothed in white robes, the habit of a Cistercian monk.

The Cistercian brotherhood was active at the time and had not yet been polluted by worldly ways to stint on their vows of poverty, obedience, and chastity. These monks reveal the secret wisdom of the Grail quest in explicit terms where each lists the hierarchy of virtues. The path to spirituality is said to be through the practice of virginity, humility, patience, justice, and charity. These are the same as the vows taken by monks.

We ought not to be surprised to discover that these monkish vows are exalted in the tales. As we said, it was written by a monk. Those knights whose efforts proved their purity achieved the impossible because they were like knights and like monks. The Vulgate Cycle was written during the time of the great monkish orders of knighthood, the Templars and Hospitalers, which provided a model.

The monks also explain the secrets of the Holy Grail. These are revealed to be curiously in line with the dogma then being proselytized by the Cistercians. The quest illustrates that the Holy Grail is Divine Grace, a force which is necessary to allow us inherently evil human beings to find God. Divine Grace can be gained through the sacrament of the Eucharist, or Holy Communion, whose miraculous complexity is shown in the tale.

One of Tom's major changes, for the better, was significantly to shorten almost all of the explanations made by Cistercian hermits who are found after every mysterious event in the

Vulgate Cycle. Thus we are not subjected to their pedestrian explanations. This has the wonderful effect of returning some of the ambiguity and mystery to the tale for us.

The quest draws towards its close. Sir Galahad, the most rarified and perfect of the questers, gets a close encounter of the First Kind and goes right to heaven, taking the Grail with him and away from us sinners. Percival fades out, rather anticlimactically, a year later. Sir Bors finally returns to Camelot, tells the tale, and hands out some final artifacts.

Sir Thomas, preparing the way for us today, questioned whether the effort was worth it. The monumental and inhuman effort required by the successful Grail questers result in nothing of value for the world, and any personal gains are totally selfish. The healing of the Fisher King and the realm are significantly downplayed. Sir Galahad, as if too ephemeral and fragile, departs the world in some sort of Dantesque beatitude. Percival just wimps out. Only Bors returns.

This last is significant: only Bors returns. Joseph Campbell has pointed out how the critical segment of the Heroic Journey is the Return phase when the quester goes back home with whatever boon he has uncovered to share it with his people. Without a Return the quest is unfinished. Bors, who is the least holy of the questers to the monks in the earlier Vulgate version, becomes, for us, the most significant success among the knights who participated in the Grail quest.

Malory's Grail quest also alters the part of Sir Launcelot, especially in his reaction to the whole affair. Launcelot is returned to his station as the Greatest Knight of the World after Galahad fails to return from his holy encounters. And Launcelot is content with the limited success which he achieved. Launcelot is not fooled by visions of immaterial realms, but finds satisfaction in his good deeds, constant love, and fulfillment in the ideals of his High Order. Launcelot may not fulfill the Best Ideals (as determined by a church whose hypocritical corruption was monumental), but he was content with Good.

Malory reorganized the hierarchy of knighthood from that in the earlier version. The Vulgate Cycle had honored the monklike spiritual knight first, then the chivalrous one, and finally the lover. Sir Thomas, a man of this world, not a dreamer in another, saw the lover as highest, the chivalric as central, and the spiritual knight as the least important.

In short, Thomas preferred life, in this world, over religious excess. He preferred the constancy of love, even with all its dangers, over the abstract and unreal Grail. He did not shun or fear the emotional and physical passions which terrorized the prissy clerical author of the Vulgate Grail Cycle. He did not degrade life, or the desire for life.

The Author

All that is certainly known about the author of *Le Morte d'Arthur* is taken from his own works: that he was a poor knight prisoner when he wrote the books, and that he finished in the ninth year of the reign of King Edward IV (1470).

Human curiosity is insatiable, and scholars have been driven to discover more about this genius. Using existing records from the Middle Ages, they have turned up four possible candidates. The most likely are: a Welsh knight; a knight from Huntingdonshire, of Papworth St Agnes; a knight from Yorkshire; and, a mercenary and outlaw knight from Warwickshire, holder of the manor at Newbold Revel.

Maybe none of these are correct. It is quite possible that the Sir Thomas Malory who wrote the manuscript has escaped the paper records which have survived the 500 years since they were compiled. It is, however, unlikely, and so we must choose one of these.

I do not find the choice difficult. Even if all other factors were equal I am drawn towards one of these candidates. Most authorities agree, on scholarly research, and I also find it emotionally satisfying, to choose the best-known candidate as our hero author.

Thus the author of *Le Morte d'Arthur* is Sir Thomas Malory of Newbold Revel. More is known about him than any other knight of his time and place. Much of it is embarrassing at best, unspeakable at the worst.

He was born sometime around 1415 in Warwickshire, in the Midlands of England. The year 1415 was when the English archers achieved their third great victory over the French knights, slaughtering them at the Battle of Agincourt. Henry V, the hero-king descendant of Henry II, began the penultimate phase of the Hundred Years War with the reconquest of France. Although this was a monumental English victory it was another great nail in the coffin of chivalry, for the knights did not take the day with their glorious mounted charge. Instead they dismounted, and peasants armed with bows brought victory that day.

When Thomas was a child, probably seven years or so, the heroic King Henry V died, and was succeeded by an infant son, later King Henry VI. Regents were appointed to oversee his childhood. Two major factions, called the Yorkists and Lancastrians, struggled to control the regency during Henry's childhood. Later the adult king was recognized to be mentally incompetent, and so the power struggle continued for years. Troubles simmered between the factions during the concluding years of the Hundred Years War, then later exploded into civil war. The 30-year civil war became known as the War of the Roses. However, the Hundred Years War still had a few years left to run while the factions accumulated grievances against each other.

In 1429, when young Thomas was of age to begin his squiring, Joan of Arc led her first victories in France, and the French began to reconquer their lands. Contemporaries thought something was very wrong with the world when that occurred. Not only was England being defeated, but all of knighthood took another great wound when it was a mystically-oriented woman who led the French war of liberation. She was betrayed by her countrymen and the English convicted her of witchcraft and burned her to death in 1431. But the damage had been done.

Sometime about 1434 Malory inherited his modest holding and was knighted. We do not know what his arms were. At that time the French had increased the pace of their reconquest. Young Sir Thomas went to France and fought, as was the custom, for pay and plunder. His presence did not significantly slow the French, and castle after castle fell to their cannon.

Newly-knighted Sir Thomas must have held few illusions of what he had inherited. He was an impoverished member of a privileged, but morally bankrupt, social class, raised in the time-honored tradition of killing men, but now ineffectual at it. The best weapon of the knight, the armored charge, had become more and more useless. The once-proud tradition of the fighting chivalry was gone. It had been replaced by titled men wearing terribly expensive regalia and going to luxurious tournaments which were becoming more of a pageant than a martial exercise.

The cost of the accouterments was beyond the means of most knights, including Sir Thomas. Thus the showiest part of knighthood mimicked the Arthurian glory with empty pomp, and left the majority of its members out in the cold.

The only alternative to the expensive empty pomp was for a knight to serve as a paid mercenary in a brutal war of siege and plunder. Many did. Thus France proved to be a training ground for disaffected young men, and taught them how to make war. This was useful to politicians during the following years of civil disorder.

After some service Sir Thomas returned to England and began a criminal career. Well, let us be objective here: he began an *alleged* criminal career. He was never brought to trial for the accusations, and never found guilty. So if you believe that some sort of *legal ruling* determines criminality, you can rest assured that Thomas Malory was innocent.

Maybe it is useful to be objective about the courts during this time of history, too. After all, the legal system was viewed as one of several ways to get revenge, and the medieval noblemen were nearly as litigious as twentieth-century Californians. An accusation was often made without legitimate reason. Releases were often political, so a release does not mean innocence, just that the man was released. In the same light, prosecution may or may not mean guilt of the accused crime. Perhaps the guilty party was actually guilty of disagreeing with the stronger party about mill rights, or where to herd his oxen.

If subjective morality is your guide then Sir Thomas was again innocent of anything which landed him in prison. He did nothing unusual for his time. He was only one of many knights who was busy at armed robbery, rustling, plundering abbeys, rape, multiple arrests, and multiple daring escapes from prison.

Despite these possible excuses, our man Thomas has such a solid jail record that it convinces me that he was certainly an outlaw, even in the disintegrating order of his own world. A misfit. Not a total misfit, however. He was certainly successful at what he did do, illegal though much of it was. And he wrote his *Works*.

The year 1443 was a busy one for our author. Sir Thomas was married, and his trail of legal papers began. The first writ for his arrest says he committed robbery, but nothing came of it. Two years later he was elected as one of two knights of the shire, and served in Parliament. At least his shiremen trusted him, making the writ questionable. It is precisely this sort of empty, unfulfilled accusation which brings so much question into the legal records of the time.

Malory, a knight of Warwickshire, was a Yorkist. He followed the lead of John Mowbray, Duke of Norfolk, from whom Malory held his land, and of Richard Neville, Earl of Warwick, who was a key figure among the Yorkists and came to be called 'Kingmaker'.

In the fall of 1449 the dispute heated up. Several Lancastrian noblemen were attacked. One ambush was against Humphrey Stafford, Duke of Buckingham, who was one of the richest and most influential men in England. The attack was led by Sir Thomas Malory of Newbold Revel, and included most of the male population of his small holding. Unlike some of the other attacks in England this one failed to kill its victim. Shortly afterwards a writ was issued for Sir Thomas's arrest.

For almost two years Sir Thomas remained free, and went upon a monumental criminal spree. Most of his activity was directed against his neighbors. Offenses include robbery and extortion.

At this time our author also committed the crime most heinous in our eyes: breaking into a house to rob, and then raping Miss Joan Smyth there. He did this not just once, but is charged with committing the same crime eight weeks later. It is possible that this rape is only the old sense of the word, meaning she was carried off with some force or violence. Analysis of the precise terms, however, makes it clear that here rape meant just what it means today, and included sexual intercourse.

More writs were issued for his arrest, but he still eluded capture. He committed more violent offenses: cattle and sheep rustling, entering and plundering a manor, and finally plundering the nearby Axholme Abbey, the first but not last of these institutions to feel his wrath.

Plundering possessions of the Church proved his undoing and another writ for his arrest was issued, this one sponsored by the Archbishop of Canterbury himself. Sir Thomas learned of its issuance, and before it could be enforced he and his men went on a rampage to exact revenge in advance. They broke into a game and hunting park owned partly by the Archbishop and destroyed much of it, even carrying off six does. The writ of arrest cites damage at the ridiculous value of £500! At last, however, he was captured by men of the Duke of Buckingham, and imprisoned.

Sir Thomas was unrestrainable. He broke out two nights after being captured, swam the moat, and rejoined his band of men who were hiding nearby. Without hesitation the gang broke into another monastery, Combe Abbey, robbed the monks, and caused great destruction. Not yet content, Tom and even more men repeated the action at the same abbey the next day, taking in triple the loot of the first day.

Sometime before 1452 Sir Thomas was apprehended and sent again to prison. He was detained only a short time, either escaping or being released, but rearrested a year later. This time severe penalties were placed on the warden if Thomas escaped again. The Church was making its charges against him stick.

In 1453 the Hundred Years War ended. All of France except Calais was back under French rule. The English had suffered a significant defeat, despite their much-praised archery. Their king was off his rocker. The noblemen, unchecked and divided into factions, turned upon each other in the Wars of the Roses.

In 1454 Malory was released, bailed out by other men of John Mowbray, Duke of Norfolk. This duke was Malory's own liege lord, and a leader of the Yorkists. The politicians needed the muscle of a loyal, experienced soldier.

Thomas immediately went to work, aiding first in an armed robbery and a great horse-stealing spree. After three months he was arrested again (his fourth capture), effected another violent armed escape (his second), but a few months later was caught again. And once again, a great fine was placed on the head of his jailer if Sir Thomas escaped, ensuring his continued imprisonment. This time his captor was the Marshal of England, a very powerful lord.

In 1456 Thomas presented a fake pardon to the courts, but it was recognized as bogus and he went back to jail. He then borrowed money, bribed a guard, and escaped. But he was unable to pay back the debt, and what the king's men could not do Malory's bondsman quickly did: he was captured and put into debtor's prison.

He was removed to the Tower of London, a stronger prison, probably because his Yorkist patrons had begun to move towards open warfare. Malory's imprisoners had interest in detaining Yorkist soldiers. So Sir Thomas was in the Tower of London when the Yorkists gained a great victory at the Battle of St. Albans. Despite the success of Malory's friends, he was denied a pardon and removed to Marshalsea Prison.

In 1457 Sir Thomas was temporarily released again. His two months of freedom were uneventful, or at least legal enough to leave no paper trail, and he peaceably turned himself back in.

In 1459 Sir Thomas was released yet again. As had occurred many years earlier, his sponsors were the Duke of Norfolk, his liege, and the Earl of Warwick, Richard Neville the 'Kingmaker'. The politicians once again needed a tried and true soldier.

On 10 July 1460 Thomas fought at the Battle of Northampton. The Yorkists crushed their foes and the Duke of Buckingham, whom Thomas had ambushed eleven years earlier, was killed. The victors persuaded their candidate to accept the crown, and England got its King Edward IV in 1461.

After this military service Sir Thomas went peacefully back to prison. He was among those pardoned by the new king in 1462. He, and presumably many others recently freed, was with King Edward at the sieges of Bamburgh and Alnwick that winter.

He seems to have gone straight for a while, and appears in several documents as a witness to legal proceedings. In 1466 a grandson of Sir Thomas was born, and his son died.

About this time the 'Kingmaker' had a falling out with King Edward. Warwick, so long a champion of the Yorkist cause, turned against the man he had made king. Sir Thomas, true to the High Order, remained loyal to Warwick, who had helped him, and so he became an enemy of the king. Sir Thomas, who was around 50 years old by now, stirred up enough trouble to be captured by the king and imprisoned again sometime around 1467. He was in prison in 1468 and 1470, when he was among those specifically excluded in four General Pardons issued by King Edward.

During this period he wrote the majority of his stories. In 1470, at about the age of 55, as witnessed by his own hand, 'in the ninth year of the reign of King Edward IV', Sir Thomas Malory finished his last work, *The Most Piteous Tale of the Morte Arthur Saunz Guerdon*.

On 9 October 1470, King Henry VI was temporarily restored to the throne and Sir Thomas was pardoned. He did not go far from his latest prison. His final days were full of talk of another upcoming battle, and he may have felt a final desire to join his leaders in the fight. He did not.

The last document pertaining to Sir Thomas records his death on Thursday, 14 March 1471, and his subsequent burial at the sumptuous Greyfriar's Chapel in London.

The Middle Ages were ending. A month after Malory's death also saw the defeat of Malory's powerful protector, Warwick the 'Kingmaker', in the Battle of Barnet. The Wars of the Roses continued without either our great author's presence, or that of his powerful patron.

In 1485, 14 years after the death of Sir Thomas Malory, Caxton published his *Works* as *Le Morte d'Arthur*. That same year the Battle of Bosworth Field ended the Wars of the Roses. The mighty Plantagenet line, started by King Henry II 329 years earlier, ended. The Tudor dynasty began its Renaissance history. The Modern Age began its inexorable grind towards today.

Conclusion

Malory's work is especially pertinent to us because we can easily understand its modern form and extrapolate from it. We, like Sir Thomas, must take the legend and remold it to access the great secrets which it holds for us.

The democratization process which helped to end the Middle Ages interrupted general interest in the Arthurian romances. King Arthur was too much associated with an embarrassing past when a corrupt noble class exploited the masses. The rising middle class staked out more economic and political territory in their rise to social power. The class of luxuried, spoiled noblemen disappeared into the souvenir chest of history. Eventually the process toppled even the desire for *any* king, and fathered our own democratic political institutions.

No more is there a small body of rich folks to listen to idealized tales read aloud over long winter nights. Instead there is a populous middle class whose lowest members are better off than any medieval king.

No more do we have special people who know all the stories and can interpret them to us as they wish. Instead we have individuals who have access to a hundred different stories, and who are responsible for choosing our own favorites.

No longer are we able to leave leadership to those individuals who want it. We are the best-informed, potentially most-empowered people to walk the earth.

History has granted us great gifts, like medicine and democracy, but it has also stolen from us. What it has stolen are our myths, which are the very food of our souls. Now something inside of us weeps with hunger, and the myths move like memories of old banquets which we heard about in our youth, but of which we remember no details. The process which brought us medicine and democracy has also given us nuclear destruction and personal isolation. We are caught in conflicting currents of blessing and curse.

Some things have not changed. We still like a good story. We still wonder, in dark moments of depression, at the meaning of death. We still respond to joy, love, anger, jealousy, and loyalty. The fight/flight reflex still works. These things cannot be quantified in concrete terms, but they exist, and have to be addressed some way or another.

Mythology is the language to define these things which cannot be pinned down. It is not rational, and must sometimes just be experienced to understand at all. Some myths, like those of King Arthur or the Holy Grail, excite us beyond all reasoning. These are the places to start our personal mythification.

These stories are like sketch maps for us. Their deepest truths, hidden from casual perusal, are the same for many of us. The details will always vary. However, any familiarity in strange territory is welcome, and I have found comfort in Malory's tales.

It is no wonder that we feel so strongly for Sir Thomas's story: his times were a lot like ours. An age ends: in his case the Middle Ages, and in ours, the Age of Waste. Except that we can look back on his time to see what happened, and we do not know what is going on now with us.

Society is in turmoil: for Tom the heretofore unknown middle class was being reborn, though he could not tell what it was; and for us something is going on, though we cannot yet recognize it.

Spirituality is in reassessment: shortly after Malory died the Church ran out of heretics to burn and the Inquisition Bull of Innocent VIII loosed the Spanish Inquisition, when thousands of innocent people (mostly women) were burned by fanatical and sadistic miscegenists in the name of God and Church. Shortly afterwards Henry VIII crushed the Catholic Church in England. Something is stirring among us now, and we do not know what it will become.

Violence abounds: Thomas contributed mightily to the murder and mayhem of his age, which was widespread enough without him. Random mayhem, street crime, and government policies keep violence active in everyone's life today as if it was just down the street.

Confusion reigns because we have no center, and we have not yet learned how to cope with that. Sir Thomas certainly felt the lack of a strong king to serve, yet loyally served his lesser lord until the end. His noble concept of chivalry as 'a fellowship controlled by the authority and example of a great king' (Vinaver, p. xxxiv) lacked a king. We have no king today, nor anyone who qualifies as a real leader who we can respect. We want King Arthur back, and if we cannot get him back in our mythology we open the way for a bogus king, the tyrant, to come to us in the political world.

King Arthur is said to come back to his people in time of need. Make what you will of literal truth, but he has in fact returned to his people during times of great trouble. (We will skip speculation about the prehistoric Sleeping God of Britain and talk only of this short trail of written references.) The sixth-century warlord certainly came during a time of crisis. The twelfth through thirteenth century started the post-Dark Ages renaissance. The fifteenth century, when Malory wrote, was the time of the Wars of the Roses, the start of the Renaissance and of modern times. Tennyson wrote his hopeful idealizations in the early twentieth century, like a mask over the cracking imperial edifice. And now, in books, and among individuals, it grows.

Arthur is coming back. Maybe he is here. Where? Among us, in you and me, in the same way that the rest of the King Arthur stuff is inside of us. Maybe he isn't in you, but he is in me and a whole bunch of other people! The dispersion of the royal power has made us all kings, and we must take responsibility for our own segment of the world. Find that King through arthuring!

What does my arthuring of the story of Sir Thomas Malory tell me? Well, I like the guy. I don't think he really raped Miss Smyth, not the same way *twice* (even though he has a fascinating penchant for repeating his deeds). I think Thomas loved Miss Smyth to the end of his days, and never once regretted ambushing the Duke of Buckingham to impress her, even if she did forget that constancy part of their love after he was imprisoned. 'It wasn't like that in the old days!'

And I like the fact that Thomas smashed up several monasteries. I am not inordinately violent, but I'd really like to tear down a church some time. The hypocrisy and lies of the Roman Catholic Church did my mother's little boy some serious harm back in those Dick and Jane days. I've learned not to complain since it helped make me what I am today, but the search has led me to also admit that, yes, I would like to trash a church. I don't plan to, thanks to my arthurizing. When I read about Sir Thomas's destruction I remembered when I was very young and watched St Joseph's church burn down, and how happy I felt about it, down there not far inside the attendant guilt. I'm really glad that Tom smashed them, in fact.

In fact, I *really like* the outlaw knight. Yes, he pushed things to extremes more than once. But he fulfilled his personal vows of loyalty and duty to his liege, and must have been pretty good at it since he was several times ransomed specifically to fight. ('Hey Neville, we got a fight coming up. Go bail out that guy who does in churches so well.') He was certainly not an ordinary character, and everyone has trouble realizing how this knight, who was like a rampaging Punk Biker of his time, was also the writer of the greatest work of Old English prose. That is because they have not met enough Punk Bikers, and because they just don't realize that everyone is a myth-maker today. And let us not forget to forgive.

I think Tom was a little bit crazy, like I am a little bit crazy, and like some of you are. One time I met someone, maybe it was Sir Thomas, who said it was not only all right to be a bit crazy today, but it is also *good for me*. So I will continue to be crazy a bit, but I will also take the lesson from Sir Thomas and not go quite so far out.

Finally, I find solace in the fact that many years of research have brought me to conclusions similar to Tom's. I do not find the imbalance imposed by chastity to be suitable for our age and our future. The rarified, detached spirituality of Christianity is unsuitable for our future, when we will require a balance between the physical and spiritual, as well as between all opposites.

Literary arthuring has dragged me through the Vulgate and other versions, and my personal investigation has stuck me out in the desert without food. I know what suffering is, and I know some things for my future. I know the Wasteland, and I have seen people from the Grail Castle. And I do not want to be like Galahad, or Launcelot, or Thomas for that matter. But all of them have shown me lessons on being myself, and I am better for that.

The penultimate thing that Sir Thomas asks for in his last book is to pray for his soul after he is dead. If you do that sort of thing, try to remember Sir Thomas next time.

Part Two:

THE CONTINUATORS

5

THE SCHOOL OF THE GRAIL

by

John Matthews

The real inner history of the Grail has yet to be written.[1] Yet there are those who have already contributed chapters to the continuing story, some of whom are dealt with in this book, and especially in the chapters which follow.

The Grail has had a part in the esoteric life of Britain for a long time. From the moment that Robert de Boron wrote how Christ spoke to Joseph of Arimathea 'holy words that are sweet and precious, gracious and full of pity, and rightly are they called Secrets of the Grail',[2] he assured that seekers would come who would desire to know these secrets, even to imagine they knew them when they did not.

In the Middle Ages, at the height of the Grail fever which attended the appearance of more and more texts dealing with the quest for the sacred vessel, both the Cathars and the Knights Templar were thought to possess the Grail in some form. In fact the idea of the saintly 'pure men' of the Albigensian heresy possessing any physical object is unlikely—though they certainly seem to have known of the inner mystery which the Grail expresses.[3] The Templars, according to more than one authority,[4] may have guarded for a time the Mandylion, a sacred relic which may have concealed the famous Shroud of Turin. It has been noted that the description of the folded Shroud, protected by a frame which showed only the face, is consistent with descriptions of 'the head in the dish' found in certain Grail works then circulating. Whether the Templars actually possessed any secret knowledge of the Grail is less easy to prove, since so much calumny was directed at them at the time of their fall, and actual documents are few and far between.

Modern Templar Orders exist which claim the wisdom of the Grail as part of their heritage:

> It is a fundamental belief of the Templar tradition, a belief backed by long experience, that if a seeker after truth begins to work seriously on himself, he will start to radiate light on the inner levels ... Every man and woman who is stirred by stories, legends or films of noble heroes is merely reacting to the promptings of the True Knight who sleeps within the heart ... The task of awakening the True Knight within us is not an easy one. We will need first of all to look honestly at ourselves and then take the first steps with courage and determination. The spiritual impulses of the Age of Aquarius will then certainly respond to the light of our aspiration and reveal to us that True Will which will guide us inevitably to the Grail.[5]

Modern Cathar movements have also made an appearance in recent times, and have declared themselves to be founded very firmly in Grail spirituality. In particular the Lectorium Rosicrucianum, founded by J. van Rijckenborgh and Catharose da Petri in 1952, has continued to grow and disseminate ideas. A full account of it is to be found in *The Treasure of Montségur* by Walter Birks and R.A. Gilbert.[6] A guiding light in its early days was Antonine Gadal, who later changed his name to Galaad, after the greatest of the Grail knights, and who founded a centre in the Pyrenees (also called Galaad) devoted to the restoration of Cathar ideals and (possibly) to the discovery of the Grail itself. His book *Sur le Chemin du Saint Graal*[7] makes fascinating reading and is full of insights into the inner meaning of the Grail mysteries.

One of Gadal's associates for a time was the Irish writer on esotericism named Francis Rolt-Wheeler, who later made his own contribution to Grail literature in his book *Mystic Gleams from the Holy Grail*,[8] in which he gave an account of the stories from a generally esoteric viewpoint, including some unprovable connections and links with the past which nevertheless have a ring of (inner) truth about them.

> The Legend of the Holy Grail glows ... with an inner light of esoterism (sic). Few, indeed, be those who have sought to follow the silver thread of Spiritual Initiation in this strange and

mysterious cycle of miracle, of faerie, of chivalry, and of a super-sacrament. Consequently, in this mystical legend, there is a glimpse of the unknown; the reader may lose his way in a thicket of visions ... This Way will lead us into the astral world and into the kingdoms of Faerie, where Merlin, the enchanter, serves as guide. Those who know how to read the Book of Nature will find the link of Celtic Initiation in these sagas, and may even hear the tread of 'the Lordly Ones'.

Despite Rolt-Wheeler's rather colourful style, there is much in his book which reinforces the fascination with the inner mysteries of the Grail among modern esotericists.

Another source of inspiration was the Rosicrucian movement, beginning in the seventeenth century from roots in the Renaissance. More than one writer has seen the Rosicrucians as the inheritors and propounders of the Grail material. In particular Manley Palmer Hall, who founded the Philosophical Research Society in the United States in 1936, linked the mysterious group with the Grail, stating that 'it is evident that the story of ... the symbolic genealogy of the Grail Kings relate to the descent of Schools or Orders of initiates. Titurel [the Grail King] represents the ancient wisdom and, like the mysterious Father C[hristian] R[ose] C[ross] is the personification of the Mystery Schools which serve the Shrine of Eternal Truth.[9]

The prestigious Hermetic Order of the Golden Dawn were working with Arthurian archetypes as long ago as 1896, and after them, several offshoots, including Dion Fortune's Society of the Inner Light (see Knight pp. 104–19), the Stella Matutina, and the Servants of the Light, have all utilized the deeply mystical elements within the story to form working magical systems.

A.E. Waite, himself one of the founding members of the Golden Dawn, first wrote of a 'Secret School of the Grail' in his 1933 volume *The Holy Grail: Its Legends and Symbolism*.[10] Here he finds the presence of a mystical body of thought, almost without form, but threading its way throughout the literature of the Grail, in some way 'a Grail behind the Grail'.

The presence of this ... Secret Church is like that of angels unawares. In the outer courts there are those who are prepared for Regeneration and in the *adyta* there are those who have attained it: these are the Holy Assembly. It is the place of those who, after the birth of flesh, which is the birth of the will of man, have come to be born of God ... it is the place of the Waters of Life, with the power to take freely. It is like the still, small voice: it is heard only in the midst of the heart's silence, and there is no written word to tell us how its Rite is celebrated; but it is like a Priesthood within the Priesthood and harmony, wherein is neither haste nor violence. There are no admissions—at least of the ceremonial kind—to the Holy Assembly: it is as if in the last resource a Candidate inducts himself. There is no Sodality, no Institution, no Order which throughout the Christian centuries has worked in silence ... it is not a revelation but an inherence ... It does not come down: more correctly it draws up; but it also inheres. It is the place of those who have become transmuted and tinging (sic) stones.

Despite Waite's words, which should be understood in a mystical rather than a literal way, other groups and individuals have continued to work along the lines which assume the existence of such a school.

The Anthroposophical Movement, founded by Rudolf Steiner as a breakaway from the Theosophists, has had the Grail at the heart of its operations from the beginning. Steiner himself wrote a considerable amount on the subject, which repays study, including this prophetic passage from his *An Outline of Occult Science*:

The 'hidden knowledge' flows, although quite unnoticed at the beginning, into the mode of thinking of the men of this period ... The 'hidden knowledge' which from this side takes hold of mankind now and will take hold of it more and more in the future, may be called symbolically 'the wisdom of the Grail' ... The modern initiatives may, therefore, also be called initiates of the Grail. [and] The way into the supersensible worlds ... leads to the 'science of the Grail'. [thus] The 'concealed knowledge of the Grail' will be revealed; as an inner force it will permeate more and more the manifestations of human life ... We see that the highest imaginable ideal of human evolution results from the 'knowledge of the Grail': the spiritualization that man acquires through his own efforts.[11]

During the 1930s and 1940s Christine Hartley and Charles Seymour worked together under the aegis of the Stella Matutina lodge of the Golden Dawn, forming a Merlin Temple and pursuing their studies of Arthurian archetypes and the Grail. A partial account of their activities is to be found in two recent books: *Dancers to the Gods*[12] by Alan Richardson and *Ancient Magics for a New Age*[13] by Richardson and Geoff Hughes. The latter also contains an account of Hughes' own more recent work in the tradition of the Merlin Temple.

More recently the Servants of the Light School of Esoteric Science have utilized specifically Arthurian and Grail materials as the foundation of their inner work.[14] Some privately issued papers give an idea of the range involved: *Grail Centres*, *Alexandria, Gnostics and the Grail* are anonymous works, while the Grail Lectures by S.F. Annett includes *The Grail Tests* and *The Gnostic Hypostases and the Grail Legend*. The former examines the initiations of Arthurian knighthood, with especial emphasis on the chivalry of the Grail, which the writer finds central to the concept of inner strength and

Self Reverence, Self Knowledge, Self Control
These three alone raise man to sovereign power.

Other esoteric groups who have continued to work with the Grail are the Aurum Solis, or Order of the Sacred Word, originally founded by Charles Kingold and George Stanton in 1897, and more recently continued by Melita Denning and Osborn Phillips, who have released some of the order's papers in the form of a series of books published under the general title of *The Magical Philosophy*.[15]

In America, the Sangreal Sodality, founded by the British occultist William G. Gray, operates a correspondence course based upon Gray's ongoing series of books. These include a study of Kabbalah, of the background to the Western Inner Tradition, and includes a series of ceremonials and sacraments loosely based on the Grail Mysteries.[16]

This is a prime example of a modern mystery school deeply founded upon the matter of the Grail. At Hawkwood College in Gloucestershire, Gareth Knight has lead a number of weekend workshops which brought into being a company very like that described by Waite above—having no constitution, sodality or initiation beyond that of simple presence and participation in the work involved. A ritual 'Catechism of the Grail', first performed in 1981, is still in regular use among those who were privileged to be present at these latter-day Arthurian Mysteries.[17]

All of this gives some idea of the richness of the tradition still in operation, not only in Britain but elsewhere in the world, which draws upon the Grail stream for its inspiration and energy.

Charles Williams, who is the subject of a later chapter in this book, himself a member of the Golden Dawn, founded the Order of the Co-inherence within an immediate circle of friends. This was something again closer to Waite's idea, and was more of a mystical brother and sisterhood than a proper magical order. Williams wrote about it at the end of his study of the Holy Spirit, in the following terms:

> The apprehension of this order, in nature and in grace, without and within Christendom, should be, now, one of our chief concerns; it might indeed be worth the foundation of an Order within the Christian Church [where ...] the pattern might be stressed, the image affirmed. The Order of the Co-inherence would exist only for that, to mediate and practise it ... the Order would have no easy labour. But, more than can be imagined, it might find that, in this present world, its labour was never more needed, its concentration never more important, its profit never perhaps more great.[18]

This is to speak of a need for the Grail to be at work in the world. That it is so seems apparent, for despite the dark times in which we live there are certain gleams of light which betray the presence of the active principle of light still at work in the world.

Notes and References

1 J. Matthews, *Elements of the Grail Tradition* (Shaftesbury: Element Books, 1990).

2 M. Schlauch *Medieval Narrative* (New York: Gordian Press, 1969).

3 J. Matthews, op. cit., 1989.

4 N. Currer-Briggs, *The Shroud and the Grail* (London: Weidenfeld, 1987).

5 G. Delaforge *The Templar Tradition in the Age of Aquarius* (Vermont: Threshold Books, 1987).

6 W. Birks & R.A. Gilbert *The Treasure of Montségur* (Wellingborough: Crucible, 1987).

7 A. Gadal, *Sur le Chemin de Saint Graal* (Harlaam: Rosenkruis-Pers, 1979).

8 F. Rolt-Wheeler, *Mystic Gleams from the Holy Grail* (London: Rider, n.d.).

9 M.P. Hall, *The Adepts in the Western Esoteric Tradition* (Los Angeles: Philosophical Research Soc., 1949).

10 A.E. Waite, *The Holy Grail, its Legends and Symbolism* (London: Rider, 1933).

11 R. Steiner, *An Outline of Occult Science* (New York: Anthroposophic Press, 1972).

12 A. Richardson, *Dancers to the Gods* (Wellingborough: Aquarian Press, 1985).

13 A. Richardson & G. Hughes, *Ancient Magicks for a New Age* (Minnesota: Llewellyn Press, 1989).

14 For further information about the Qabalistic correspondence course, write to Servants of the Light, PO Box 215, St Helier, Jersey, Channel Islands, UK.

15 M. Denning & O. Phillips, *The Magical Philosophy*, 5 vols (Minnesota: Llewellyn Press, 1974-9).

16 W.G. Gray, *Western Inner Workings*, 1982, *The Sangreal Sacrament*, 1983, *Concepts of Qabalah*, 1985, *Sangreal Ceremonies and Rituals*, 1986, (Maine: Weiser).

17 This esoteric work is continued and visually portrayed in *The Arthurian Tarot* and *Hallowquest* by Caitlín & John Matthews (Wellingborough: Aquarian Press, 1990).

18 C. Williams, *The Descent of the Dove* (London: Faber & Faber, 1939).

6

DION FORTUNE AND THE GRAAL

by

Gareth Knight

Of all the many esotericists who have worked with the matter of Arthur, Merlin and the Grail, perhaps the most important was Dion Fortune (Violet Mary Firth). The details supplied by Gareth Knight, himself a sometime member of the Society of the Inner Light, the order founded by Dion Fortune in c.1922, show something of the depths and power of the work she undertook. Much of that work has since become public property through her own publications and those of her associates—including Gareth Knight's own seminal books *The Secret Tradition in Arthurian Legend* (Aquarian Press, 1983) and *The Rose Cross and the Goddess* (Aquarian Press, 1985).

At another level altogether, her insights have filtered through to popular fiction, such as Marion Zimmer Bradley's *Mists of Avalon* (Micheal Joseph, 1987) and more recently the trilogy of works by Stephen Lawhead: *Taliesin, Merlin* and *Arthur* (Lion Books, 1987-9). Each of these works has picked up on Dion Fortune's connection of the Arthurian Grail tradition with the ancient concept of Atlantis. Whether or not this is accepted by the more sceptical readership of our own or these later books is not important. What matters is that from this synthesis comes a degree of inner contact rarely equalled. The Grail has from its beginnings lent itself easily to esoteric interpretation; in the future it must surely become more widely developed in this area, with what results we must wait to see.

❧

Dion Fortune is a key figure in the history of modern occultism, for she marks a transition from nineteenth-century to late twentieth-century occult thinking and practice.

She was born in the early 1890s, when the attitudes of occult fraternities in the West still reflected the past. On the one hand they tended to be antiquarian discussion groups with a mystical symbolic bent, or enclosed orders with secret ceremonies of initiation that borrowed much from the Freemasonry of the previous two hundred years. Of these, the Hermetic Order of the Golden Dawn exercised a considerable influence, and it was within an offshoot of this organization that Dion Fortune received much of her early training.

Most of the secret ceremonies of the Golden Dawn have now been exposed to the public eye, and for the practising occultist they have a certain period charm. The rituals do have a considerable residual power within them and there remain small groups of enthusiasts who apparently derive some benefit from working them.

No one in those days could have foreseen the present widespread interest in altered and expanded states of consciousness. Nowdays, what was once reserved for the innermost inner of the old time fraternities is relatively freely available in books, cassettes, videos, and a whole host of weekend workshops and conferences.

Much of this is presented under the banner of psychology, as indeed much of it is, although the subject is rather more extensive than psychology in the narrower sense. It is the opening of doors of perception into very real 'inner worlds' that have an objectivity of their own, and are by no means confined to the contents of one's own head—any more than the physical world is despite the fact that it comes to us filtered by the interpretations of the mind upon what is received by the physical senses. The inner worlds are sources of equally objective events that happen to be perceived by inner or psychic senses. These psychic senses are more common, and natural, than many people realize.

Dion Fortune was attracted to occultism via psychology, through the study of Freudian psychoanalysis. She later stated that she sought in occultism the key to certain phenomena of the mind that psychology failed to explain. Two of her early works, under her maiden name of Violet Firth, were in fact books of popular psychology—*The Machinery of the Mind* and *The Psychology of the Servant Problem*—although their very titles indicate that they are now somewhat dated.

Her first works of fiction, however, under the pen-name of Dion Fortune, were short stories under the title of *The Secrets of*

Dr Taverner, where the protagonist was a very special kind of psychologist, who ran a strange nursing home for the treatment of psychic disorders. In this, and her related non-fiction work, *Psychic Self-Defence*, it might well be thought that she wrote up the cases with considerable artistic licence to make a good story. She always maintained, however, that she toned them down to make them acceptable to the general public. However, her main contribution to occultism lay not in the psychopathologies of the subject, which in fact are relatively rare, but in the more positive field of psychospiritual development, to which end she strove to re-establish, as well as she could, the ancient mystery tradition of the West.

She did indeed, as other leading occultists of the time such as Israel Regardie, welcome the developments of Jungian psychology, which came very much to public notice in the early 1930s, with its psychological interpretation of much traditional symbolic material. Indeed, when I joined her society in 1953 one of the essential textbooks was on Jungian psychology. However, analytical psychology was never an end in itself, but rather a means to an end.

In any practical occult work that is more than what W.E. Butler used to refer to as 'pussy cat occultism', its practitioners have to learn to cope with quite considerable psychic pressures that may come up from the subconscious or from inner objective sources. Failure to cope with such forces results in phenomena that are usually termed in psychoanalytic circles 'transference' or 'projection', i.e. quite disproportionate loves, hates, obsessions or antipathies directed towards individuals or groups. The history of occult and spiritual movements is littered with anecdotes of the bizarre behaviour of its protagonists, much of which is diligently recorded by biographers for the titillation of their readers. Often the reporting itself is inaccurate because the evidence is taken from one of the parties who is suffering from such a bout of transference or projection. Hence no leader of any group is likely to stand much chance of a good press if left to the memoirs of discontented associates. The main problem of such psychological unbalance is that it takes a great deal of experience to discern when it is happening. Hence the Delphic injunction 'know thyself'.

After her death, the group which Dion Fortune founded continued to try to improve the quality of its members by various psychological techniques, but gradually Jungian psychology was abandoned, a full analysis being both too time-consuming and expensive for practical purposes, and all attempts to train a member to be a kind of resident group analytical psychologist foundered for one reason or another. There is in fact a profound gap between the basic premises of practical occultism and Jungian psychology, despite the common interest in traditional symbolism. The one is firmly based on spiritual philosophy, the other on scientific materialism. The Divine Ideas of Plato or of the Qabalistic Rabbis are a far cry from the archetypes of the unconscious of C.G. Jung.

However, this problem was little understood in Dion Fortune's day, and has only become apparent in the light of more recent experience.

Another powerful influence upon the occultism of her time was that of the East. There has always been a strong tradition of occult theory and practice in the Orient because the various religions lend themselves more to direct inner experience than has ever been countenanced by the institutional churches in the West, where even great mystics of unimpeachable orthodoxy have been regarded with considerable suspicion, and those outside orthodoxy have been roundly persecuted.

Madame Blavatsky's *The Secret Doctrine*, published in 1888, did much to open up a flood of popular interpretation of Eastern esoteric doctrines, which was given even greater impetus by the efforts of pioneering stalwarts to the Theosophical Society such as Annie Besant and C.W. Leadbeater. So pervasive was this influx that most esoteric students in the West have taken in various concepts from it lock, stock and barrel. One will, for example, hear even pagan loyalists of the old Western native traditions happily chattering about *karma*, *kundalini* and *reincarnation*.

Dion Fortune, no less than most others of her generation, took this on board, but she stuck to the fundamentally important line that there is also a Western Esoteric Tradition which, although fragmented through historical circumstance, is every bit as valid and important as anything coming from the East.

She was also one of the first to take a stand against the obsession with occult secrecy that was perhaps a natural consequence of the long tradition of persecution of unorthodox belief and practice in the West. One will, nonetheless, find it difficult to find precise practical instruction in any of her classic textbooks, whether *The Mystical Qabalah*, *The Esoteric Orders and their Work*, *The Training and Work of an Initiate* or *Sane Occultism*, although there are plenty of hints. However she did go out of her way to try and make some of the practicalities evident in her novels, particularly the later ones, *The Winged Bull*, *The Sea Priestess* and *Moon Magic*, although how far she succeeded in this is open to debate. Certainly the public did not beat a path to her door to buy them; the second had to be published by herself out of her own pocket, and the last one did not see the dignity of print until after her death. It was indeed only in her series of weekly War Letters, during the period of national emergency from 1939 to 1942, that she came out with specific practical instruction in an extended meditation group. This type of work might be considered fairly commonplace now, some half a century later, but it marked a considerable milestone then. Oddly enough, the letters have not, to this date, been published in volume form, but they tell a lot of Dion Fortune and of practical occultism in her day, despite being obviously dated as to some of the references to contemporary events.

The great strength and contribution of Dion Fortune was her synthesizing ability, and this was not always apparent even to her contemporaries—some of whom saw her as too mystically Christian, and others as too obsessed with power lines and sacred sites, while to yet others her concern with ceremonial magic seemed to dominate all else.

She saw three strands to the Western Esoteric Tradition, which had to be worked together into one strong thread. These three strands were sometimes referred to by colours, as the Green Ray, the Blue Ray and the Purple Ray. That is respectively, the Nature contacts, the Hermetic or magical tradition, and Christian mysticism.

Each has its various modes of expression. The Green Ray can be said to include all the neo-pagan movements, yet also nature mystics such as Richard Jeffries, and in its most modern manifestation it would certainly include ecological concern and the appreciation of the planet as a living organism. Indeed most aspects of 'the return of the Goddess' come under the Green Ray, including the current interest in ley-lines, sacred sites and centres, megaliths and so on. Above all, as far as Dion Fortune was concerned, were the powerful Elemental contacts she picked

up, not only at Glastonbury, where she lived, but in the great
parks of the city.

The Blue Ray or Hermetic Tradition is more of an intellectual
approach that seeks to categorize the inner dynamics of creation
and to formulate various ground maps and plans for inner
exploration. Such maps are for instance the Tree of Life of the
Qabalah and its associated symbolism. An important side of it is
the practical, however, without which all theory is useless, either
in physical ceremonial ritual or in similar patterned formal work
by directed meditation upon an inner level.

The Purple Ray is that of devotional mysticism, which in the
West is predominantly Christian, and is certainly of major
importance to us in our consideration of Dion Fortune as a
member of the 'Household of the Grail.' In the native traditions
of the British Isles it embraces the insights of the old Celtic
Christianity and the Glastonbury legends of Joseph of
Arimathea coming to these islands, and even the Christ child
too.

Her Green Ray work is, perhaps because of its very nature, the
least well documented. An important plank not only within it
but in the foundation of all her work was an Elemental contact
that came to her at Pentecost in 1926, on Glastonbury Tor, at
the foot of which she had founded her small group a few weeks
earlier at Easter.

In those days she had tended to work in full trance, and her
colleague C.T. Loveday, who wrote up the occasion, records
that the Fire and Air contacts came through with considerable
power, the repetitions gliding up the scale in quarter tones and
ever increasing volume, whilst those of Earth and Water were of
a soft and sweeter nature, tending gradually to diminish in tone.

Short excerpts of the repetitive chant of the Fire and Air
Elementals run as follows:

The wind and the fire work on the hill.
The wind and the fire work on the hill.
The wind and the fire work on the hill.
Invoke ye the wind and the fire ...

And of the Earth and Water Elementals:

Earth and water are friendly and kind.
Earth and water are friendly and kind.
Earth and water are friendly and kind ...

This eventually broke into declamatory prose that concluded:

> Com in the Name of the White Christ and the Hosts of the
> Elements. Come at our bidding and serve with us the One Name
> above all Names—the Lover of Men and of the Elemental
> Peoples—the Great Name of JEHOSHUA—JESU!

In later exegesis that same evening they were told:

> You must develop the Green Ray contacts. You need them.
> Without them your group is imperfect ... The time has arrived
> when you can handle it. That is why you have been given this
> house at the very centre of these Forces. It is not for nothing that
> you came to the Tor, and have built on the Tor, not for nothing
> believe me. Here you have the Air and Fire contracts. You will
> have your devotional aspect in the city, and you will have your
> Nature contacts here. The Elemental Forces will co-operate with
> you and give you the aid of their Powers.

The prophetic statement that they would have a devotional
centre in the city came to pass four years later in the foundation
of the Guild of the Master Jesus (also called in those early days
the Church of the Graal), of which more anon. But the
relevance of the Christian mysteries to the Elemental powers was
further elaborated upon in the statement that in the three days
between the Crucifixion and the Resurrection, when Christ is
said to have preached to the spirits in prison, these spirits
included the creatures of the Elements and to them also the
Christ gave the power to become 'sons and daughters of God'.
Thus, in Elemental eyes, the Risen Lord loved the Elementals,
and so it is in the sign of the Risen Lord that human beings can
and should contact the children of the Elements.

All this became part of a system of allocating the various hills
of Glastonbury to the Elemental contacts; the Tor to Air and
Fire, Chalice Hill to Water, and Wearyall Hill to Earth.

With regard to Dion Fortune's commitment to the Blue Ray or
Hermetic Tradition, little need be said, as her published work
remains as a permanent memorial. *The Mystical Qabalah*,

published in volume form in 1936, remains a classic and certainly one of the most readable books on the subject of the Tree of Life. She was also well into the practicalities of the subject with the system of initiation that she founded with graded rituals for progress through the Fraternity. On a more philosophical level her cosmological treatise *The Cosmic Doctrine*, although by no means easy reading, is a continuing source of inspiration and study to discerning Hermetic students. This she also received at Glastonbury in an impressive display of mediumship, which she always claimed was the source of power for any practical occult group, although this *modus operandi* is generally regarded now as somewhat passé, and the tendency now is to work a round table rather than Bee Hive formula, i.e. to develop group intuitive insights by mutual interchange, rather than have a group of lesser workers relying on the psychic contacts and abilities of one central individual.

As to the Purple Ray of devotional mysticism, Dion Fortune's commitment came largely from inner experience and somewhat against her natural inclinations. This stemmed, as in so many cases of Christian conversion, from a deeply impressive vision that she had, wherein she was taken to a high place by one of the leading magical figures of the day, the inner plane adept known as the Master Rakoczi, and given firmly into the keeping of the Lord Jesus, somewhat, it should be said, to her chagrin!

This commitment brought her into conflict with certain members of the Theosophical Society of the day in whose eyes the Lord Jesus was a minor master inhabiting a physical body somewhere in Syria. It was felt that the Eastern conception of the Lord Maitreya had rendered Christian mysticism somewhat outmoded. Dion Fortune was quite unable to accept this view, and withdrawing from the Christian Mystic Lodge of the Theosophical Society she formed the Guild of the Master Jesus which held public services at her headquarters. This was in one sense a fulfilment of what had been predicted at Glastonbury some four years earlier from the unlikely source of the Elemental contacts. It also emphasized the threefold basis of her work in that it was conducted in its services on classical Hermetic lines. To revert to the earlier instructions at Glastonbury, it was said:

> You must balance the Rays in your training, and you will find in
> each tradition the elements which connect it with all the other
> traditions.

On the Green Ray—the Celtic nature Ray—you will find the connection with the Purple Ray through the Celtic Saints, such as St Bride, St Columba and many others. You will find the link with the Hermetic tradition also, through the Mage Merlin, who is very important, and is the Master of the Celtic Ray in these islands.

Correspondingly it is stated:

On the Christian Ray you will find the link with the Celtic tradition through Grail legends and the Arthurian cycle; and with the Hermetic tradition through the Mysteries.

And thirdly:

In the Hermetic tradition you will find the link with Christian aspects through the Rose and the Cross, and with the Celtic aspect through Merlin again.

Thus, particularly through the Arthurian cycle we find common ground, and to follow Dion Fortune's personal Quest for the Graal we should perhaps start back at the beginning again—in Glastonbury.

Dion Fortune's interest in the Graal tradition had its most obvious foundation in her commitment to Glastonbury. It was there that she founded her headquarters at the foot of the Tor, on a plot of ground called Chalice Orchard and just across the lane from the famous Chalice Well where the water runs red from the Chalybeate spring which in those days used to run freely down the side of the road.

Her appreciation of Glastonbury and of the Graal tradition with which it is inseparably entwined is to be found at length in the series of articles she wrote that were published in 1934 in volume form as *Avalon of the Heart*.

Indeed, in her opening chapter to this book she recalls the legendary role of Chalice Hill, and tells how it is reputed to have been the home of the guardian of the Graal, the Fisher King, who kept it in his secret treasury at the heart of the hill.

She goes on in fact to identify two traditions in Glastonbury that have intermingled. One she refers to as Avalon of the Cup and the other as Avalon of the Sword, the Cup being the Holy Graal, and the Sword, King Arthur's Excalibur.

The Excalibur tradition she identifies with the pre-Christian faith of the ancient Britons before the legends of the Fisher King became associated with Chalice Hill. Then, she says, 'dark Morgan le Fay, half-sister of Arthur and pupil of Merlin' dwelt there; and she conjures the vision of the still surface of the well 'with its great gouts of blood stained fungus' used by Morgan as a magic mirror for her visions.

This is very much a primitive and evocative vision that shows Dion Fortune's awareness of the dark forces of the Inner Earth as well as the spiritual insights and revelations of Christian mysticism. We may well conclude that she was speaking from practical experience when she says, 'that spirit it is that broods over the well and wakes the eyes of vision in the souls of those who gaze into it.'

In Avalon she also sees the Lady of the Lake and her sister queens as guardians of the Magic Sword and forerunners of the three pure maidens who later guarded the Sacred Cup of the Fisher King.

Avalon of the Cup is enshrined in the legends of Joseph of Arimathea who came to Glastonbury bearing the Cup of the Last Supper in which had been caught the drops of blood that fell from the side of the Saviour of the World, wounded by the spear of the centurian Longinus. Thus was Glastonbury fittingly called 'the holyest erthe in Englande', where the first little mud and wattle church bore the Cup of the Last Supper, or the Holy Graal with the Sacred Blood, upon its altar.

Later, as the legend told by Dion Fortune goes, the Dark Ages encroached and the relic was withdrawn from the outer world by the Fisher King, to be kept in an underground chamber, guarded by three pure maidens who watch over it day and night. Whoever drinks from it will never thirst again for it is a well spring of the Waters of Life of the soul.

Here, in Dion Fortune's vision, came the questing knights who, after an all-night vigil at the chapel of St Bride at Beckary, just over the Pons Perilous on the River Brue, came to the secret chamber to drink of the Cup. Many were never seen again, for they were translated by this very act into another world.

Then as times became more evil the Sacred Cup was concealed at the heart of a spring that rises between Chalice Hill and the Tor, which is why the waters, rising from an immense depth, run blood-red into the sacred well.

This is the legendary background that helped to draw Dion Fortune to Glastonbury, and it was here that she made her own first important contacts with inner power sources that led her to establish her own group. The gist of much of these contacts was contained in a series of papers called 'The Words of the Masters' in her society's magazine *The Inner Light*, and also in the cosmological treatise published much later as *The Cosmic Doctrine*. They were also the background inspiration to much of her other works and papers reserved for members of her group.

It is from this source that she put forward the idea that the ancient tradition of the legend of lost Atlantis was part and parcel of the Mysteries of Britain. To this end she devotes a chapter to it in *Avalon of the Heart*, where she links the memories of a lost land of Lyonesse off the coast of Cornwall with the legend of a far more ancient land in the mid-Atlantic.

This engrafting process builds resonances of old legend onto those yet more ancient, on a thesis that one is a folk memory of the other. Thus we have the idea of Merlin being an emigré of the lost continent, arriving in these islands of Britain soon after the cataclysm, and embarking upon a plan to engender a dynasty of priest kings or god kings after the manner that is well known in the history of the Orient and even Ancient Egypt.

This does not conflict with the idea of Merlin also being a much later Druid, or one who was a confidant of a legendary historical Romano-British Arthur. Rather they are all resonating parallel strings upon the harp of the legends of ancient time.

However, is the streak of psychism, the second sight, she asks, that particular gift of the Celtic people, a strain of the old Atlantean blood that gave clairvoyant gifts to its aristocratic priesthood and thus the ability to be guided by superior intelligences—thus giving another dimension to the conception of the San Graal, or *Sang Real* as 'blood royal'.

Merlin, in this scenario, which closely follows the standard tale that has come to us through Sir Thomas Malory, is the guardian and teacher of Arthur Pendragon and Morgan le Fay. In Malory it is Merlin who brings about the conception of Arthur by enabling King Uther Pendragon to lie with Ygraine, the wife of the Duke of Cornwall, and who claims the child immediately after its birth so that he can oversee its upbringing. This was a uniting of the ancient British royal line with the Atlantean blood-line of the Duchess of Cornwall, who according to this tradition was originally a princess of Atlantis. Her daughter Morgan le Fay is rather quaintly described by Malory as being sent to a nunnery so that she can study 'nigromancy'. This strange nunnery for the study of the black arts would seem to be a garbled medieval interpretation of an ancient school of initiation, run by such as Merlin—at any rate, so Dion Fortune chooses to think, and she melds the figure of Morgan with other legendary characters, describing her as 'the dark Lilith of our island legend, sometimes identified with the Lady of the Lake'.

Although this apparently free interpretation of ancient legendary material may seem somewhat arbitrary and even fantastical, it does have a degree of validity for occultists working with this level of tradition. In such a context we cannot use the same criteria as the outer rules of material evidence. As Dion Fortune wrote in an early note upon her group and its work:

> I had to teach a great many things I could not verify, but which I could not afford to scrap because I should have brought the whole structure down if I had pulled them out ... there was, moreover, always the saving grace of intuition which sensed the presence of light and power behind the tumbledown structure of conventional tradition. This faith was ultimately justified, for I eventually discovered that historical fables were psychological truths, and merely required to be re-stated in terms of modern thought to be accurate working models of things ineffable. Trouble comes, however, when the fables and the framework are taken at their face value, for then they are very misleading and hampering.

This is very much the statement of an empirical working occultist, and another reason why she chose to couch a proportion of her teaching in the guise of fiction. It is an attitude that puts results before accepted theory, and is in line with the ancient navigators who discovered new worlds by ignoring the accepted and seemingly obvious reasoning that those who sailed too far south or west would either be roasted or fall off the edge of the world. It might also be viewed as a fitting attitude for any who are actively on the quest of the Graal.

Anyhow, it was an aid to those who sought the direct experience of the Graal that Dion Fortune founded her Guild of the Master Jesus. This was an inherent part in the work of her Fraternity, which she went out of her way to stress in the following words:

> ... the Guild is not a thing apart in the system of the Inner Light, but simply a different set of symbols applied to the elucidation of the same ineluctable truths and to the guilding of the soul by the same paths of immemorial mystical experience. It is exceedingly important to our concept and method that the Guild should be seen as part, or aspect, of an undivided whole. All the ministrants of the Guild have been through the Hermetic training which teaches them the technical methods of the Mysteries. These methods, applied to the traditional Christian symbolism, make the Way of the Cross a true initiatory Path of the Lesser Mysteries, precisely paralleling the coveted Hermetic training.

Thus we see that we have a *magical* technique being applied to induce, in those who might not otherwise come to it, a *mystical* experience. (We use the term 'mystical' to refer to an experience of the Uncreate Realities, the direct experience of God, or Eternity, whilst 'magical' refers to techniques of the visual imagination and other inner faculties of the adept. These same techniques were used by Ignatius of Loyala to train his Jesuits and it is also the *modus operandi* of Rosicrucian symbolism as correctly understood.)

In the Guild ceremony the heart of the matter was the building of a mighty Chalice upon the higher ethers, about which Dion Fortune writes quite categorically, 'We are functioning as adepts in a magical ceremony; we are making a channel of evocation.'

And she advised those who attended to assist in the building of this imagery by visualizing a mighty golden chalice, greater than the stature of a man, suspended in the air over the celebrant, who stood in the centre of a zodiacal circle in the midst of the sanctury. It was to be seen at such a height that a man standing upright could reach up and lay a hand on its base at arm's length. Thus it would be seen there throughout the whole ceremony, above the heads of the participants in the sanctuary, where, she said 'those who have psychic powers will be interested to observe the astral phenomena connected with it.' And the nature and power of its contents would be experienced in the charged atmosphere at the giving of the bread and wine across the sanctuary rails which represented the divide between the inner and the outer planes.

Of its function and symbolism Dion Fortune wrote:

> The Cup is the mystically exalted soul of man, held up to receive the influx of the Holy Ghost; and when receiving this influx from on high we stand with our feet set firm in the very heart of Nature, thus affirming the natural basis of all things in the Earth our Mother.

At the outbreak of war in 1939 the public meetings of the society had to come to an end, and Dion Fortune started a system to meet the exigencies of the war situation. This was to have a private Sunday meeting of a few chosen members consciously linked up with all those, scattered across the country, to whom her weekly letter had been sent the previous mid-week. This letter contained a subject for meditation and a couple of quarto sides of comment about it.

This started off as something of an experiment but quickly gathered power and momentum during the winter of 1939 and spring of 1940. Certain images began spontaneously to arise, at first in the form of a triangle, with a powerful figure at each point.

At one point in a sphere of red was the figure of a mailed warrior on horseback wielding a drawn sword. This was identified as King Arthur. At an opposite point in a sphere of blue was a figure seated on a throne wielding a diamond sceptre, and this was identified as Merlin. And at the third point, in a sphere of purple, there built up the figure of the Christ holding a chalice, or the Graal.

Students of the Qabalah may note that we have here a figure that will fit readily upon the Tree of Life, with the points of the triangle at Geburah, Chesed and Yesod, the red, blue and purple spheres respectively.

After a while the image took on a three-dimensional aspect, with the figure in the purple sphere holding the Graal becoming the Virgin, and the figure of the Christ forming the apex of a pyramid in a sphere of bright light. Again, Qabalistic students will see how this also fits the Tree of Life, with the figure of the Christ in the Sun sphere of Tiphereth.

This work with spontaneous magical images that built up in the group mind that they had formed continued through the duration of the national emergency, and included also the co-operation with an angelic patrol about the shores of Britain which it may be recalled is traditionally known as Merlin's Enclosure.

After the middle of 1942 the weekly letters had served their practical purpose and became more philosophical in tone. Eventually they were reduced to a monthly basis, and reverted to a more generalized teaching role. The Graal and Arthurian work went on, however, within the confines of the group. Here the gifted mediation of Margaret Lumley Brown played a part, and a considerable amount of material was brought through and worked with, known as 'The Arthurian Formula', the greater part of which was used, with permission, as source material in my book *The Secret Tradition in Arthurian Legend*, published in 1983.

Much of this material was the work of the later war years and after, and again when I joined in 1953 another of the required textbooks was *Le Morte d'Arthur* of Sir Thomas Malory. A number of the inner group were known by Arthurian nicknames, 'Morgan', 'Merlin', or 'Dragon', and until the early 1960s a staple ritual of the Greater Mystery group was the Graal Ritual, which has been constructed by Dion Fortune's successor as Warden, Arthur Chichester. This was based upon a familiar four-fold pattern of Lance, Cup, Sword and Stone, and had as a basic principle the same legend espoused by Dion Fortune in her early Glastonbury writings, about how the new Christian faith was welcomed by the Druids and flourished in the Celtic Church.

Thus it is possible to trace, from the first contacts of Dion Fortune with Glastonbury, how the Graal and Arthurian tradition developed in her mind and work, to be taken up by her group after her death, and thence by those yet to come and those beyond it. For now we see a running tide of interest in the whole field, extending it ever further. Thus apart from my own public workings concerned with the calling of King Arthur and the raising up of Merlin from the enchantment of Nimuë, Bob Stewart has brought new insights with his Merlin Festivals and his work on the *Prophecies* and *Life of Merlin* by Geoffrey of Monmouth, so long neglected. John Matthews has edited and collated material on the Graal itself, of which this book forms a part, and Caitlín Matthews has done much to elucidate and reconstruct the ancient mysteries of Mabon enshrined in *The Mabinogion*. There have been many others contributing to this work, each in their own way, and with varying degrees of power and direction of emphasis. No one has a monopoly on any of this universal material. And yet, if truth were told, all this published work and even the practical work associated with it, some known and some known only to a few, is but the tip of a mighty iceberg, whose bulk floats deep in the hidden memories, historical and paradisal, of the Mysteries of Britain, of Arthur, Merlin and the Holy Graal.

7

'DOCTOR STONE': WALTER STEIN AND THE HOLY GRAIL

by

Charles Lawrie

The subject of this next chapter is one of the least known (in this country at least) of the Household of the Grail. Yet he was almost certainly one of the most important modern commentators on the Grail, seeing beyond the evidence of the stories to deeper truths.

For Walter Johannes Stein, the Grail was a reality which stood for far more than the sum off its parts. He saw it as (among other things) a political, socio-political and economical force, as well as a generator of spiritual energy unequalled in the world. And he was the first to penetrate behind the intricate imagery of Wolfram von Eschenbach's *Parzival*,* to a historical underpinning. In his neglected masterpiece *The Ninth Century and the Holy Grail*† he identified actual historical figures who had been allegorically re-created in Wolfram's poem.

Thus the Grail was seen to have been an active principle in the shaping of history. As Charles Lawrie demonstrates, Walter Stein was always a Grail seeker. He found new and challenging insights into the quest which have still to be followed up by those who are themselves in pursuit of the Grail.

Prologue

'What does it really *mean* that Christ has become the Spirit of the Earth?' This was the Grail-question at the core of the life and work of Walter Stein. He knew how on Friday 3 April A.D. 33 at c.3 p.m. the Blood of Christ first flowed from the cross on

---

* Translated by A.T. Hatto, Penguin Books, 1977.
† Published in English by Temple Lodge Press, 1989.

Golgotha into the Body of the Earth. It is said that Joseph of Arimathea caught some of the God-permeated fluid in the cup which Christ had used at the Last Supper, as He shared His living substance with the circle of 12 disciples in an archetype of Christian Communion. And gospel writers record Joseph as the man who bade Pilate permit him to take Christ's body from the cross, and lay it, ceremonially embalmed and wrapped, in a tomb in a rock, carved at his own expense and intended for himself. Across the mouth of that tomb he rolled a mighty stone. But on Easter Sunday, and by another power, the stone was rolled away.

L'Estoire de Saint Graal relates how, later, Joseph of Arimathea was released from immurement in Jerusalem by Vespasian, and that he possessed a book composed by Christ, in which was described the history of the Holy Grail and the lineage of the people connected with it. Here we glimpse the Household of the Grail. It is interesting that a similar tale appears in the introduction to the *Book of Jashar*, which the Grail-servant Alcuin of Tours (c.A.D. 735-804) is reported to have obtained on a journey to the East. The old man, who is there rescued from immurement with his life-wisdom of the blood-lineage of Jesus Christ, was brought to Seville by that account. But the figure of Joseph of Arimathea—and his link with the Body and Blood of Christ Himself—leads us still further, to the tin-isles of Britain, and to Glastonbury. Said Dr Stein on 29 May 1949: 'Joseph of Arimathea collected the Blood of Christ in the Holy Vessel, after taking His Body down from the Cross. He is the central figure of the Holy Grail.'

Of what is the Blood of Christ the actual expression? It is that substance of the Earth which bears the very Self of God. It is the quintessence of humanity, warmed and permeated and indeed transubstantiated through the indwelling power of the solar Logos. No wonder a great change was wrought in creation by the coming of God to earth, by the birth of God in human form, by the divinization of the human form and of the earth in Christ. A new aura of the earth flamed out into the macrocosm in the moment of Golgotha, but this new seed of creation had yet to ripen and grow within the body of humanity and the earth.

In Christ was revealed, bodily, the fullness of the Godhead. In Him, through Him, the Father-Ground of all Creation is revealed, the selfless giving Will which gives us all and each our very being. This selfless Creator-Will is what works in the refashioning of Christ's øúois (physical nature) in the Resurrection-Body. And this Resurrection-Body is what forms the foundation of Grail-Christianity, and the creating of a new Heaven and a new Earth. We are in a cosmological, a cosmogenetic process when we awake to the aims of the Grail. And it was to these aims that Walter Johannes Stein once more awoke in the course of his recent life.

Upbringing

Stein was born in Vienna on 6 February 1891, at 5.30 a.m. His earliest memory is of a governess leaving him to cross a road by himself in the Vienna woods and hiding behind a tree. The challenge awoke his spirit. He saw his little body which he was to guide alone across the road, but simultaneously he perceived his self as 'I' who lived in a sphere which included awareness of the one who was hiding behind the tree. 'I still remember the inner feeling of delight it gave me to know that she imagined she was hidden from me, while actually my self was spread over the space in which she was.'

Around the child were loving parents and an elder brother, Friedrich, born in 1886. Pictures of Leonardo's *Last Supper* and Raphael's *Disputa* were on the walls. His mother had taken piano lessons from the young Mahler. Viennese life and culture came through their doors.

'My father I remember as a man of active, happy temperament, teaching me to be thankful for the gift of life.' Hungarian Dr Wilhelm Stein practised law, became a naturalized Austrian, and had a profound love of languages. 'When he came home of an evening I often found him quite early on his sofa or even in bed, surrounded by huge tomes—the well-known dictionaries of Sachs-Villate, Muret-Sanders and others ...

His mother was Viennese. Once they waited for a train. He lay asleep on her lap. She woke him 'so tenderly and gently that her lovingness rather than the actual fact of being awakened entered my consciousness. It was the picture of "the woman full of love, who is awakening me" that remained before the little child's soul as "mother" and this became a lasting memory-picture for the rest of my life.'

'As to my brother, my first important impression seems to be myself biting him in the arm.' The shock led Walter to vow never to be unkind to his brother again, and he kept his word.

His favourite game was turning a table upside-down and voyaging off on uncharted seas.

Following a protracted cold in the winter of 1900, his father sent him to recover at Ospedaletti near San Remo. Here he met 'a young German-American girl about 6 years older than myself, to whom I looked up with untold reverence and tenderness. It was my first love, utterly childlike, ethereal, remote from the world.' Beholding her soul with love, his eyes opened to Nature: 'Not until then did I begin to see the beauty of the sunrise and the sunset, the wind and cloud, the rocks and trees.'

School came at the Schottengymnasium in Vienna, run now by Benedictine monks. Once, inspired by his history lessons, he went down into the tomb of Heinrich Jasomirgott, founder of the Schotten Church. 'As a memento for all time I took a leaf from the wreath of his tomb, and in a mood of infinite reverence brought it up with me to the light of day. In my childlike soul I felt eternal thankfulness to the man to whom we owed what we were learning.'

A child with such rich inner experience awakens only gradually to intellect. But visiting a shop selling newspapers and postcards, at the age of 10, he saw a card that seemed to represent a death's head: 'Closer, it revealed itself as a boy carrying two baskets of flowers. Moving backwards and forwards I noticed first one, then the other, and realized what my own thinking was doing—and in that moment I first became a philosopher!'

In Maths and Greek, he fell behind. His teachers decided to keep him in Class 3 for a second year. And so, in 1904, he met Eugen Kolisko, two years younger, who became his closest friend. When he passed out of the Schottengymnasium on 11 July 1911 it was with grades of 'good' or 'very good' in Mathematics, Physics, Geography, History and Philosophic Studies. On a trip to Germany to widen his outlook he wrote to Kolisko from Munich on 27 August 1911: 'We have both known long enough that I'm a philosopher, and not a mathematician, but that need not prevent me from studying Maths. For here lies the beginning—and the end, as well, which means the goal—in life—in rosy, sunny, work-rejoicing life.'

Meeting His Teacher

When his father died in 1908, Walter Stein had a significant experience. Having rushed down to the chemist for an oxygen cylinder, he tore upstairs and entered the room just as the doctor was informing the family that his father was dead. 'My brother, in despairing grief, fell on his knees beside the bed ... What with bodily exhaustion and being out of breath ... with absolute composure, I stood before my dead father and surveyed the scene. At this moment it became clear to me that the human being can lift himself in mind and spirit into a world that abides eternally in silence, far beyond the surging waves of pain and passion...' He became aware that every human being lives in a threefold way. 'First, we live on earth in our earthly body. Then we express our life ... in all our passions, our pains and joys, our hopes and fears—in the world of soul. Thirdly we reach out into a spiritual world, a world beyond all personal emotions, through our membership of which we with our true Being are rooted in the objective spirit.' He was to grasp these three worlds ever more clearly in the rest of his earthly life.

After a year of military service, qualifying as a Reserve Artillery officer, Walter Stein enrolled at Vienna University in October 1912. Taking Mathematics, Physics, History of Philosophy and Psychology, he adopted a scientific materialism. This was shattered when he observed the work of a tutor in the engineering laboratories of the Technical High School who was researching the influence of the form of materials upon their strength. 'For the first time I learned that a material can be made even stronger by taking away some of the matter. A rectangular plate of glass, for example, will under certain conditions carry more weight if two semicircles have been cut out of it on either side. Such experiments convinced me that it is form and not matter which supports us, and from which we receive the sense impressions we sum up as "the material world".'

Yet mechanical science was in his mind when he picked up a copy of Rudolf Steiner's *Occult Science—An Outline* (1909) from his mother's desk. He read an account of a stage of cosmic evolution in which a condition of pure 'Warmth' or 'Heat' prevailed.

To a physicist it seemed impossible to regard heat as a quality having an independent existence of its own. I threw the book down on the table and said to my mother: 'This man must be asleep to the whole trend of modern physics.' Wishing to follow up my statement, I opened the book once more and read: 'The author of this book can well imagine that anyone who reads what he has to say on Heat or Warmth will conclude that he is ignorant of the first elements of modern physics ... the author would certainly never have ventured what is here said about "Heat" and "Warmth" if he were not conversant with ... the historical development of all the explanations and lines of thought associated with J.R. Mayer, Helmholtz, Clausius and Joule.'

Stein decided to study Steiner's works, and for 10 hours a day, for two months or more, he read everything he could find.

Stein saw that Steiner's views were consistent, but was 'well aware from mathematics that a system of thought need not represent any reality just because it is logical and free of contradictions.' He began to compare Steiner's teaching with other philosophic, religious and mystical systems, and found 'it contained the key to all'.

'Still it may be,' he thought to himself, 'that these spiritual world conceptions do not represent any reality at all.' So he studied the relation of Steiner's teaching to all the branches of natural science available to him. 'Where he diverged from the orthodox teaching I found he did so for good reasons. He was indeed further advanced than the official science, and his system did in fact represent a reality ... the reality of nature.' And what was this teaching? Stein noticed Steiner's words in Chapter VI of *Occult Science*: 'The pathway into the spiritual worlds, the first steps of which were set forth in the preceding chapter, culminate in the "Science of the Grail". '

On 19 January 1913, Rudolf Steiner gave a public lecture in Vienna on 'The Supersensible Worlds and the Nature of the Human Soul'. Stein attended. 'As I listened to his lecture, I said to myself: "This man Rudolf Steiner is giving instructions for the development of a threefold faculty of clairvoyance." '

He began to ask questions in his mind. The lecturer answered. Perhaps it is simply the logic of the theme, thought Stein. He continued the test.

'Which came first, human language or human reason?' he asked in a written question at the end, inspired by Lazarus Geiger's book he had found on his father's shelves. Steiner answered from the viewpoint of child development, rather than from the evolutionary perspective Stein sought. Stein was bitterly disappointed. His heart was thumping.

Steiner picked up the paper again: 'What I have just been saying is one point of view; there is another aspect which the writer of the question had in mind.'

'And he went on to tell how in the evolution of mankind language and reason had evolved by means of one another.'

Stein went up to him afterwards: 'I know who you are, and I would like to become your pupil.'

Said Rudolf Steiner: 'I take it you know English.'

'No.'

'Read the philosophical works of Berkeley, who denied the existence of matter, and of Locke, who based everything on the senses. Then write a theory of cognition for spiritual knowledge, avoiding both of these one-sided points of view. Do it as I have done: learn to know the fullness of the world through Aristotle, and the act of cognition itself through the philosophy of Fichte.'

'So,' wrote Stein in 1936, 'I became Rudolf Steiner's pupil, and the remainder of my life has been lived in the sign of this discipleship.'

Initiation

War broke out. Friedrich Stein had already gone to the Eastern Front. Walter followed, in August 1914, serving like Ludwig Wittgenstein as an Artillery Observer, guiding the fire. Like Wittgenstein, his philosophical treatise was 'worked out on the battlefield, in daily meditation and constantly in the face of death.' Both were decorated repeatedly for bravery. Wittgenstein was known to his fellows as 'the one with the *Gospels*' (by Tolstoy); Stein as 'the one with *Theosophy*' (by Rudolf Steiner), which passed up and down the lines twice. The regiments of both were shocked to hear on 22 March 1915 of the fall of Przemysl, when Friedrich Stein was killed in battle.

Death approached Walter. 'Under heavy artillery fire, a shell landed in front, another behind, a third directly to left, a fourth to the right exploded. I thought "Now I have only seconds left."'

Suddenly, inwardly, 'Rudolf Steiner stood before me, laughing genially, in sunny peace. "There won't be a fifth," he said. And as I heard this in spirit, an infinitely restoring peace filled me.'

'All officers who have been in the firing-line continuously for the past 18 months are to retire at once,' came the order. Stein returned to Vienna. A telegram reached him from Steiner: 'Am in Berlin for three days longer; can discuss dissertation, if you can come.'

As they met, Count Ludwig Polzer-Hoditz was hurrying from Steiner's door. 'I have to get an important document across the frontier,' he explained to Stein. 'A letter to the Emperor Karl.'

'Give it to me,' said Stein. And so it came about that he delivered to Polzer-Hoditz's brother Arthur, Kabinettschef to the Austrian Emperor, Rudolf Steiner's first Memorandum concerning the *Dreigliederung* or Threefold Social Organism, in response to Austria and Europe's social need. But it was not delivered to the Emperor until too late.

Stein served the rest of the war as an instructor in officer's training schools in the land of Rudolf Steiner's youth—Wiener Neustadt, Brunn and Vienna. In Vienna, he asked Professor Arthur Stöhr to supervise his doctoral thesis. 'Theme?'

'I want to compare the ideas of Nature and theories of knowledge of Goethe and Rudolf Steiner. I want to show that human consciousness is only a special kind of consciousness, that there are other forms of consciousness to which we can evolve. I want to clarify the possible forms of consciousness and examine their relation to what science teaches us about the real world. I want to show the middle way between Locke's one-sided sensualism and Berkeley's denial of matter.'

He wrote the dissertation over 10 days during September 1917 in Magyarkerztur, Hungary, in the home of Nora von Baditz, who became his wife in August 1918. He received his doctoral grade in Summer 1918, as Wittgenstein completed his *Tractatus* in Vienna.

Steiner was about to make the unemployed 'Doctor' his secretary, when Polzer-Hoditz rang. So Stein went back to Vienna to help the Threefold social movement. He collected signatories for Rudolf Steiner's 'Appeal to the German people', and asked the Ludwig Wittgenstein Trust unsuccessfully for funds. On 15 May 1922, in Munich, he helped to protect Rudolf Steiner from attack by the Hitler-garde.

Meanwhile, requested by Stuttgart industrialist Emil Molt, Steiner had started the original Waldorf School at Uhlandshöhe in 1919. Stein was asked to join the staff. Though a trained philosopher and scientist, he was given History and Literature. 'I still remember my despair when Rudolf Steiner told me at two o'clock one night that I should have to take a history lesson next morning. "But I do not even know in what century Charlemagne lived." "Begin by teaching what you know" said Steiner, "Give them the history of the World War, for there you surely were yourself, were you not?"'

It was typical of Dr Stein that by Easter 1928 he was publishing his magnum opus—incomplete as he knew it to be—*World-History in the Light of the Holy Grail*, with particular reference to the centuries in which Charlemagne lived!

His wife came to join the staff and in 1920 their daughter Clarissa was born. Stein looked back later on '13 happy years of active work and study' as a pioneer Waldorf teacher among a staff of 64.

On Sunday, 9 March 1924, at the age of 33, half-way through his life, a turning-point occurred. His friend Dr Karl Schubert was conducting the children's service. 'There was something deeply impressive in this Sunday morning service, and on this occasion I was moved by it more deeply than ever before. The experience became so concrete as to merge at last into spiritual vision. I could experience quite clearly how I was entering into a more or less unaccustomed condition, becoming free of the bodily nature. From that time onwards I knew by my one experience what it was to enter the spiritual world free of the body and to perceive without the bodily sense-organs ... Rudolf Steiner, who explained the experience to me, gathered it up into a meditation which he gave me.'

My head, it bears the being of the resting stars
My breast is harbouring the life of the wandering stars
My body lives and moves amid the elements
All this am I.

Like Pascal on 23 November 1654, part of his experience included the spiritual encounter with Jesus Christ, the Son of the Living God. Further genuine spiritual experiences followed, as Stein gained orientation in his new spheres of consciousness. These qualified him to interpret the esoteric meaning of the Grail.

'In Dr Steiner's life-time,' recorded Stein, and it was on 27 June 1924 that this first occurred, 'these experiences had ... taken on a form which enabled me to look back' into a previous life on earth. By 28 August he had confirmed what he had seen through external historical research.

But on 30 March 1925 Rudolf Steiner died.

The Vision of the Earth

Students of the Grail sometimes believe they must look backwards to unite with it. Not always do they realize that the Household of the Grail is ever-present and evolves rhythmically in new community forms. The key to this evolution is reincarnation, on the one hand, and the nature of the Grail itself on the other. It exists as a companion to all humanity for all earthly time.

Walter Stein showed himself competent to know the truth of reincarnation, as witnessed in his writing of 1932 and 1938, *The Principle of Reincarnation* and *The History of the Idea of Reincarnation*. And, particularly through the help of his friend Rudolf Steiner, he came to know the essence of the Grail—for the Grail is nothing less than the form in which Christ makes Himself perceptible to humanity at a given time. In Palestine, at the turning-point of time, He had come in the form of a human being. Now, at the hour of the twentieth century, He is returning within the life-sphere of the earth as a whole, in the form of an Angel-Being, an Angel of Light.

In a lecture concerning 'Christ' that Dr Stein gave in his later years—when he was giving as many as 300 lectures a year—he referred to Rudolf Steiner's *Occult Science* (1909) as 'an abbreviated cosmology, which holds the teaching of the Grail—the Angel of Christ which approaches the earth'. Now, just as Joseph of Arimathea may have brought the tidings of the Grail to Albion's shores after the First Coming and planted a staff of thorn which has flowered at Christ-Mass ever since, so he was to bring an important contribution from Albion to the evolution of the planetary economy and the crucial recognition of the Staff of Life within it, which he came to develop in the form of a Gold-Wheat Standard. This took place at the start of the Second Coming in A.D. 1933.

At Glastonbury in July 1932, Dr Stein spoke these words in his fifth lecture to an Anthroposophical Summer School:

The many-sided knowledge concerning the nature of the earth given by Anthroposophy (the method of Rudolf Steiner's spiritual science) makes us realize that the Earth is much more than a celestial globe floating in space, much more than an object of dry, abstract study. We feel the Earth not merely as a structure composed of continents and seas, rivers and lakes, mountain ranges and plateaux, but also as a friend, as a being of intelligence and soul. It is our duty in this age to carry *the wisdom of the Earth herself* into our economic arrangements. We must, in fact, be able to perceive that *a moral form can only be given to the economic system by the recognition that the Earth is the Body of Christ*. For inasmuch as the Blood of the Redeemer flowed into the Earth, the Earth became His Body.

He saw the problems of the modern economy, which were then critical, as a matter of the death throes of an outdated system and the birth pangs of something unrealized and new.

The idea of using political frontiers as economic frontiers—a conception originating in the East—is obsolete and ought to be abandoned. Political frontiers are justifiable only in the form of boundaries enclosing psychological entities—the souls of the peoples.

World Economy must arise out of the conditions indicated by the *Earth*—goods should be produced where production is most economical. Our system of world trade enables everything to be easily distributed; the needs of every human being can be satisfied. The Earth is rich enough and the peoples are industrious enough. It is only obstinacy inspired by outgrown and obsolete ideas that is driving mankind into crises.

The creation of a system of World Economy is the real mission of the Anglo-Saxon/Germanic people ... If we had courage enough to begin the organization of trade and industry on a world-wide plan, we should very soon see that this is precisely the way in which war could be prevented.

Walther Rathenaw had thought the same.

One of his hearers did have this courage: Daniel Nicol Dunlop OBE, founder in 1911 of the British Electrical and Allied Manufacturers Association, and in 1924 of the World Power Conference, whose aim was to unite those involved in production, distribution and consumption of the earth's energy resources in conscious collaboration. (This is now called the World Energy Conference, and had its last meeting in Montreal in 1989.)

On 8 June 1933, Dunlop wrote to Stein from the London Office of the World Power Conference:

> I have been awaiting a suitable opportunity to start a Research Bureau in association with the World Power Conference for the collection of data and statistical information in relation to World Economics, with the twofold object of:
> a. Preparing for an International Conference and
> b. Publishing in a suitable form, conclusions arrived at based on the data and information collected.

Would Stein help with the collecting, concluding and publishing?

And so for the last 24 years of his life, Walter Stein became a Londoner. And only now did he resolve, at last, to learn English!

Plan II

In this brief essay we cannot describe Walter Stein's work for the world economy in detail, e.g. for the *World Survey* journal and the 'World Power Conference' in London; and via King Leopold III of Belgium, for a Research Institute for World Economy in Brussels, linking to the International Statistical Agency at the Hague. Perhaps a few quotes will show how he saw the question of global economy as a Grail-question—indeed, as a modern quest for the Household or Temple of the Grail. For this is his unique contribution to us all. And this work is still more pertinent today, East and West, North and South, when the planet is seeking its voice in a single *oikonomia* or humanely planned household as never before.

Preparing his keynote speech to an international conference for world economy planned by Dunlop for Chicago in 1936 (which never came about since Dunlop died on 30 May 1935), Stein developed and wrote (in the British Museum Library á la Karl Marx) a remarkable picture of 'The Earth as a Basis of World Economy', to move from nation-economies based on gain and competition to a single economy based on knowledge and mutual interest.

> Unfolding the panorama of the Earth from its well-defined contours, over the oceans, through the air and the surrounding atmosphere of warmth, we have passed on to the influences of

sun and planets, which are woven through the rhythms of the living earth. Here we come upon the influence of the rhythms of nature on economic life. In crops and corn prices we saw how the earth and the cosmos, working into the life-processes of the Earth, actively enter into the course of economic development. Our knowledge in this field was admitted to be elementary as yet, because in consequence of the fact that the organization of our educational system tends to specialization, nobody is in a position to gauge the universal field where these problems alone can be solved. Here we have been able to do no more than to show this universal field, emphasize its importance, and point out that only through the real co-operation of all sciences and of all nations can *knowledge* be born which will serve as a foundation for the building up of a world-embracing economy. What we most need is a form of organization, directed from the *universal* point of view, in the realms of education and research.

To help, he founded the monthly *The Present Age* (1935–39), whose cover came to show the planet earth. Here he published his discovery that the major step towards the founding of commercial towns in England and on the Continent in the tenth century derived from the historical prototype of Lohengrin—Athelstan's chancellor and eventual Abbot of Croyland, Turketul. Now, one thousand years later, it was time for servants of the Grail to take the next major step and found the global economy, fulfilling the aims of the Templars as Christian bankers of Europe, and of the Order of Christ who succeeded them.

What stood against them?

A system of economy conducted by experts along true economic lines is capable of embracing the whole world, but a system of economy conducted by politicians along political lines can never do so. Hence it is essential to have bodies for world-wide research and administration of a quite non-political nature ... The separation of economics from politics is an economic necessity. Those nations who have acquired great possession of gold, for instance, are checking, through the power of gold, the just and effective administration of the economic system. The gold function which adjusted the balance between the separate national economies through re-coinage and the timely import and export of gold must be replaced by something else in a system of world-economy which, *being a complete unit with no frontiers*, knows nothing of import and export.

These were world-embracing views.

The essence of his reforms was to introduce a mobile *time-conception* to the handling of processes formerly conducted in space. For example, by organizing a global stabilization fund for the timely purchase, storage and sale of surplus wheat, we could stabilize prices, for the price level of other commodities follow the price of wheat, and we could feed the starving millions who depend upon the earth as a whole, and not only on the accidents of their natural and political climates and purchasing power. The cost of the fund would balance out over not more than seven years. And who could distribute the wheat? The peace-time navies who were paid in any case to travel the globe.

Of unemployment? 'We have always to face the fact that there are unemployed people. We close factories, we do not know what to do with the large masses because we have no research institutions covering the whole economic field to tell us in what branches the economic life will prosper, or decay, so giving us an opportunity *in advance*, to educate people and fit them to take part in other ways.'

Instead of the cross-currents of internecine business and trade war, '... in a fully developed system of world-economy, embracing the whole earth, its universal character would enable such a division of labour among all peoples that each would be able to produce precisely those things for which they are best fitted and to adapt the methods and tempo of production to their particular national temperament.' He would have thought well of Dr Schumacher. In his booklet *West-East: a Study in National Relations*, Stein studied these temperaments and revealed their secret connections.

Let us end with inflation.

As we know, inflation occurs when bank-notes have decreased in value between the time of their receipt and their exchange for some commodity. The individual author of a commodity is thereby defrauded of the money equivalent of what he has produced. It is quite reasonable that this should be considered a great wrong. If, however, we realize how this wrong has been got over and so-called 'stabilization' achieved, we see that it has been at the cost of the ruin of the small businesses ... Shares are consolidated—as the saying goes. Many shares are made into a single share. But this is the same phenomenon as inflation. The burden has merely been transferred to another pocket ... Bread fulfills its purpose when it is eaten and while the bread diminishes, the money, which to begin with was there as a draft against the commodity, remains. Inflation, therefore, is merely the counter-image of the consumption of commodities ... There must always be inflation, and to imagine that it has been done away with is merely a sign of living in illusion. *Our task is to bring rhythm into it, to see that it occurs in the right degree, at the right time, and at the right place.* But where is this right place? It is not in the bank-notes in the pocket of the capitalist, but it is where the Earth gives her uninterrupted flow of gifts to the social organism. The gifts of the Earth are coal, metals, the fruits of the field. And when the whole process of circulation, when production and consumption are brought to a true balance in a healthy social organism, new issues of bank-notes will be regulated by production, and decrease in the money-value by consumption. Instead of hitting the individual, the balance is set up by the free gifts of nature, by the free gifts of the Earth. It is the Earth which takes away from human beings what is now leading to suffering, but the Earth can only take away this suffering when human beings, by dint of true ideas and organizations which must be kept flexible and adaptable, maintain intact the link between the social organism and the planet Earth.

These things demonstrate the intimate connection which exists between the most practical affairs of life and lofty spirituality. When the whole Earth—not the little territories we call States— but the whole planet Earth, permeated as it is with the Christ Impulse, is truly incorporated into the social process, a sublime Nature takes the burdens of inflation upon Itself, takes upon Itself all that it is beyond the power of the individual to endure. The whole planet Earth then becomes part and parcel of the economic process. The whole of mankind today is struggling, unconsciously, to bring this about and is, furthermore, on the way to realize it consciously.

Epilogue

If the first half of Walter Stein's life was a gradual coming to the Grail, the second involved the quest to share the Grail with as many others as possible—through lectures; through writing books, pamphlets and in journals; through direct action in economic and political events; and from the Second World War until his death in 1957, by personal consultation as a medical practitioner (homoeopathic) and counsellor. He advised Kemal Ataturk and Winston Churchill, his work was known to

General Smuts and supported by the King of the Belgians (who wrote to him in longhand as 'Dr Stone'). And for countless people whose names were less often in headlines, his help and care were crucial.

It is not just the great and public figures who matter in history. It is not even merely those who succeed. It is also those who fail, who leave things uncompleted. Without Amfortas, without Kundry, without Trevrezent, would Parsifal have come, with Fierefis, to the Grail?

We are all interwoven, and therefore there is no one who is not in some way related to the Household of the Grail. But not all of us are aware how. One who did become aware in the course of his recent earthly life between 6 February 1891 and 7 July 1957 (when he died in London's Middlesex Hospital at 1.20 a.m.) was Dr Walter Johannes Stein.

Comments on *The Spear of Destiny*

'The actual history of the Spear is a novel in itself' wrote Dr Stein of the so-called lance of Longinus. 'For the history of the Spear,' he added, 'see *Jahrbücher der Deutschen Geschichte Konig Heinrich I*, by George Waitz, Leipzig, 1885, p. 67.'[1]

His friend Trevor Ravenscroft, who died in January 1989, set out to present this novel, after the death of Dr Stein. But he left history behind.

There are elements of historical truth in his *The Spear of Destiny* (Neville Spearman 1973, and Samuel Weiser 1982/3/5/6). But central things claimed as historically true were not.

In particular, W.J. Stein first heard Hitler's voice, *by his own account* in a lecture in London on 12 October 1943,[2] while taking to Walther Funk about the problem of the gold standard in the Hotel Kaiserhof, Berlin. This must have been in 1932. Ravenscroft has Stein meet Hitler in dramatic circumstances in Vienna some 20 years before the above encounter took place.

Again, Ravenscroft asserts that Stein knew something of his own earlier incarnations already in 1916. But Stein records the first memory of any such as occurring in June 1924, as mentioned above.

Further, Ravenscroft asserts that Stein 'in the Spring of 1912, when he had completed his first full year of research, ... had already come to the conclusion that the Grail romance of Wolfram von Eschenbach had been written against the background of the ninth century and that the host of weird and wonderful names in its pages veiled actual physical-historical characters who had lived during the age of the Carolingian Emperors (p.44). This scarcely squares with Stein's comment to Rudolf Steiner in 1919: 'But I do not even know in what century Charlemagne lived,' nor his account in his Grail-Book of the provenance of his quest into the ninth century for historical prototypes of Wolfram's character which began in earnest in January 1923.

No, Trevor Ravenscroft changed history to suit the purposes of his novel. He told me himself he had 'hotted up' the initial draft on the advice of his publisher. Possibly in some remorse for the protest that ensued from other friends of Dr Stein, no less than to meet the many requests he received in the post, he set out 'to develop and expound the Grail teachings of Dr W.J. Stein' in cooler mood in his *The Cup of Destiny* (Rider 1981).

What he did now, as Mr John Hogervost of Leiden has faithfully shown,[3] was more or less précis or reproduce Dr Stein's *World-History in the Light of the Holy Grail*. Though, even here, some of his wilder hares scamper across the pages.

But we should not accuse Trevor Ravenscroft of plagiarism. He felt genuinely indebted to Dr Stein, and wanted to make his work known to a far wider public. He sensed the real drama of the Grail. And to many, he has conveyed it.

What he has perhaps principally obliged us, by his efforts to do, is to learn to discriminate painfully once again in our own selves between the ways of the raven, the magpie, and the dove.

Notes

1   *The Present Age*, Vol. 1, No. 3, p. 9.
2   c.f. *Shoreline* journal No. 2, 1989, p. 22.
3   Mr Hogervost has noted no fewer than 69 specific 'transplants'.

8

THE GRAIL QUEST AS INITIATION

Jessie Weston and the Vegetation Theory

by

Prudence Jones

Of the writers discussed in this book only one truly deserves the ascription 'Grail scholar', and that is Jessie Laidley Weston (1850-1928). Others, such as C.G. Jung and Joseph Campbell, were learned in the extreme, but none devoted so much of their time to the explication of a single theme. 'Miss Weston' (as she was universally called by her peers) brought an entirely new spectrum to the study of the Grail in the twentieth century. Her scholarship is impeccable—despite occasional flights of fancy which she was never afraid to make, and she paved the way for a whole generation of investigators to come. Her books and articles, now at last being republished,[*] still make exciting and challenging reading, and she deserves to be remembered as someone who caused an entire generation—those who disagreed as well as agreed with her—to look again at the Grail, and to see new possibilities—possibilities which are still being followed up.

❦

The Vegetation or Ritual Theory of the origin of the Grail is long overdue for consideration at the present time, when the pagan reigions of Western Europe are being reborn in a new form for the twenty-first century.

The Ritual Theory claims that the Grail was originally conceived as the mysterious source and origin of life, both of physical life—the renewal of crops, of animal and human existence sought in the fertility rituals of Nature religions world-

*The Romance of Perlesvaus, Janet Grayson ed. (Holland, Michigan: Studies in Medievalism, 1988).

wide—and of spiritual life—the immortality of the soul, or our potential for union with the Divine, which is sought by the inner, esoteric practitioners of all religions, whether pagan, Christian, Buddhist, Moslem or any other. Because all religions share this search for personal knowledege of the source of spiritual life, the theory claims, it was possible in the twelfth century for a Celtic tale from the native pagan religion to be assimilated, in its mystical aspect, to the mystical practices of Christianity. Thus a magical tale about a folk-hero who renews the failing spirit of vegetation each year could give rise to a mystical tale about an initiates's hard-won knowledge of the source of both physical and spiritual renewal. This source, the Grail, could also be described as a Christian relic, both as the vessel of the earthly feast, the cup of the Last Supper, and as that of the Mystery of the Incarnation, the cup which had caught the blood of the incarnate God, the dying Christ.

The theory thus involves a definition of the Grail which, in the earliest text we have, the *Perceval* of Chrétien de Troyes, is described only as an object 'wrought of fine gold and having many sorts of precious stones', whose brilliance outshines the candles just as the sun and the moon outshine the stars. It is 'a very holy thing' and it serves the Fisher King's father with a single Host. The description is tantalizingly vague, but it may well describe some kind of platter. Most people nowadays understand the Grail to be the cup of the Last Supper, the object of a disastrous quest by the Knights of the Round Table in Arthurian romance, something that is of uncertain practical value but no doubt highly spiritual for those of a mystical bent. This too is an over-concrete definition, for not only does the Grail appear in many forms, including a cup, a dish, a stone, etc., but it is not always of Christian provenance. After many years' study of the manuscripts and commentaries, Dr Jessie L. Weston, originator of the Ritual Theory, chose to define the Grail conceptually, rather than identifying it with any particular relic, as 'the mysterious source of physical and spiritual life.' This precise and yet broad definition allowed her to harmonize many conflicting features of the texts which have come down to us, to give them a coherent meaning, and also to propose a possible history of their development in the world not of concepts but of facts.

Jessie Laidlay Weston was born on 29 December 1850, and was

educated at Brighton, Paris and Hildesheim. She also studied art
at the Crystal Palace School. Her background was that of a
scholar of medieval literature, but in her leisure hours she was
keen on Wagner's operas. Their source legends, from Saxon
poetry and Icelandic saga, were little known in England at the
time, and at the Bayreuth Festival of 1890 she conceived the idea
of rendering Wolfram von Eschenbach's *Parzival*, the original of
Wagner's Grail opera, into English. The verse translation was
published in 1894, followed by a retelling of the *Lohengrin* story
in ballad form, and then in 1896 came *Legends of the Wagner
Drama*. These renderings were for a popular readership, but the
following three studies of Arthurian romance, *The Legend of Sir
Gawain* (1987), *The Legend of Sir Lancelot du Lac* (1901), and the
two-part *Legend of Sir Perceval* (1906 and 1909) were textual
analyses of the origin and development of the story concerned.
It was in these, however, that the groundwork and first
formulation of the Vegetation Theory appeared.

Writing with all the tools of literary scholarship at her
disposal, including, from her background at the Sorbonne, the
rigorous French method of *explication de texte*, a far more detailed
analysis of style and argument than the English usually
undertake, Dr Weston began trying to solve some puzzles in the
presentation of Sir Gawain in the Arthurian romances. She
eventually concluded that Gawain—Gwalchmai, the Hawk of
May—had originally been a Celtic solar hero, a mythical figure,
son of Lugh the light-bearer, and that his function had been to
restore the spring after winter's cold. Even after he developed
into a fully human figure, the first of Arthur's knights, Gawain
always retained his connection with the Otherworld, his Faerie
mistress and his magic horse and sword. As a character, he was
particularly favoured by medieval English ballad-writers, and
although in the later, highly ecclesiasticized Arthurian romances
he appeared as a treacherous libertine, eclipsed by Lancelot,
Perceval and the others (no doubt because he still represented
the pre-Christian order of things), in the early French and
German stories he retained his original heroic status as the
bravest and most courteous of all the king's knights.[1]

Jessie Weston's research was the first systematic attempt to
establish the relative dates and origins of the multitude of
Arthurian stories. Previously, it had been assumed that since
Chrétien's *Perceval* was the oldest manuscript, it represented the

oldest version of the story. By careful analysis of the texts, Dr Weston showed that this was not the case. On the contrary, it eventually appeared that the Gawain version, attributed by Gautier to Bleheris, represented the earliest attainable form of the story. Her discoveries about the Gawain texts surprised the author as much as they surprised her readers. 'I had formed no definite conclusion on the subject,' she wrote in the preface to *The Legend of Sir Gawain*, 'the results, such as they are, have evolved themselves naturally and inevitably in the course of careful study and comparison of the different stories.' This combination of open-mindedness with utter clarity and ruthless adherence to the evidence characterizes all of Jessie Weston's work and even today makes it extremely exciting to read. At the time, it reduced some of her critics to incoherent frenzy.

Her next study, on Lancelot, again vindicated some unpopular theories. She demonstrated the late arrival on the Lancelot tales in the Arthurian canon, and suggested that his love affair with the queen was probably modeled on the already popular romance of Tristan and Iseult. Although he supplanted Gawain as the king's best knight, because of his adulterous relationship with the queen, Lancelot could not similarly replace Perceval as Grail winner in the popular but increasingly moralistic Grail cycle. As the Lancelot tales show signs of having been influenced by the Perceval tales, and vice versa, some rivalry between the two heroes would have been inevitable, and it was for that reason, our author suggested, that the sketchily-drawn figure of Galahad was introduced, a pure and holy Grail winner who would bring his father vicarious glory in this most compelling of quests. Many adherents of the Christian theory of origin were not happy to see Galahad relegated to the status of an after-thought, perfect example of the *genre* though he undoubtedly was.

Already, Jessie Weston's interest in the folk-tales of northern Europe evidenced in her Wagner studies, had allowed her to recognize the origin of the Arthurian tales in Celtic legend, at a time when many scholars still thought them to have been mere literary imitations of Chrétien. Dr Weston's main concern at this stage was to untangle the developmental threads of the whole Arthurian corpus. The Grail was not, in itself, a prime source of interest. But while writing the next volume in the series, the first part of her Perceval study (1906), her emphasis shifted decisively.

Recognizing that Perceval was not in his origins a Grail-winner (the Anglo-Norman poem *Syr Percyvelle* making no mention of the Grail), and investigating other possibilities as to his origin, she realized that the original Grail-winner, the hero who appeared in the earliest versions of the story, those attributed to Bleheris or Blihis the Welshman (whom she later identified as a historical personage), must have been none other than the Celtic solar hero, Gawain.

This theory caused controversy until her death in 1928 and beyond. 'In its origin, of which the *Gawain* stories are the survival, the Grail was purely Pagan,' she wrote at the end of the first volume of the *Perceval* studies.[2] This was of course heresy. The Grail was generally thought to have been the container for the Holy Blood, a cup or cruet, supposedly brought from Jerusalem to Glastonbury by Joseph of Arimathea or one of his descendants. In the more literary of the Arthurian romances it was treated as an object of high Christian mysticism, and its Pagan origins are loftily ignored by many of its commentators even today.

However, Jessie Weston argued, ordinary textual investigation revealed the earliest versions of the Grail stories to be those containing the Celtic elements of the magic stag hunt, the challenge by the Green Knight, the welding of the broken sword, etc., rather than any Christian element. Why then had a Christian interpretation been added to what would ordinarily have become an entertaining secular adventure? Why too had so many distinctly non-Christian elements been retained? Why was the Grail always kept in a castle, associated with a king, rather than in a temple, associated with a priest? Why did it miraculously and automatically provide people with the food and drink they most desired; and why did the successful hero's question about its nature miraculously restore the Wasteland or its king to health? Such features argued for the Grail's origin in a Pagan fertility religion rather than in Christian iconography. Why was the Grail always carried by a maiden rather than by a priest? This would have been sacrilege to medieval Christians.

Furthermore, the story called the *Elucidation* is utterly unilluminating from the standpoint of a Christian origin. Added as a prologue to the Mons MS of Chrétien's *Perceval*, it tells how once in the land of Logres, a King Amangons and his men raped the mysterious maidens of the hills, who had previously offered refreshment to all travellers. As a result, the court of the Rich Fisher disappeared from view and the Grail was seen no more. However, if we see the story as explaining how the priestesses of a Pagan fertility cult, responsible for the prosperity of the kingdom, were driven out of public life and their cult reduced to an underground existence, then the *Elucidation* is precisely what its name implies. Once more, this argues for a Celtic Pagan origin to what had already become a Christian tale. Now what was it about the original story that had made it susceptible of Christian development?

Jessie Weston's researches into the adventures of Gawain, Carados and Bran de Branlant in Chrétien's poem, stories which seemed to have been interpolated randomly into the Grail narrative, which described the winning of a magic castle and a lady associated with it, soon convinced her that here too were meaningful parts of the original narrative. These 'interpolations' were all modelled on the same archetypal theme, important enough in its own right to have retained an air of numinosity. Here at last was the Pagan forerunner of Perceval's Christian Grail adventure.

This was not some single folk-tale containing all the elements of Perceval's story. No such original had been found. It was rather 'the confused remembrance of a most ancient and widespread form of Nature worship ... which underlies many of the ancient Mysteries';[3] the cult of the dying and resurrected god, the spirit of vegetation and ultimately of prosperity, once known to Greeks as Adonis, but personified in what we now call Native religions throughout the world. The ailing Fisher King of the Grail romances was originally the vegetation god, the Lance which dripped blood, the symbol of his wounded virility, and the Cup, where this appeared, the corresponding female symbol. The hero who asked the question about the nature of these objects had won the sacred kingship not by valour alone, but by entering into conscious awareness of the instinctive process of renewal. He was thus entitled to supplant the King, or, by restoring the latter to conscious awareness of his role, to heal him.

This is, in essence, the Vegetation Theory. The Grail is a Life talisman, bringing fruitfulness to all who have the right relationship to it. The theory relies heavily, and explicitly, on the theories of Sir James Frazer in *The Golden Bough*, newly

published at the time and which made sense of what had
previously seemed to be barbaric and primitive superstitions the
world over. The theory also highlights features of the native
European religion, and Frazer's examples of modern Fertility
Cult survivals, such as mumming plays and Easter celebrations,
delighted folklorists all over Europe. (Jessie Weston had joined
the Folklore Society in 1897.) The healing of the land, however,
and the hero's winning of the divine Kingship, while no doubt
giving rise to a compelling adventure story, are not in themselves
enough to justify the legend's conversion into the more personal
spirituality of Christian mysticism. It was this shift from the
physical to the spiritual aspect of healing which now engaged
Jessie Weston's attention.

In her 1906 paper to the Folklore Society, 'The Grail and the
Rites of Adonis',[4] Dr Weston explained in detail how the
Vegetation Theory accounted for otherwise inexplicable features
in the texts, such as the weeping women in the Grail Castle, the
greening of the land when the King is healed, the presence of
doves in the ceremonies, and other features too numerous to
mention here. The Grail ceremony itself would thus have been
a standard ritual of the fertility cult, perhaps carried on secretly
in some corner of the Christian kingdom—presumably Wales,
from which the story's author, Bleheris, was said to come. The
experience of the visiting knight, however, the Grail quester, was
of the nature of a test, which he must pass in order to learn the
nature of the marvels he had seen. Could it therefore have been
an initiation?

Medieval scholars do not usually think in terms of initiation,
and they certainly did not in the days before Jung gave a
psychological gloss to esoteric ideas. But a footnote to the first
Perceval volume[5] runs: 'Having lent the Volume of *Gawain-Grail* visits to one whom I did not then know to be connected
with Occult views and practices, [6] it was returned to me with
the remark, "This is the story of an Initiation told from the
outside." ' Jessie Weston took her informant's evidence seriously.
The Grail stories, so it seemed, described the experiences of one
who had happened unawares on a ceremony for which he was
unprepared, either through blundering in by accident, or else
through replacing the rightful candidate, as when Gawain took
the place of the knight who had been slain while under his
protection.

Now an initiation presupposes a body of secret knowledge, which only prepared souls are able to witness without harm. In her Adonis paper, Jessie Weston cautiously assumes that the Grail rituals were secret simply because they were forbidden relics of the Old Ways surviving in a Christian land. In Volume 2 of the Perceval studies, however, she distinguishes between the outer, public practice of religion and its inner Mystery cult, containing teachings suitable only for a few. The annual ceremony of the restoration of greenery to the land by the coming of the Hawk of May, for example, was not important enough to occasion a link with the Mysteries of the new religion. However, the inner ceremony, the initiation into the secret not of physical but of spiritual life, could indeed have lent its setting and its symbols to the equivalent teachings of Christianity.

The means of transmission, though, was obscure. Granted that any modern initiate could recognize that the Grail romances made esoteric sense, granted that the Celtic background described in their more primitive versions was that of a fully Frazerian Nature religion, how was she to prove that an esoteric core of Celtic Pagan teaching ever existed, and even if it did, how could she show the original story-teller had actually understood it? We have no easily accessible record of the hypothetical Celtic Mystery teachings; there is no Celtic Plato, no Plotinus, no Apuleius with his story of initiation. In recent years, initiates and psychologists have been piecing together the scattered fragments of evidence, but in Jessie Weston's time, before Jung, before the Human Potential Movement with its workshops on breakthrough and transcendence, the task was almost impossible.

Nevertheless, the Ritual Theory stands as a hypothesis. The story of the finding of the Grail, having its origin in Celtic fertility religion, was thus told by Bledri the Welshman to his Norman allies in the early years of the twelfth century. As (what we would now call) an archetypally powerful story, it caught its hearers' imagination, was embellished as a romance by poets at the court, and was then reworked by a handful of other initiates who understood its significance, such as Robert de Boron and Wolfram's source, Kyot. The outer Pagan teaching about the source of physical life had been refined, in the hypothetical Mystery cult whose story Bledri transmitted, into an inner and universal teaching about the source of spiritual life. This source,

the vessel of the Divine outpouring, was what the poets called
the Grail. It was something which Christians could recognize, on
the mystical level of the higher emotions, as easily as Pagans
could, and it was something which could be equated with the
chalice of the Eucharist as easily as with the magic feeding vessel
of Celtic symbolism.

As well as providing an explanation for particular features of
the Grail stories such as the weeping women, etc., Dr Weston
was the first to mention in print that the four Grail Hallows were
identical with the four Treasures of the Tuatha de Danaan, and
with the four suits of the Tarot pack. Drawing on Classical and
Hermetic sources as well as on her Western Mysteries informant,
she was also specific about the nature of the initiation described.
This was a twofold process. The Grail in its lower, animal aspect
was the Cup, paired with the Spear, associated with the colours
black and green, and ruled by the King of Castle Mortal. To pass
beyond this mortal realm of impermanence and attain to the
earthly Paradise, the red land of the 'rich Grail', the feeding
vessel, ruled by the Maimed King, the spirit encased in flesh, the
initiate had to brave the ordeal of the Chapel Perilous, the
meeting with the Black Hand of Death. (This was the point at
which Arthur's squire Chaus, in the *Perlesvaus*, failed.) Having
attained to the Castle of the Grail, and seen the wonders there,
the initiate was next required to re-solder the Sword, symbol of
conscious awareness, and/or to put the Question which signified
his recognition or his desire for awareness of what this earthly
richness signified. If he was able to do this, he had won to the
'Holy' Grail proper, the Grail on the highest level, invisible to
mortal eyes, source of spiritual life and blessedness, whose
kingdom was the white land ruled by the Fisher King.

Though we know little about Jessie Weston's personal life, it
would seem that she was never an initiate. She criticized the
sloppy scholarship of most 'occult' writing of the time as freely as
she gave credit where it was due. Her loyalty to 'our faith', the
Christian religion, remains unquestioned in all her writings. Yet
clearly she understood the mystical realm of insight where all
religions meet and can communicate their different approaches
to the truth. The tone of commitment and enthusiasm in the
passages referring to this realm would suggest that she knew it
from personal experience.

The two volumes of the *Perceval* studies were followed by a little book for esotericists, *The Quest of the Holy Grail* (1913), which summarized her ideas to date for an audience which was willing to look for their inner coherence rather than simply for external evidence in support of them. The more academic business of editing and commenting on medieval poetry continued (see Bibliography), and she also contributed the section on Arthurian legend to the *Encyclopaedia Britannica*. By the second decade of the twentieth century, she was in her 60s, working as hard as ever, still based in Paris, still attending the Bayreuth Festival, and still fascinated by the universal Mystery embodied in the myth of the Holy Grail.

The search for proof of an esoteric pagan cult in Britain continued. In one of his volumes of Gnostic fragments, *Thrice-Greatest Hermes*, G.R.S. Mead had published an account of a Christianized Pagan Mystery cult in first-century Asia Minor. At last there was proof that in centuries long past at least the Christian Mysteries and the Pagan Mysteries had combined. An early Christian Gnostic sect, the Naassenes, had based their rituals on those of the Great Mother Cybele and her dying and resurrected son, the vegetation god Attis. 'These Naassenes frequent what are called the Mysteries of the Great Mother,' thundered their third-century adversary, Bishop Hippolytus of Portus,[7] believing that they obtain the clearest view of the universal Mystery from the things done in them.' They had a lower initiation 'into the mysteries of the fleshy generation', and a higher initiation 'into which no impure man shall enter', to which the Christians added a third, that of Jesus: 'for we alone are Christians, accomplishing the Mystery at the third gate'. Such an outlook, while anathema to the orthodox of any faith, is in perfect accord with Dr Weston's own view in 1906: 'I do not think it matters in the least whether or not the Grail was originally Christian, if it was from the first the symbol of spiritual endeavour ... the symbol and witness to unseen realities, transcending this world of sense.'[8]

It is also suprisingly similar to the attitude which, she had argued, would have characterized the initiates who transformed the pagan story of the Grail into its later Christian form. Perhaps for this reason, although there is again no evidence that the cult was transmitted from Asia Minor to Britain, much less remained intact until the twelfth century, the Naassene document underpins the argument in her last book, *From Ritual to Romance*

(1920). This book received wide popular acclaim. It summarizes her previous arguments, presents the evidence of the Naassenes, and so challenges the reader to deny that such a coherent development of religious thought, which had a document prototype from an earlier age, and which alone gave the fullest explanation of the conflicting features of the Grail romances, was the true background to the Mystery of the Grail.

From Ritual to Romance exercised a profound influence on the thought of the twentieth century. The poet T.S. Eliot took it as his theme for his 1922 poem *The Waste Land*, describing the barrenness and anomie of the early twentieth century, the Waste Land, where there is plenty of expediency but neither true love nor true purpose, has become a commonplace image of the century. 'What shall we do tomorrow? What shall we ever do?' ask the hopeless characters in his barren scenario. This is the land of existential futility, where the passions have no place and where every occurrence is arbitrary. In the years since the Nazi terror and Second World War, Europeans and Americans have perhaps integrated their passions better into the routine business of everday life. The inner sickness, anomie, is no longer an urgent problem. The problem now is the outer manifestation of Europe's earlier hopelessness; the Waste Land is here in fact. Our ecological crisis can no longer be ignored, and in no uncertain sense we must rediscover the secret of the Grail in order to restore greenness to the earth.

How ironical that Jessie Weston should have left us with the image of a curse, the Waste Land, when the whole aim of her work was to point the way to its solution.

In 1923 she was awarded the D.Litt by the University of Wales for her services to Celtic literature, and on 29 September 1928 she died in London, having not quite finished what she considered would be her final volume on the Grail mystery. Her obituary in *The Times* spoke of her many friends world wide, and of the students to whom she had also devoted much of her tremendous energy and impartial commitment to the truth. Her books are now required reading for students of medieval literature, and the theme of the Waste Land has passed into modern literary studies through commentaries on Eliot.

But Jessie Weston's influence does not end there. The Ritual Theory has not been prominent in Grail studies recently, but the historical link left unforged, the demonstration of a Pagan

Mystery cult in twelfth-century Europe, has been worked on from quite a different direction, by those who laid the framework of a religion for the New Age. Unlike her exact contemporary Jane Ellen Harrison, whose work she acknowledges warmly in *From Ritual to Romance*, Jessie Weston did not emphasize the female aspect of deity, so obvious in ancient Paganism and also, as she acknowledges herself, in the Grail cult. The Cup as a female symbol, the importance of Perceval's sister in the versions where he is unmarried, the female Grail bearer and the prototypes of all these figures in Irish legend and folktale, were all mentioned by Dr Weston, but not presumably seen as important. She describes both the Cup and the Spear as 'phallic symbols'; the female principle is as invisible in her commentaries as it was at the time in the culture at large.

The new versions of Paganism which have emerged in the twentieth century, based partly on the native folklore heritage, partly on classical models documented by such as Jane Ellen Harrison, and partly on new inspiration, have, however, taken the Goddess as a central figure. In her form as Earth Goddess, the Great Mother is a powerful symbol for those who are working to restore the ravages of technology and inspire a new philosophy which will no longer desecrate the earth. The feminine aspect of deity is currently more effective here than her masculine counterpart, the Green Man, Great Pan, Adonis—the Spirit of Vegetation in his many cultural guises.

So the outer philosophy of Paganism, which we would see but few would name as the practical work of the Grail in the world, the healing of the Wasteland, has reinvoked the ancient power of the Goddess. The Mystery core of Paganism, the secret world of initiation, is correspondingly unambiguous. The Goddess *is* the Grail, both the feminine principle symbolized by the Cup, and the mystical principle of fulfilment. Passages from Mead's Gnostic fragments, paraphrases of Jessie Weston and of the Cambridge Ritualists—Harrison, Murray, Cornford—dot the handwritten pages of modern witches' Books of Shadows. Someone, somewhere in the twentieth century, took up the unfinished research of Jessie Weston and her contemporaries and discovered the missing inner Mysteries of Paganism, no mere relic from the twelfth century, but already existing in potential as a framework for the spirituality of the twentieth.

Notes and References

1   The full theory, summarized here, was not completed until the *Perceval* volumes; *Gawain* simply laid the groundwork.
2   p. 322.
3   *The Legend of Sir Perceval*, vol. 1, p. 330.
4   In *Folk-Lore* V, xviii, now reprinted in John Matthews *An Arthurian Reader* (Wellingborough: Aquarian Press, 1988).
5   p. 253.
6   This informant is generally thought to have been G.R.S. Mead, to whose volumes of Orphic and Gnostic fragments Dr Weston refers throughout the second volume of her Perceval studies. A footnote attributed to 'A.N.' (Alfred Nutt, the folklorist and Grail Commentator) on p. 314 of that volume describes the four treasures of the Tuatha de Danaan, and footnotes on pp. 78 and 79 of *From Ritual to Romance*, 2nd ed., credit A.E. Waite and W.B. Yeats respectively with information concerning the corresponding four suits of the Tarot minor arcana.
    From Ritual to Romance, p. 157.
8   *The Legend of Sir Perceval*, vol. 1, p. 336.

Select Bibliography

Books by Jessie L. Weston

1894   (Tr.) *Parzival: A Knightly Epic*, Wolfram von Eschenbach, 2 vols., (London: David Nutt).
1896   *The Legends of the Wagner Drama* (London: David Nutt).
1896   (Tr.) *The Rose-Tree of Hildesheim, and other Poems* (London).
1897   *The Legend of Sir Gawain: studies upon its original scope and significance* (London: David Nutt).
1899   *King Arthur and his Knights: a survey of Arthurian Romance* (London).
1900   *The Soul of the Countess and Other Stories* (London).
1901   *The Legend of Sir Lancelot du Lac* (London: David Nutt).
1901   *The Romance Cycle of Charlemagne and his Peers*.
1905   *Sir Gawain and the Green Knight*.
1906, 1909   *The Legend of Sir Perceval*, 2 vols. (London: David Nutt). Reprinted 1988 as *The Romance of Perlesvaus*, ed. Janet Greyson (Holland, Michigan).

1907   *Sir Gawain and the Lady of Lys.*
1910   *A Hitherto Unconsidered Aspect of the Round Table.*
1911   (Tr.) *Old English Carols from the Hildesheim MS.* (London).
1912   *Romance, Vision and Satire: 14th century English alliterative poems.*
1913   *The Quest of the Holy Grail,* (London: Bell).
1914   (Ed.) *The Chief Middle English Poets* (London).
1920   *From Ritual to Romance* (Cambridge Univ. Press).

Articles by Jessie Weston

Arthurian entry in *Encyclopaedia Britannica.*
Same in *Cambridge History of English Literature.*
Articles in *Modern Quarterly for Language and Literature, Romania, Révue Celtique, Athenaeum, Modern Language Quarterly, The Quest,* and *Folk-Lore,* including 'The Grail and the Rites of Adonis' (1906), since reprinted in John Matthews, *An Arthurian Reader* (Wellingborough: Aquarian Press, 1988).

Her Predecessors

Sir J.G. Frazer (1890) *The Golden Bough,* 2 vols, 1st ed. (London).
(1907) *Adonis, Attis, Osiris,* published as separate volume of 3rd, expanded, edition of *The Golden Bough,* (London).

Leroux De Lincey (1840) *Essai sur L'abbaye de Fescamp,* Rouen. Contains Fescamp *Saint-Sang* legend.

W. Mannhardt (1877) *Antike Wald- und Feld-Kulte, aus nordeuropäischer Ueberlieferung erläutert,* 2nd ed. (Berlin).

Alfred Nutt (1989) *Studies in the Legend of the Holy Grail.* (London).
'The Ayran Expulsion & Return Formula', in *Folklore Record,* vol. iv.

Gaston Paris (1881, 1883) 'Etudes sur les romans de la Table Ronde', in *Romania,* vols. x & xii.
(1988) *La Littérature Française au Moyen Age* (Paris).

K.J. Simrock (1842) *Wolframs 'Parzival' übergesetzt,* with introduction (Stuttgart).

G. Waitz (1890) *Die Fortsetzungen von Chrétiens 'Perceval le Gallois'* (Strasburg).

Her Contemporaries

Adolf Birch-Hirschfeld & H. Suchier (1900) *Geschichte der Französischen Litteratur von den ältesten Zeiten bis zur Gegenwart* (Leipzig & Vienna).

F.M. Cornford (1914) *The Origins of Attic Comedy* (London).

F. Cumont (1909) *Les Religions Orientales dans le paganisme romain*, 2nd ed. (Paris).
(1894) Textes et monuments figurés relatifs aux mystères de Mithra (Brussels).

Jane Ellen Harrison (1903) *Prolegomena to the Study of Greek Religion* (Cambridge).
(1912) Themis, a Study of the Social Origins of Greek Religion (Cambridge).

S. Langdon (1914) *Tammuz and Ishtar* (Oxford).
(1909) Sumerian and Babylonian Psalms (Paris).

G.R.S. Mead (1900) *Fragments of a Faith Forgotten* (London).
(1906)Thrice-Greatest Hermes (London).

Sir G. Murray (1912) *Four Stages of Greek Religion* (New York).
(1913) Euripides and his Age (London).

W.A. Nitze (1909) In *PMLA*, 'The Fisher King in the Grail Romances'.

L. Von Schroeder (1908) *Mysterium und Mimus im Rig-Veda* (Leipzig).

A.E. Waite (1909) *The Hidden Church of the Holy Grail* (London).

Her Heirs

A.C.L. Brown (1943) *The Origin of the Grail Legend* (Cambridge, Mass.).

J.D. Bruce (1923) *The Evolution of Arthurian Romance* (Göttingen, Baltimore). [Antagonistic comments.]

T.S. Eliot (1922) *The Waste Land* (London: Gollancz). (Reprinted many times since.)

Prudence Jones (1988) *The Path to the Centre: the Grail Initiations in Wicca* (London: Wiccan Publications).

Sir W. Ridgeway (1915) *Dramas and Dramatic Dances of non-European races in special reference to the origins of Greek tragedy* (London). [Criticism from alternative anthropological theory.]

9

JULIUS EVOLA: AN ITALIAN INTERPRETER OF THE GRAIL

by

Robin Waterfield

The place of the Grail in what has been variously called 'Inner' or 'Cosmic History', 'supra-historical reality' or 'Primordial Tradition' is a tremendously important one. As yet, few attempts have been made to trace this thread of mystery and wonder from its beginnings; however, certain authors, in their explorations of the inner side of history, have recognized the presence of the Grail and given it due acknowledgement.

Among the foremost of such writers are René Guénon and his one-time pupil Julius Evola, the subject of this fascinating essay. Both men see the transcendent quality of the Grail-Myth, and acknowledge the part it has played in the infrastructure of world development. What follows only begins to touch upon some of the profounder aspects of Traditionalist views on the Grail, which would certainly repay further investigation.

Of all the figures dealt with in this collection, Evola is perhaps the least well known to the English speaking world. This is a pity, because his writings are filled with luminous thoughts and provocative assertions. It is to be hoped that before too long *The Mystery of the Grail and the Imperial Ghibelline Ideal* will find a publisher in England or the United States, where it is sure to find a large and interested readership.

Julius Evola, whose book *The Mystery of the Grail and the Imperial Ghibelline Ideal* is the subject of this chapter, was a student of the great French metaphysician and hermetist René Guénon and of his Italian disciple Arturo Reghini. To some, the point of view of the expositors of what is called the Primordial or Hermetic

Tradition in the West may be unfamiliar and so calls for a word of explanation.

The peculiar nature of the Western Tradition is that quite early on it became fragmented and certain historical tensions developed, which some would say date back to the conversion of Constantine and the taking over by the Roman state apparatus of the young Church and their subsequent uneasy co-existence.

For reasons of state the Church rapidly became exclusive and dogmatic; correctness of doctrine was more important than living a life according to the teachings of the founder. Nevertheless, heroic efforts were made by a minority to retain the primacy of the spiritual individual, as opposed to the overruling of the ecclesiastical hierarchy who wished to maintain an overall conformity in an obedient flock. Those who did not toe the Church's line were to be excluded. Those who maintained that underlying all the diverse expressions of religious truth in the different great world religions there lies a substratum common to them all were frequently condemned or pushed to one side.

Perhaps it would be fair to say that this split is found in all of us; on the one hand we long for certainty and the guidance of an infallible superior who will tell us just what to do, and on the other hand our truest self seems to tell us that each one of us individually has to find his or her own way from darkness to light and that the path we have to tread and the difficulties and dangers we have to overcome are unique to us, even as we too in our essential selves are unique. It is this personal struggle towards the truth about ourselves which forms at least part of the underlying significance of all myths, including that of the Grail.

For Guénon the struggle was a totally personal one and he rigorously eschewed any attempts to extend the personal search to one for an ideal social and political state. Not so Evola, who was all his life involved in the search not only for a personal truth but also for the social and political system which could be derived from his understanding of the Primordial Tradition. This concentration on the social and political aspects as well as on the personal was due to his particular temperament and upbringing and to the particular circumstances prevailing in Italy after the First World War. We will come back to this in greater detail shortly.

But before we do so we have to see the Grail legend as Evola did, in the light of the Traditional understanding of history. If we trace the history of any nation backwards, we shall eventually reach a point where the available evidence for what we call history is exhausted and we find ourselves in the realm of myths and symbols. However far back, chronologically, archaeological research may push this date, we shall eventually find ourselves peering into the darkness engendered by lack of factual knowledge. History becomes mythological and the distinction between men and gods becomes blurred. What is remarkable is that all the mythological and symbolic formulations at this period can be seen to have an underlying unity. This unity is not apprehended by reason or logic, which have no place here, but rather by imagination and intuition. These two faculties lead us to apprehend what has been called Cosmic History or as Evola calls it, supra-historical reality.

To understand this aright two dangers must be avoided: first, that of reducing all myths to Jungian archetypes resident in the human psyche; and second, the danger referred to by Dr D.R.R. Owen in his book *The Evolution of the Grail Legend*. When writing of the early composers of the sagas he says: 'There was a particular proneness, already seen at work in the earliest writings, to euhemerize the old gods, to deprive them of their divinity and treat them as human heroes of bygone days.' (p.6)

The above dangers are all too evident in the works of many writers on the Grail and are in direct contradiction to the Traditional view of history which has two fundamental tenets: first, 'As above so below'; and second; 'The Higher (Cosmic) history can and does influence the Lower, but the Lower can never influence the Higher'. At certain crisis points in human history the intervention of the Cosmic process becomes manifest.

For Evola the flowering of the Grail legend with Chrétien de Troyes was one such moment, about which he wrote:

> The particular form in which all is described in the Grail legend corresponds to the moment when supra-historical reality irrupts into the historical process by uniting in the most direct way the symbols of the Mystery with the living but confused apprehensions which the effective application of the Mystery required so that it might achieve the solution of the temporal and spiritual crises of the Middle Ages and beyond.

In brief, true formulations of the Primordial Tradition such as the Grail legend are always pertinent but their relevance only becomes obvious at certain moments of crisis. Perhaps the renewed interest in the Grail legend today may be seen in this light. The fundamental teaching enshrined in its matter and manner is still relevant for us today. The Grail can and does form a symbolic vehicle by means of which we can, both as individuals and as a society, overcome the manifold perils which lie before us and find our way through the dark wood into the light of a new age.

We have referred to Evola's particular temperament and personal history, and now seems to be an appropriate point to fill in the details of his life and personal history.

Julius-Césare Andrea Evola (1898–1974), better known as Baron Jules Evola, was the son of an old Sicilian family who, at the time of Evola's birth, were living in Rome. Evola, like Guénon, consistently refused to provide any detailed information about his family background. In his only autobiographical work *Il Cammino del Cinabro*, he says virtually nothing about his childhood but a good deal about his early intellectual development. From his earliest years, he tells us, he felt within him two related impulses: first, an impulse towards transcendence, and second, a disposition akin to that of the Hindu caste of *Kshatriya*, the Warrior caste whose duty it was to guard the highest caste of Brahmins or spiritual leaders.

In his early years these tendencies were manifested in extreme egotism and self-assertiveness. Eventually they were internalized into great powers of self-discipline and courage, and an admiration for traditional society, which he conceived of as hierarchical, aristocratic, feudal, the antithesis of both the bourgeois democracy of the right and the Marxist communism of the left. Of himself at this time he wrote: 'I felt a kind of intellectual intrepidity, a willingness to risk all in pursuit of truth, recklessly and without hesitation.'

From a very early age Evola embarked with passionate intensity on a wide course of reading in European literature, in French, German and Italian. As might be expected, Nietzsche was the main formative influence of these years, but he also read with great interest the works of Michaelstädter and Otto Weininger, both of whom had committed suicide while still young. Throughout his early life he was clearly pushing everything to its limits. He was also attracted to the early writings of Giovanni Papini in his first iconoclastic, polemical and very individual phase, soon alas, to burn out and give way to a banal Catholicism. For Evola, Papini was above all others the lost leader.

In spite of his disgust with the jingoistic attitude of Papini and many of his followers, Evola did join up at the outbreak of the First World War and served in a crack regiment of mountain artillery. After the war Evola, like many other intellectuals who had fought in it, felt lost and out of place in peace-time Italy.

His desire for some absolute, some totally transcendent path lead him to the verge of mental breakdown and even suicide. It was his study of Buddhism that saved him and provided him with the clear aim that he needed: that of enlightenment in the Buddhist sense, and showed him that his obsession with extinction and self-destruction was the attitude of a slave, not of a free man.

About this time he also had certain psychic experiences of a very profound nature that opened to him the possibilities of psycho-physical control, hitherto unimagined. After some years of collaboration with a group of Hermetists, many of whom had Anthroposophical antecedents, Evola decided as had Guénon to follow his own path and not attempt to join any other group or associate himself with any individual leader.

In his desire to break through every convention and all the accepted ideas of his time, Evola had been interested for a short time in Marinetti's Futurist Movement but he had soon tired of its admiration for America and the Machine Age and its noisy exhibitionism. The same was true for his contacts with Dada and its founder Tristan Tzara, who nevertheless remained a friend, as did Marinetti.

His attempt to find in painting something akin to the experience of *Kenosis*, or the self-emptying of the mystics, resulted in the publication of his book *L'Arte astratta* and publication of a number of poems in French and Italian. But by the age of 23 he had abandoned poetry and painting, and after his experiments with the group of magicians already referred to, he began to study on his own. He formulated his ideas under the rubric of Novalis' 'magical idealism' and the concept of the Absolute Individual, all of which was closely allied to Taoist notions of the transcendent man and of *wu wu-wei* (active inactivity). These ideas crystallized for Evola in the idea of *L'uome come potenza* and the belief that it was necessary and possible for man to recover and centre within himself all the dispersed elements of his personality. In this, Tantric Yoga played an important part. For Evola believed that the function of the mind by the exercise of knowledge is to recover its primordial unity: to restore to the 'I' all that which appears to be other than it; to reanimate within the world of objects, which are only elements of our consciousness, which have become opaque, that clarity of consciousness which has been as it were buried or coagulated in the mind.

All these ideas, which are in essence Vedantist, were pursued by Evola with a fanatical consistency which placed him in clear opposition to all that he found around him in the bourgeois society of the Italy of the time. Like his mentors Novalis and Guénon he had found that 'he who travels towards the truth will eventually find himself travelling alone'.

On completing his university course, he refused to take a degree, he cut all family ties, he never married, he never took any paid work, he never exercised his right to vote and he never joined any political party. It was as if his mastery of himself cut him off from all the normal commerce of life and, like Walter Savage Landor, he strove with none for none was worth his strife; all power was to be concentrated within his own person.

The emphasis on power, or better, potency (*potenza*) was the mainspring of Evola's life and drove him ever onwards. But as Evola himself pointed out:

> Detachment and a fully-lived life can co-exist in a continuous union between the calm of Being and the activity of living. Existentially this conjunction produces an intoxication of a very special kind; clarity of vision which one could almost call an intellectual fascination; the very opposite of exposure to the elemental instinctual forces of nature. This special kind of intoxication which is both subtle and clear can achieve the necessary vital support for a genuinely free life lived in a chaotic world abandoned to its own devices.

Here we can see the two elements which Evola himself discerned in his own character, fusing into a personality which was at one and the same time rock-solid in its heroic strength and yet also always seeking to move forward into new areas of self-transcendence.

Unlike Guénon whom Evola reproached, as have others, with being too unworldly and obsessed with the East as opposed to the West, Evola was not afraid of the world since now he felt he was its master. He embraced it in all its manifestations, determined to subdue them and to use them in his search for the 'beyond beyond all possible beyonds'.

Although Mussolini had assumed power in 1922 it was not until considerably later that Evola showed any overt interest in his movement. It was possible in its early days to believe Fascism to be a truly radical departure from both Capitalist and Marxist thought. Evola always maintained that Fascism must give primacy to the spiritual or it would be nothing. But it did seem to have this potential and to correspond in some way with Evola's doctrine of awareness or what the French call *Eveil* (*consapevolezza*)—'A state of being resulting from purification of will and imagination, detachment, freedom from all personal, subjective misrepresentations, bringing clarity of vision, light without shadow.'

During the succeeding years Evola was sought out by many younger enquirers and had a number of groups whom he taught. He himself became more and more interested in traditional studies, especially alchemy. Alchemy he defined as the science of the Self in all its potentialities. He understood it as the symbolic expression of traditional teaching: first, the Black Art leading to the death of the ego-consciousness; second, the White Art and the opening in ecstasy to the Light from on high; and third, the Red Art of purification, leading to pure power in action and being.

Naturally, Evola's studies of Buddhism and Vedanta brought him in contact with the thought of the Aryans. Buddhism was their *credo*, that of a pure aristocratic and noble race to whom all ideas of a God who punishes, or of sin and redemption as in the Christian doctrine, would seem a creed more suitable to slaves than to free men.

Eventually Evola's researches led him to Tilak's theory of the Arctic origin of the Aryan race and of the Vedas, spreading southwards and bringing with them solar symbols and a masculine patriarchal society, based on the Laws of the Fathers and the cult of Fire and the Sun. As it penetrated further south it encountered the matriarchal feminine Mediterranean or Middle Eastern cultures. Evola saw the culture of ancient pre-Christian Rome as an expression of the Northern Tradition and Christianity as the expression of the Middle Eastern lunar feminine culture.

Within Italy itself with its Roman heritage these two opposing forces have always existed in a state of tension and the history of Italy in the Christian era has been the history of this struggle. For many Italians from Dante onwards the Papacy and the Church are seen as the destroyers and usurpers of the old Roman *Imperium*. Did not Beatrice promise Dante 'Here thou art a stranger for a brief day but of that Rome where Christ is a Roman, then shalt thou a citizen be for aye' (*Purgatorio* xxxii, 101-2). Dante and many other great Italian writers sought to reverse the appropriation by the Papacy of all the old pre-Christian Roman festivals and sites.

This struggle polarized around the two great factions, Guelph and Ghibelline, who over the centuries struggled to dominate Italy. The Guelph aimed to establish a Christian theocracy with the Pope at its head, and the Ghibelline wished to maintain and later restore the old Roman Imperial rule. These loyalties were later revived and redefined in the nineteenth century by the politics of neo-Ghibelline and neo-Guelph ideologies. Both were to assert their claims to be the true heirs of ancient Rome. The Guelphs saw the Papacy as the head of the new *Holy* Roman Empire both *continuatio* and *restauratio*, whereas the Ghibellines saw papal pretensions as a perversion of the true Roman *Imperium* and of that particularly Italian form of ancestor worship which is *Romanita*.

Naturally enough, Evola was a Ghibelline, hence the title of his book *The Mystery of the Grail and the Imperial Ghibelline Ideal*. His belief in the greater value and potency of the northern pagan solar masculine myths as opposed to those of Christianity lead him to view with a certain degree of approval certain theories about the origin and virtues of the Aryan race which were in vogue at the time. Evola had corresponded with Alfred Rosenberg well before the rise of Hitler.

Here a word must be said about Evola, Fascism and Nazism. Certain sensational articles have appeared in France and elsewhere denouncing Evola as an arch-Fascist and anti-semite and a more recent paper has called him the 'guru of the extra-parliamentary right' in Italy and 'the single most creative and influential thinker in this tradition'.

The appropriation of the Grail legend as support for a certain extreme form of nationalism has been a persistent, if minor, feature on the fringes of the Hermetic and occultist movement in Great Britain also. The matter of Britain and the Once and Future King have on occasion been misused by such people in what can only be described as an ignoble attempt to gain political power in a manner totally inappropriate to the Grail tradition of personal sacrifice and heroic self-denial.[1] Such a perversion was a constant temptation for Evola.

There is no doubt that his influence in Italy and Germany both before and after the Second World War was considerable. Some of his books were translated into German and he was invited to speak in Germany and Austria, but his audiences were puzzled by his insistence on the spiritual nature of the Fascist revolution and his rejection of biological arguments for racial superiority. Mussolini read and approved of his book on race but in the end did not support him, apparently because of his refusal to join the Fascist party. During the war he worked for a branch of the SS in Vienna but only in a scholarly backwater translating Masonic and other documents connected with occult societies. In 1945, having escaped injury all through the war, he was blown up by a bomb and henceforward was crippled from the waist downwards.

After the war his lodgings in the Corso Vittorio Emanuele in Rome served as a meeting place for many right wing extremists. The crippled figure of the ageing sage no doubt impressed the throng of young right wing activists disgusted by the venality and corruption of both right and left. But Evola's hearers took from him only what they wanted to hear, namely, justification, as they thought, for violence. They understood little and cared less for what lay behind and beyond Evola's gnomic utterances, and his even more pregnant silences.

Evola's tragedy was that his sense of frustration lead him to attempt to be both Brahmin and Kshatriya—sage and warrior. He thus displayed some at least of the qualities he most disliked in his fellow Italians—lack of balance, emotionalism, a penchant for exaggeration and hyperbole—and in so doing, he made it easy for his disciples to misunderstand him and eventually betray him. In this he was unlike his master Guénon who rigorously avoided the cult of personality and adopted a public stance of rebarbative obscurity. For Guénon the message was all-important, not the messenger. Evola would have agreed, but in practice was not so successful in hiding the messenger.

Perhaps this was inevitable for all attempts to apply the fundamental traditional principles to concrete political and social situations are fraught with danger. But perhaps also the metaphysical purity which Guénon so esteemed was no better than the risk and fact of contamination and misunderstanding that Evola experienced.

Evola's particular situation as an heir to the Italian Ghibelline tradition, an exaltation of the pagan *Imperium* as the supreme repository of spiritual power, as opposed to the Church and the Papacy, lead him to discount the Christian versions of the Grail legends and to stress their Nordic pagan elements.

The Grail legends as we know them now are undoubtedly of Celtic or better Irish (Aryan) origin in their exaltation of the masculine virtues of heroic loyalty to a supreme ruler by members of an aristocratic nobility pledged to unswerving loyalty. Their duty is twofold: first, to engage in a spiritual quest for a mysterious object symbolizing spiritual transcendence; and second, to be united to one another as an elite group who would by their unceasing efforts save the world from chaos and destruction by the negative powers of the evil by which it is constantly threatened.

In his book Evola traces the origins of the Grail legends to Celtic (Aryan) northern sources and links them to the more comprehensive symbol of the *Rex Mundi* and the *omphalos* or central point of the universe as described by René Guénon in his masterly work *Le Roi du Monde*. He also, as many others have done, sees the transformation of the Grail legend in the history of the Cathars and the Templars who essentially were pursuing the same heroic tasks of quest and preservation. One other point in connection with the Grail legend that Evola stresses is the importance of the feminine in this predominantly male world. In this tradition Evola believed that every transcendent power was a union of male and female. The female element is the *Shakti* of the Vedantists, a term meaning both spouse and power. The union to be effective must be spiritual and not physical. Hence the emphasis on chastity and the virginal purity of the spiritual spouse.

The feminine element Evola says is a 'vivifying and transfiguring power by means of which men are enabled to transcend the human condition', or, as Denis de Rougement puts it in *Passion and Society*, '... Woman in the eyes of the druids was a being divine and prophetic, she is typified by the Germanic Vellada ... Eros has taken the guise of Woman, and symbolizes both the other world and the nostalgia which make us despise earthly joys.'

The whole Western concept of chivalry and romantic, unattainable love stems from such concepts as these—concepts of a divine Womanhood, pure, chaste and sacred, which inspires the knight, her servant, to deeds of heroism and enables him to overcome all the hazards and difficulties in the way of the attainment of his unattainable goal, which is achieved not by reaching but by the striving to reach.

But for Evola the Grail legends have significance on another level, that of the restoration of a kingdom which is in essence separate or distinct from the spiritual hierarchy of the visible actual world and must be subsumed within it. It is for this reason that both Evola and Guénon rejected all the exclusive claims of the Roman Catholic Church and, above all, papal claims to dominion over all other sources of authority. For both of them the Primordial Tradition was supra-religious in the sense that all the great enduring religious systems were but the local form and manifestation of the one universal Truth.

Guénon does not go nearly as far as Evola in his rejection of Christianity and thereby shows his more profound understanding of the metaphysical relationship between the one and the many. But Guénon did stress the balance represented by the tension between the two sources of power, the sacred and the secular, as one more example of the dualism inherent in a 'fallen' world.

Evola's rejection of Christianity made it easier for him to be mistaken about the nature of the Aryan myth which whilst having deep significance cannot be simply transferred to the sphere of practical politics and the reformation of our decadent society at the end of the Kali-Yuga.

Evola, whilst sharing in the commonly agreed elements of the Grail legend, stressed its Luciferian nature, the epic of the fallen angel and the Grail being the stone which dropped from Lucifer's crown in his expulsion from heaven. This stone or stone vessel was entrusted to Adam who had to leave it behind on his expulsion from Eden, whence it was recovered by Seth, who became the guardian of the occult tradition handed down in parallel with the Torah by Moses when he received the two revelations on Mount Sinai.

For Evola this pagan element in the Grail legend was of paramount importance since it stemmed from the ancient Scandinavian mythology and was transmitted to ancient Rome, where it was again enshrined in the tradition of the Emperor. Christianity and Papal claims were thus seen as usurping and perverting this earlier and purer tradition. Evola sums up his views thus:

> The inner decadence and eventual political collapse of the ancient Roman ideal marks the end of the effort to mould the West in the Imperial form. The influence of Christianity, because of the particular form of dualism which it teaches and because of its purely religious outlook, greatly hastened the process of dissociation referred to above, until the period of the invasion of the West by Nordic races took place and medieval civilization took shape and the symbolism of the *Imperium* arose again. The Holy Roman Empire was *restauratio* and *continuatio* ... which in its ultimate meaning implies a restoration of the Roman movement towards a world-wide 'solar' synthesis, a restoration which logically implies transcending Christianity.

Evola may well have misunderstood the profundity and the future role of Christianity in our world, but what he stood for were virtues in noticeably short supply today. Discipline, loyalty, unceasing effort, backed by great intellectual insight and a very widely based erudition, were all put to the service of a vision of a world very different and very much better than our own—the emergence of an *élite* foreseen by Guénon.

One of Evola's French students, Philippe Baillet, has summed up his status very well:

> An authentic anti-conformist, quite unostentatious and unrelenting, indifferent to fashion, despising slogans, and their associated rabble, a pilgrim of the Absolute, torn between myth and history. Evola is revealed to us as the Watchman, the 'guardian of the horizon'; the horizon of the cosmic cycle which is to come, the initiator of heroic new beginnings after the decease

of a world which already smells of putrifaction and the restorer of that imperishable Norm forever regnant in the Heavenly Places.

Note

1 cf. N. Webster, *Secret Societies and Subversive Movements* (London: Britons Publishing Co., 1964).

Bibliography

Evola's most important works are more easily obtainable in French than Italian at the present time.

*c.*1980 *Le Fascisme. Vu de Droite* (Paris).
Symboles et Mythes de la Tradition Occidentale (Milan).
1982 *Le Chemin du Cinabre* (Milan).
1982 *Chevaucher le Tigre* (Paris).
1982 *Les Hommes au Milieu des Ruines* (Paris).
1983 *L'Arc et la Massue* (Paris).
1985 *Le Mystère du Graal et l'Idée Impériale Gibeline* (Paris).
1985 *La Tradition Hermetique* (Paris).
1987 *La Doctrine Aryenne du Combat et de le Victoire* (Puiseaux).
1988 *Orientations* (Puiseaux). (With a long and valuable introduction by Philippe Baillet.)

D. Cologne *Julius Evola, René Guénon et le Christianisme* (Paris: 1978).

Collective Work: *Julius Evola, le visionnaire foudroyé* (Paris: 1977). (Contains three important texts by Evola as well as commentary.)

R. Drake, *Julius Evola and the Ideological Origins of the Radical Right in contemporary Italy.* (Part of an unidentified collective work.)

A. Romualdi, *Julius Evola. L'Homme et L'Oeuvre* (Paris, 1985).

Other Works Consulted

H. d'Arbois de Jubainville *Le cycle mythologique irlandais* (Paris, 1884).

_____ *L'épopée celtique en Irlande* (Paris, 1892).

C.-A. Gilis, *Introduction à l'enseignement et au mystère de René Guénon* (Paris, 1985).

R. Guénon, *Le Roi du Monde* (Paris, 1927, and many reprints).
_____ English translation: *The Lord of the World* (Coombe Springs Press, 1983).

R. Guénon 'Le Saint-Graal', in *Voile d'Isis* 170 (1934), pp. 47-8.

L.E. Iselin, *Das morgenlandische Unsprung der Graal-Legende.* (Halle, 1909).

D. Nutt, *Studies on the Legend of the Holy Grail* (London, 1888).

D.D.R. Owen, *The Evolution of the Grail Legend* (Edinburgh, 1968).

M.J.C. Reid, *The Arthurian Legend. Comparison of Treatment in Modern and Mediaeval Literature* (London, 1970).

Denis de Rougemont, *Passion and Society* (London, 1940).

B.G. Tilak, *The Arctic Home of the Vedas* (Pune, 1983).

R. Waterfield, *René Guénon and the Future of the West* (London, 1987).

10
CHARLES WILLIAMS AND THE ARTHURIAD

by
John Matthews

Charles Williams was a poet, novelist, historian, biographer and theologian with equal skill and remarkable perception. He was also a long-time student of the Arthurian myths, who delved deeply into their origins and from there projected his own unique vision of the Grail. Through the medium of poetry, he produced two extraordinary volumes, *Taliessin Through Logres* and *The Region of the Summer Stars*, which together form a cycle unequalled for its sensitivity and depth among any Arthurian or Grail text in the present age. Working from the thousand-and-one clues scattered throughout the literally hundreds of medieval re-tellings, Williams formed many new and exciting theories, which together gave a wholly new dimension into the matter of the Grail. Without his work, which deserves to be better known than at present, our view of the Grail would be very different, and so much the poorer.

I

When Charles Walter Stansby Williams was born in London in 1886, William Morris was still living and had not long since written his *Defence of Guinevere*. The pre-Raphaelite School of painters and designers were still active, recreating, in their own unique terms, the world of Arthur and the Grail. It was a world that Williams was to make his own, both in what he wrote and in the way the myth interpenetrated his own life. He was to leave behind a legacy unique in Grail literature since the Middle Ages, and which changed the shape of the myth so profoundly that once one has encountered his work it is no longer possible to see the old stories in quite the same way again.

Williams worked for most of his life at the Oxford University Press, first in London and later in Oxford itself, where he came into contact with a group of writers who met regularly to discuss their work in progress. Known as the Inklings,[1] the most famous and influential members of the group were undoubtedly J.R.R. Tolkien, author of *The Lord of the Rings*, and C.S. Lewis, Christian apologist, critic and novelist. Charles Williams has not attained anything like the status of the above named, but his work has continued to attract attention and to find an increasingly enthusiastic readership.

Without doubt the majority of this readership comes from among students of the Arthurian legends, and of the Grail in particular; and although Williams wrote over 40 books, in the fields of fiction, criticism, theology, and history, as well as several brilliant and much neglected plays, it is the four titles in which he dealt with Arthur and the Grail which are most likely to survive.

These four books, in order of publication, are a novel, *War in Heaven*,[2] two volumes of poetry, *Taliessin Through Logres*,[3] and *The Region of the Summer Stars*,[4] and a posthumously published prose study of the Arthuriad entitled *The Figure of Arthur* which was edited, along with a commentary of the poetry, by C.S. Lewis as *Arthurian Torso*.[5] To these must be added an essay, 'Malory and the Grail Legend', originally published in *The Dublin Review* in 1944,[6] an early volume of poetry, *Heroes and Kings*,[7] in which many of the ideas developed in the later volumes first appeared, and several poems printed in William's *Three Plays*[8] in 1931.

But his first foray into the realm of the Grail comes in the novel, and we should begin by looking at this in detail, since it gives an in-depth idea of Williams's thinking at this point in time.

Williams wrote seven novels in all—he called them 'spiritual shockers' and dismissed them as money-spinners. But they are much more than that—in fact they are probably the finest examples of modern occult fiction to date, better written than either Dion Fortune or Dennis Wheatley, and more steeped in the reality of the inner worlds and higher powers. They are, in fact, commentaries on the action of magic and the supernatural in the everyday world.

Williams peoples his stories with everyday people, familiar objects and characters which have a *symbolic* reality—for example the policeman in his novel of the Tarot, *The Greater Trumps*,[9] who stands for Justice. In another novel, *The Place of the Lion*,[10] Platonic archetypes enter the world through a magical accident and are let loose to create havoc—their sheer reality is too much for our dimension, which is mere shadow compared to the huge aliveness of the dwellers in the archetypal realms. In *War in Heaven*, the Graal is the archetypal object found within the world. Its actions are the subject of the book, together with the struggle for its possession by the forces of good and evil.

The book begins memorably: 'The telephone bell was ringing wildly but without result, since there was no one in the room but the corpse.' This corpse is the beginning of a fantastic modern quest, undertaken by a publisher's clerk, an archdeacon of the Anglican Church and a member of the peerage, who each, in his own way, corresponds generally to the three most famous Grail knights—Galahad, Perceval and Bors.

We are introduced to these three in turn. First there is Kenneth Mornington, who works for the publisher in whose office the corpse is found. He is a pleasant enough chap, with a fine disregard for everything, no obvious religious beliefs and a rather superior manner. Yet he is nonetheless an essentially 'good' man, a lover of poetry and literature and a believer in the moral standards of the time (the novel is set in the 1930s). He is, perhaps, the Bors of the book.

The second member of the group is Julian Davanant, Archdeacon of Castra Parvelorum, the Camp of the Children, which has become more widely known as Fardles. He is a simple, almost saintly man, though with a very human sense of humour and a sharp eye for the darker side of human nature. He is given to singing little snatches of hymns of psalms aloud to himself—he is most clearly identified as Galahad.

The third member of the group is the Duke of the West Ridings, a staunch Catholic from an old family which numbers both the Norfolks and the Howards in its ancestors. He is also a poet and a deeply religious man—perhaps nearest to the figure of Perceval in Williams' scheme of things.

Ranged against this unlikely trio are three servants of the

negative side of creation: Gregory Persimmons, a long-time practitioner of small evils, petty hateful things which have finally drawn him to become part of a greater evil. He seeks the left-hand path with a great willingness, desiring to become one with the God he worships, who is Satan, leader of all the hosts of darkness. He is the murderer of the man found in Kenneth Mornington's room at the start of the book, and he desires the Graal to use as a talisman of power to bind the soul of a child to his own perverted way.

Persimmons' associates are Manasseh, a Jew who is dedicated to the destruction of the Graal, and a mysterious Greek, Demitri Lavrodopolous, who is so far down the path of destruction that he has almost no human characteristics at all—he is simply an expression of the supreme negativity of evil, which desires nothing unless it be total absorption into the dark nothingness of Hell.

Each of this trio of anti-Graal figures represents to some extent Williams' depiction of evil. For him it was complex, intricate, convoluted; good was simple, direct, uncluttered—above all ordered. Order was the most central part of his hieratic world. As C.N. Manlove puts it in his book *The Impulse of Fantasy Literature*:[11]

> His vision of reality is of an ordered dance in which all things, from the most evil to the most good, and from the most magnificent to the most sordid, offer in their own modes delight to the beholder and praise to the Creator.

In *War in Heaven*, the balance between good and evil is maintained by the Graal itself, which is capable of being used to destroy as well as to create; in the hands of the 'good' people of the book it can heal and defeat the forces of darkness; in their hands it could, potentially, destroy...

After the discovery of the corpse in the publishing house the police declare themselves baffled. The murder seems totally motiveless, and there are no identifying marks either on the body or its clothing. But stranger things are afoot. By chance Kenneth Mornington makes the acquaintance of the Archdeacon, who has a book to offer for publication, and by chance when he visits the publishing house to discuss this with Kenneth, the Archdeacon happens to catch sight of a set of uncorrected proofs of a book called *Historical Vestiges of Sacred Vessels in Folklore* by Sir Giles Tumulty. In fact Tumulty is a friend of Gregory Persimmons, who also happens to own the publishing company. He is a thoroughly unpleasant man who has travelled the world and seen, and possibly been involved with, many strange and not always pleasant things. He has stumbled on the fact that in all probability the Graal is now kept in the Archdeacon's own church at Fardles. He has conveyed this fact to Gregory who has requested him to remove the reference from his book. By chance the Archdeacon sees a set of proofs which still have the passage. His thoughts about the Graal at this time are that it is unimportant, though undoubtedly interesting for the energies it may have absorbed from its use as the Cup of the Last Supper and for having received the blood of Christ after the Crucifixion.

Immediately after this, Persimmons himself, who has taken a large house close at hand, visits the rectory and tries unsuccessfully to buy the chalice from the Archdeacon. When this fails an attempt is made to steal it, causing the Archdeacon finally to believe there might be something more to the suggestion that the chalice is indeed the Graal.

Meanwhile, Persimmons visits a strange chemist's shop somewhere off the Finchley Road, where he encounters the Greek and purchases a strange ointment. That night he uses it to send him on a terrifying interior journey to meet his master. Williams' description, here as elsewhere, conveys a disturbingly real sense of what it actually feels like to work magic. (He was an active member of the Hermetic Order of the Golden Dawn for five years.) In this case it is a dark magic, and we are left in no doubt as to its effects or to the nature of the man working it.

Meanwhile, the Archdeacon, having decided that the chalice may indeed be the Graal, decides to take it to London, and to his Archbishop. Within sight of Fardles, however, he is knocked unconscious by Persimmons' chauffeur and the Graal is stolen.

Kenneth Mornington, having decided to take a walking holiday in the country and to call upon the Archdeacon on the way, encounters the Duke of North Ridings in a storm and the two arrive together at Fardles in time to hear of the Archdeacon's adventures. The police subsequently arrive, having been called to investigate the attack on the Archdeacon. He, reluctantly, tells of his suspicions and is even more reluctantly persuaded to go to Persimmons and confront him. Once there, events move fast. The Archdeacon, along with Mornington and the Duke, steal back the Graal and flee to London, where the cup is subjected to an occult attack and is successfully defended by the Graal's new guardians.

This latest attempt having failed, the enemy set about obtaining the Graal by other means. But a new character is now brought into the action, in the shape of a young man in grey, who appears without warning in Gregory Persimmons' garden and addresses him in such a way that it is clear that he knows what is afoot and that he is the Graal's true guardian.

Unshaken by this, Persimmons continues with his plan. He has invited to stay, in a cottage in the grounds, another employee of the publishing house named Lionel Rackstraw, together with his wife, Barbara, and their young son, Adrian. Gregory's desire is to use Barbara as a means of obtaining the Graal, and at the same time to steal Adrian in order to bind his soul to the ways of evil. He manages to inflict a small wound on Barbara Rackstraw's arm and anoints it with some of the evil ointment. Its effects on the innocent woman are as one would expect; faced with interior images of evil too subtle for her innocent nature, she appears to go mad.

Having taken charge of Adrian, Gregory attempts to use him as a medium to find out more concerning the young man in grey, but finds that he encounters a force greater and stranger than anything he knows.

Undeterred, Gregory suggests to Lionel that if the Graal were to be offered to a certain doctor he knows of (who is in fact the Jew Manasseh), a cure might be found for Barbara, and a desperate Lionel calls on the Archdeacon for help. He of course responds willingly, though not without grave doubts on the part of the Duke. In the end, another agency releases Barbara, though in the confusion of the moment the Archdeacon still gives Manasseh the Cup.

Meanwhile, Sir Giles, who is about to leave, having realized that all may not be going Persimmons' way, meets the young man in grey, who finally reveals his identity:

> I am Prester John, I am the Graal and the Keeper of the Graal. All enchantment has been stolen from me, and to me the vessel itself shall return.

In the outside world, a series of small clues have led the police investigating the murder of the man found in Mornington's office towards an unlikely suspect, the publisher Mr Gregory Persimmons. The police begin to close in on the chemist shop, where plans continue to pervert the Graal to evil use. At this juncture the Duke and Kenneth arrive on the scene, bent upon retrieving the Graal. They are unprepared for the strength of the evil face, and Kenneth dies in the attempt to win back the Cup. But other and higher matters are yet to come. The enemy themselves are scarcely aware that they are caught up in a greater struggle than that for the Graal—war in Heaven has indeed been joined ...

The police search now for the house where the chemist shop should be, but it has been hidden. The Archdeacon, called to the aid of his fellows and not knowing of Kenneth's death, is now held captive. A terrible fate awaits him as Gregory and his associates prepare to 'marry' his soul to that of the murdered man, whom Gregory had slain as an offering to his god. Then the police, still searching for the house in a strange fog, receive a surprise. For suddenly, the strange mist concealing the shop parts and Gregory emerges to give himself up for the murder.

How has this come about? The last two chapters of the book are required reading for all who wish to see Williams at his best and most powerful. They contain some of the most powerful descriptions of magical acts ever written. For, as the Archdeacon is about to be sacrificed, the young man in grey appears and overcomes all opposition. The forces of evil are utterly overthrown and the Archbishop, the Duke and the innocent Adrian are returned to their homes, together with the Graal.

Next day in the church of Castra Parvelorum the Archdeacon, the Duke, and Lionel Rackstraw and his family gather, there to perceive, each in his or her own way, the Higher Mysteries once perceived by Galahad, Perceval and Bors in the Holy City of Sarras, which we see now is also the Kingdom of Prester John. Here the Final Things take place, as the Priest King (who is also in some senses Christ) celebrates the Mass of the Graal.

He stood; He moved His hands. As if in benediction He moved them, and at once the golden halo that had hung all this while over the Graal dissolved and dilated into spreading colour; and at once life leapt in all those who watched and filled and flooded and exalted them. 'Let us make man,' he said, 'in Our image, after Our likeness,' and all the church of visible and invisible presences answered with a roar: 'In the image of God created He him: male and female created He them.' All things began again to be. At a great distance Lionel and Barbara and the Duke saw beyond Him, as he lifted up the Graal, the moving universe of stars, and then one flying planet, and then fields and rooms and a thousand remembered places, and all in light and darkness and peace.

Heroes and Kings appeared in the same year as *War in Heaven*, showing that Williams had already advanced far upon the path to the Grail even though his poetic establishment of it had still some way to go. These poems display the strengths and weaknesses of Williams' early writings—the rhythms are less sure and the verse style is still that of the Georgian school of the 1920s rather than the harder, more sinewy line which he developed later on, but the sense of the numinous is already present. It is, however, to the later works that we must turn for a full appreciation of Williams' work on the Arthur myth.

II

Williams' poems are often described as difficult, and, to be sure, they are not light reading. However, most of the complexities disappear once a working knowledge of the underlying story is arrived at. C.S. Lewis's commentary is invaluable, as are the various (sadly, fragmentary) clues scattered throughout Williams' own writings.[12]

Lewis gives a list of the poems in the order which he believes they should be read in order to best understand the structure of the cycle:

From *The Region*: The Calling of Taliessin
From *Taliessin*: The Calling of Arthur
                   The Vision of the Empire
                   Taliessin's Return to Logres
                   Mount Badon
                   The Crowning of Arthur
                   Taliessin's Song of the Unicorn
                   Bors to Elayne: the Fish of Broceliande
                   Taliessin in the School of the Poets
                   Taliessin on the Death of Virgil

                              Lamorack and the Queen Morgause of
                              Orkney
                              Bors to Elayne: on the King's Coins
                              The Star of Percevale
                              The Ascent of the Spear
                              The Sister of Percevale
From *The Region*: The Founding of the Company
                              Taliessin in the Rose Garden
                              The Departure of Dindrane
                              The Queen's Servant
From *Taliessin*:   The Son of Lancelot
                              Palomides Before His Christening
                              The Coming of Galahad
                              The Departure of Merlin
                              The Death of Palomides
                              Perceval at Carbonek
From *The Region*: The Son of Lancelot
From *Taliessin*:   The Last Voyage
From *The Region*: The Prayers of the Pope
From *Taliessin*:   Taliessin at Lancelot's Mass[13]

This gives an idea of the richness and detail of the work, which
will bear more than one such rearrangement of material.
Williams' own statement, in the preface to *The Region of the
Summer Stars*, states the 'arguement' of the work as clearly as one
could wish.

> The Theme is what was anciently called the Matter of Britain;
> that is, the reign of King Arthur in Logres and the Achievement
> of the Grail. Logres is Britain regarded as a province of the
> Empire with its centre at Byzantium. The time historically is after
> the conversion of the Empire to Christianity but during the
> expectation of the Return of Our Lord (the Parousia). The
> Emperor of the poem, however, is to be regarded rather as
> operative Providence. On the south-western side of Logres lies
> the region of Broceliande, in which is Carbonek where the Grail
> and other Hallows are in the keeping of King Pelles and his
> daughter Helayne. Beyond the seas of Broceliande is the holy
> stare of Sarras. In the antipodean seas is the opposite and infernal
> state P'o-l'u.

Another quotation, from *The Figure of Arthur*, might stand as an introduction to the whole of the work as it would have existed if William had lived to complete it.

> [The] theme is the coming of two myths, the Myth of Arthur and the Myth of the Grail; of their union; and of the development of that union.[14]

We should realize at the outset that for Williams the Grail was, beyond question, a Christian myth. It may have subsumed elements from Celtic story and oriental symbolism,[15] but the essential story 'came from, and with Christ, and it came with and from no one else'.[16] This is an extreme view and one which many scholars would question, but it sets Williams's Grail myth firmly in context. He intended it to serve as a paradigm of the union of Christianity with the civilization of the West—Hellenic, Roman, Indo-European.

For Williams the way of the Grail was made straight by the complexities of doctrinal argument throughout the period immediately before and during the growth of the Grail in literature. The attempt to define the doctrine of the Blessed Sacrament, culminating in the Doctrine of Transubstantiation, whereby the species of Bread and Wine used at the Mass were said to contain the actual body and blood of Christ, is central to the manifestation of the Grail in the medieval world as Charles Williams saw it.

Another essential set of keys to an understanding of Williams' Arthurian works is a knowledge of certain symbols and characters which run throughout the entire cycle. The most important of these is the Forest of Broceliande, in which it could be said that most of the events described take place. Williams himself described it in *The Figure of Arthur* as a Western forest which 'was to expand on all sides until presently it seemed as if Camelot and Caerleon and even Carbonek were both temporary clearings within it'.[17]

It lies to the West of the Arthurian kingdom of Logres, with its feet in the sea and touching the terrible land of P'o-L'u, Williams' image of Hell, where the 'Headless Emperor' walks in a place where land and sea, forest and water merge.

The second important aspect of Williams' vision is centred not in an abstract symbol but in the figure of Taliessin, the King's poet, who is called to visit first of all Byzantium, where he has a vision of the future and is sent back to Logres-in-Britain in search of the great events to come.

The bard Taliessin (or, as he is more usually spelled, Taliesin) is known to have lived in sixth-century Wales, and thus to have been more or less contemporary with the historical figure of Arthur. He left behind a body of extraordinary lapidary verse which has only recently begun to be properly understood.[18] There is no doubt that his writings influenced Williams in a remarkable way, for although the latter eschews the Celtic element within the Grail myth, images such as 'the Region of the Summer Stars' are taken directly from the work of the Welsh bard—albeit transformed.

In the opening poem Arthur defeats the opposing forces which threaten his new, young kingdom, concentrated into the figure of King Cradlemas, one-eyed and leering, in 'a mask o'ergilded' which covers 'his wrinkled face'. The kingdom is established and the Round Table Fellowship, the 'household of Arthur' comes into being.

An important aspect of Williams' symbolism is that of the human body, which is equated with the landscape of the poems throughout the later part of the cycle. The endpapers to the original edition of *Taliessin Through Logres* depict the naked body of a woman superimposed upon the map of the Western world. The head is Logres, the breasts are at Paris, giving the 'milk of learning'; the hands are at Rome, signifying those of the Pope dispensing blessing; the navel is Byzantium, the centre of the Empire; while the loins, which generate life, are at Jerusalem, the buttocks are at Caucasia, and the feet rest on or in the anti-realm of P'o-L'u. The importance of this plan is that it enables Williams to relate the various zones within the forest to the events taking place both at Camelot and Carbonek, cities at once of chivalry and of the Grail.

The unified Catholic world of the Emperor lies East of Logres; West is Broceliande, the Forest of potentialities. Here Nimue (Nature) lives and rules through her children Merlin (Time) and Brisen (Space), who perform a magical operation to bring about the foundation of the Kingdom of the Grail. In effect they seek to unify Carbonek (the Grail) with Byzantium (the Emperor) in Camelot (Arthur). Britain (or Logres) is an important part of the Empire, its foundation resting upon Byzantium in the East and Rome, the place of the Pope, in the West. These two points control the rest, seeking an 'organic whole', of which Logres represents the head, where will come about the 'union' of mind and spirit.

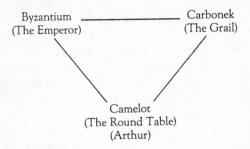

Byzantium — Carbonek
(The Emperor)   (The Grail)

Camelot
(The Round Table)
(Arthur)

If the plan had been successfully carried out, and all the perfections of the kingdom been established as the great powers intended, the intention then was that

> ...the King Pelles, the Keeper of the Hallows, was at the proper time, when Merlin had brought Arthur into his royalty and Logres had been cleared and established, to emerge from Carbonek into Logres ... [as] the prelude of the Second Coming. Logres was to be blessed thus, and he who said Mass in Sarras would say it in Caerleon and Camelot as he did in Jerusalem.[19]

Within Broceliande lies the Wounded King. He receives his hurt from the pagan knight Balin le Sauvage, who rides in search of vengeance. In the castle of Carbonek he seizes the Spear which wounded Christ on the Cross and strikes a blow in self-defence which brings about the wound which will not heal and the Waste Land which surrounds the place of the Grail until the Quest is achieved. The Dolorous Blow, as this is called, becomes for Williams the image of the Fall, and is followed by Balin's death at the hands of his own brother, the coming of the Waste Lands, and, somewhere, the beginning of the Quest.

> Balin the Savage in ignorance kills his own brother Balan, and Balan him. The natural pieties begin to be lost, and there is incivility in the blood. It is in fact the further externalization of the Wounded King. But the disorder spreads further. In the first

tales Mordred was the king's nephew, in later versions he became the King's son by incest, but unknown incest. The Queen Morgause of Orkney, the wife of King Lot, was Arthur's sister. But he does not know this when she comes to the court, and he tempts her to lie with him. The birth of that incestuous union is Mordred, and the fate of the Round Table comes into the world almost before the Table has been established ... (AT 86)[20]

From here on the pattern is set. Arthur must choose between power (the Kingdom) and spiritual love (the Grail). He chooses power. Lancelot, on the other hand, must choose between carnal love (Guinevere) and the Grail. He chooses the Queen. Arthur becomes, as nearly always in the myth, passive; while Lancelot, his soul's twin, becomes active both in his love of the Queen and the power he exercises on behalf of the Round Table. Guinevere herself fails to represent fully 'the glory [of herself] to the Women of Logres' (Rose Garden) and instead, as Williams puts it, has nothing to do but 'sit and work at embroideries and love'. She is contrasted infavourably with Dindrane, Perceval's sister, who gives her blood for the healing of another, while at best Guinevere can only rise to the level of remarking to Taliessin, in 'The Poet in the Rose Garden', 'Has my lord dallied with poetry among the roses?'

Dindrane indeed is Taliessin's great love—though we would suppose hopeless since he says of himself 'no woman would wish to bed me'. Dindrane is Williams' ideal of womanhood: saintly yet human, an almost Beatrician figure who is alone permitted the grace of being buried in Sarras, the Land of the Trinity and the place of the Grail. Williams conflates her with the unusually unnamed sister of Perceval, and Blanchfleur, the Woman of the Tent, with whom Perceval falls in love in Chrétien de Troyes Conte del Graal (see Paxson).

Williams' use of the three knights, Galahad, Perceval and Bors, to show three very different approaches towards wholeness is fascinating. Galahad is made for his task, but both Perceval and Bors have to struggle on the long journey from the temporal to the spiritual order. The Quest

... is the tale of the mystical way; but it is also the tale of the universal way ... Bors is in the chapel at Sarras as well as Galahad and Perceval. This is what relates the Achievement to every man. The tale must end, and that part of it when the holy thing returns again to earth—when Galahad is effectually in Bors as Bors is implicitly in Galahad—cannot be told until the cause of the Lord's Prayer is fulfilled and the kingdom of heaven is come upon earth...[22]

The union of opposites, which is one of the themes most consistently dealt with by Williams, takes place within the Grail. There, Galahad and Bors 'exchange places' and act out each other's roles and experiences. Finally, the Grail can only manifest through the intermediary of the Atonement, which Christ enacted for all men. Galahad, as a type of Christ, brings the Grail into manifestation and takes it back out again, leaving the way open for others as yet unborn who will one day set out upon the Quest. Thus Williams hints that Galahad is indeed a manifestation of the Parousia, the Second Coming, mentioned in the introduction to the poems.

Behind this lies Williams' idea of 'co-inherence'. It implies, simply, that all things in creation, no matter how large or small, are intimately connected, so that no single act can take place which does not have its concomitant effect elsewhere. Thus the acts of the Emperor, or the Pope, are what holds the Empire together in a kind of temporal stability—a stability which is broken when the Round Table and the realm of Logres is 'broken' by internal strife, the head no longer knowing what the hands are doing, acting in estrangement from the laws of the heart.

The second important theme, and an extension of the first, is that of 'exchange', which is defined as the ability of all created beings to take upon themselves responsibility for the lives and deaths of each other. The Incarnation of Christ is the prime example of this. Christ 'exchanges' the love of God for Man, and of Man for God through the act of the Crucifixion and the Resurrection, of which the Grail is an outward symbol. As the Archdeacon in *War in Heaven* notes, the Grail 'had been nearest the Divine and Universal heart'.

In the re-worked myth, the coming of Galahad is a supreme example of the way of Exchange. Even as early as the poems contained in *Heroes and Kings* we find this theme expressed in a poem entitled 'The Song of the Riding of Galahad', in which the Grail knight speaks of his coming to the court of Camelot, and of his parentage.

Though I be in great fame
Who hath called me by name?
Though I sit at the Table Round
Who hath seen me or found?
What Bishop or King or Knight
Hath spoken of me right?
Though I be greatly styled
The Champion, the Merciful Childe,
The High Prince Dom Galahad,
Yet most shall they be glad
That none have at all forgot
I am also Lancelot.
I am no faery's son,
No ghastly myrmidon
Loosed from the thick profound
Shadows of underground
Wherein Apollyon roars,
Nor cherub from the doors
Of heavenly beauty sent
To herald God's advent,
Not elemental Knight
Made human but to right:
I am all men, I wot,
And born of Lancelot.

For my lord Sir Lancelot
In a marvel me begot
On my mother the lady Helayne,
Whom, our fair Christ did ordain
For a covering and a shrine
For the body that is mine:
From his joy and agony
Then I began to be,
His love being a fair thing
Had holy assoiling
By the heaven's council and plot
I also am Lancelot...[23]

Already the importance of Galahad's relationship to his father is established. This was to remain a central image of Williams' work. He wrote of it again in *The Descent of the Dove: A Short History of the Holy Spirit in the Church.*[24]

There was built up, in the romances called the *Lancelot* and the

Queste del Saint Graal, a world of chivalry and love in order to be overthrown by the creation of another world of religion, contrition, and sanctity; and as in that world the Grail shone defined, the same and yet (in effect) other than the Eucharist, so in proportion to its pure glory Lancelot was barred from achieving it. But by what has been one of the greatest moments of imagination ever permitted to man, he was allowed and compelled, in an enchantment and supposing himself to be with the queen, to beget upon the predestined mother the shape of the High Prince.

Thus the 'sin' of Lancelot and Guinevere is transformed, 'exchanged' into good. Galahad comes. The Quest begins. And Taliessin, standing outside the castle sees:

through the unshuttered openings of stairs and rooms the red flares of processional torches and candles winding to the king's bed; where instead of Arthur Galahad that night should lie, Helayne's son instead of the king's, Lancelot's instead of Guinevere's...[25]

Here an entire complex of themes is brought together. Galahad should have been Arthur's and Guinevere's son; instead he is the product of Lancelot's obsession with the Queen, which is caused to bring about the creation of Galahad. Thus do Merlin and Nimue prepare for the possibility of failure in the perfect kingdom they have helped establish, arranging the begetting of Galahad who, even though the rest fail, will bring about his own apotheosis and move beyond—perhaps, like Christ, experiencing the joy of the Grail for the sake of all. (Thus in Williams' version the final achievement takes place as Arthur prepares for battle with Mordred. The dream of the kingdom is over, but the dream of the Grail continues.)

We see only fragmentary glimpses of the quest from here on. Through the experiences of the quest knights we watch the development of the development of the myth, remaking some, all but destroying others.

In the end, Logres, the ideal world devised by Merlin and Brisen, fails. Lancelot and Guinevere are discovered, Arthur banishes his greatest knight and condemns the Queen to the stake. In the inevitable rescue operation Lancelot accidentally kills two of Gawain's brothers, setting in motion a vendetta

which culminates in Arthur following him to France and making
war upon him. Meanwhile, Mordred dreams of taking power
from his father and thinks of the Grail that he needs no such
'faery mechanisms' and that if it existed he would send a dozen
of his knights to destroy it. Once his father is away he
overthrows the kingdom and declares himself king. It is a victory
for the anti-Grail powers, and the Pope, awaiting good news
from the West, hears only

> ... of bleak wars between Arthur and Lancelot.
> Gawain set to seek his heart's vengeance,
> The king's son gone whoring with fantasies,
> and mobs roaring through Camelot...'[26]

Williams' theme of the unification of the ideals of Christianity
with those of civilization proves to be unattainable in Arthur's
Logres, which slips back to 'mere Britain'. Charles Moorman, in
his valuable study of Williams' Arthuriad, sums up:

> ... this order is constantly frustrated by man's desire for self-
> sufficiency and independence. The main theme of the cycle thus
> becomes the battle between order and charity and cupidity, lover
> and pride, exchange and possession.[27]

Charles Williams was a remarkable man by any standards. It was
not enough for him to recreate the myths of Arthur and the
Grail in written form. He wished to bring the insights he
possessed into the spiritual lives of his characters to the world of
everyday existence. To this end he formed 'The Company of the
Co-inherence', made up of friends and colleagues. He saw Sir
Humphrey Milford, the then head of Oxford University Press,
very much as he saw Arthur in the myth. Others were allotted
other parts. He himself seems to have identified with Taliessin.
Lois Lang-Sims, in Letters to Lalarge, her as yet unpublished
account of her friendship with Williams, describes the way in
which this worked, and describes him as 'a writer so passionately
and personally involved in his own thought-world, even to the
extent of manipulating his friends into fulfilling the roles created
for them in his private myth'.[28]

Alice Mary Hadfield, who worked with Williams at the Oxford
University Press, notes also that his office life 'was always on the

point of becoming the opening of one of his own novels. Every morning when I went to work I had a fluttering feeling that it might happen, and although my office was on the floor below I would make sure I got into the plot.'[29]

In his *The Descent of the Dove*, which is dedicated to 'The Companions of the Co-inherence', appears the passage quoted on p. 102 of this book. It shows the depths of the idea as it permeated all of Williams' life and work. This extraordinary sense of identification with the spiritual realities represented by the Arthurian characters, as by real people, are what gives Williams' work such power and immediacy. There is a constant sense of urgency behind all that he wrote, as though he indeed awaited the Second Coming at every moment (as perhaps he did in truth). For him the myth of the Grail was a reality which transcended the world of form. Of all the multitude of modern writers on the subject he perhaps more than any has re-shaped the myth in which the Grail resides, making it different for all who come after. As his work becomes gradually better known, its influence will certainly be keenly felt in the lives of those who still seek the wholeness implicit within the stories of the divine vessel.

Notes and References

1 Humphrey Carpenter, *The Inklings* (London: Allen & Unwin, 1978).

2 Charles Williams, *War in Heaven* (London: Gollancz, 1930).

3 _____ Taliessin Through Logres (Oxford Univ. Press, 1938).

4 _____ *Region of the Summer Stars* (Oxford Univ. Press, 1944).

5 C.S. Lewis, 'The Figure of Arthur' in *Arthurian Torso* (Oxford Univ. Press, 1948).

6 Charles Williams, 'Malory and the Grail Legend' in *Dublin Review*, April 1944.

7 _____ *Heroes and Kings* (The Sylvan Press, 1930).

8 _____ *Three Plays* (Oxford Univ. Press, 1931).

9 _____ *The Greater Trumps* (London: Gollancz, 1932).

10 _____ *The Place of the Lion* (London Gollancz, 1931).

11 C.M. Manlove, *The Impulse of Fantasy Literature*.

12 Charles Williams, *The Image of the City and Other Essays*, ed. Anne Ridler (Oxford Univ. Press, 1958).

13   C.S. Lewis, *The Arthurian Torso* (Oxford Univ. Press, 1948).

14   Ibid.

15   John Matthews, *Elements of the Grail Tradition* (Shaftesbury: Element Books, 1990).

·16   Lewis, *The Arthurian Torso*.

17   Ibid.

18   John Matthews, *Taliesin: Shamanic Mysteries in Britain & Ireland* (London: Unwin Hyman, 1990).

19   Lewis, *The Arthurian Torso*.

20   Ibid.

21   Ibid.

22   Ibid.

23   Williams, *Heroes and Kings*.

24   _____ *The Descent of the Dove* (London: Faber & Faber, 1939).

25   _____ *Taliessin Through Logres*.

26   _____ *The Region of the Summer Stars*.

27   Charles Moorman, *Arthurian Triptych* (Russell & Russell, 1960).

28   Lois Lang-Sims, *Letters to Lalage: a Correspondence with Charles Williams* (unpublished MS).

29   Alice Hadfield, 'The Relationship of Charles Williams' Working Life to his Fiction', in *Shadows of Imagination*, ed. M.R. Hillegas (Southern Illinois Univ. Press, 1969).

11

IN SERVICE TO THE PSYCHE
The Grail Legend in C.G. Jung's Individuation Process
by
Pedro de Salles P. Kujawski

The position of Carl Gustave Jung in the history of twentieth-century thought is beyond calculation. His work in the field of psychoanalytical studies changed the direction of thinking in this area for the second time in a few years—the first having been the theories of Freud. But Jung's approach was very different to that of his old colleague—he recognized the importance of the inner spiritual truth which he saw as present within the psyche of everyone, whether they were patients or not. Since that time, the revolution in personal therapies, self-help, vision-questing, and the inner search have grown and multiplies until there are numberless ways to discover and realize the deep mythical core of being within the individual. Many of these have drawn, either consciously or unconsciously, on the work of the great Swiss analyst, whose own writings continue to inspire and challenge all those involved in the inner quest.

The Grail legends were of considerable importance to Jung. Although it was left to his wife, Emma, to publish the results of her own considerable researches into the meaning of the Grail (*The Grail Legends*, reprinted by Element Books, 1987), the matter of the quest continued to influence Jung's work for the rest of his life. Pedro Kujawski, himself a practising Jungian analyst, has chosen to examine the way in which the Grail legends illuminate significant stages in Jung's own inner development, and how this in turn spread outwards into the broader reaches of his thinking. This in turn leads to the realization of the way in which the spiritual traditions established a contact with those of the great twelfth-century 'renaissance', including the work of Joachim de Fiore, who recognized that of the three ages of men he promulgated, the third would be of the Holy Spirit, and hence of the Grail.

The work of Jung thus emerges as of primary interest for those presently engaged on the Quest, and he earns a high place at both the Table and the Household of the Grail.

In 1911 the Swiss psychiatrist C.G. Jung, then in his thirty-sixth year, reached a turning point in his life. He had been working in collaboration with Freud for some years and had become the first president of the International Psychoanalytical Association. Independently from Freud, his own scientific research had already brought him international recognition and had led him to America, where he had lectured on his work-association studies at Clark University of Worcester, Massachusetts. He was also a lecturer in psychiatry on the medical faculty of the University of Zurich. In short, at a relatively young age Jung had won for himself a solid position in the processional and academic world of psychiatry and medical psychology of that time.

However, he was also at an age which marks the beginning of the second half of life, when a metanoia, a mental transformation, not infrequently occurs.[1] An increasing urge to become what one really is confronts one from within, and the values of personality become more important than achievement in the outer world. In an article about the stages of life Jung uses the image of the course of the sun in the sky to illustrate this process of inner transformation: 'After having lavished its light upon the world,' he writes, 'the sun withdraws its rays in order to illuminate itself.'[2]

It was certainly a deep need to follow the law of his own being that made Jung feel less and less comfortable within the confines of psychoanalysis and of academic teaching. For soon he had to abandon both and strike out on his solitary path, in a confrontation with his inner daimon or, in psychological terms, with the unconscious.

A landmark in this development was his book *The Psychology of the Unconscious*.[3] The book is an extended commentary of the fantasies of a young American, Miss Miller, which had been published in Geneva by Théodore Flournoy. The fantasies presented an unmistakable mythological character, thus revealing a layer of the unconscious psyche which was far from being personal or purely a product of repression, as in Freud's view. With the help of the young woman's fantasies Jung was able to show that it was possible to understand the unconscious as an objective, collective psyche. This new idea created in fact a wider setting for medical psychology, bringing within its purview that creative side of the human psyche which expresses itself in the language of myth.[4]

Why was it so important to bring the myth-creating activity of the human spirit under the scrutiny of medical psychology? Certainly not to explain the myth away as a derivative of repressed sexuality, but rather to take it as an expression of an activity *sui generis*, belonging to the normal functioning of the mind. Because it reflects in its images the ancient and instinctive modes of functioning of the psyche, the myth-creating or, as Jung called it, the archetypal mind is also the natural vehicle for the healing potentialities in the psyche. For most of our psychogenic illnesses originate precisely in a deviation from our original, instinctive pattern. The archetype is the instinctive, natural man, as he has always been, and it expresses itself in mythological formations.

Jung observed that a conscious, living connection with the mythopoeic imagination had a healing and vivifying effect on the whole of the personality. It is as if one carried within oneself one's own medicament, like the spring of Merlin which came to life spontaneously and cured him of his madness. Jung emphasized this fact in his foreword to the fourth Swiss edition of the book mentioned above:

> Hardly had I finished the manuscript when it struck me what it means to live with a myth, and what it means to live without one ... The man who thinks he can live without myth, or outside it, is an exception. He is like one uprooted, having no true link with the past, or with the ancestral life which continues to live within him .... So I suspected that myth had a meaning which I was sure to miss if I lived outside it in the haze of my own speculations .... So, in the most natural way, I took it upon myself to get to know 'my' myth, and regarded this as the task of tasks ...[5]

Thus started Jung's quest for his own myth. What deeper chord had been struck in him at that time? A dream he had while writing *The Psychology of the Unconscious* gives us a hint. In this dream he found himself in an Italian city, around noon. It was the midday rush hour and a crowd came streaming past him. In the midst of this steam of people Jung saw a *knight in full armour* walking slowly towards him. The knight wore a helmet and chain armour. Over the armour was a white tunic into which was woven, front and back, a large red cross. Jung asked himself what that apparition meant, and it was as if someone answered him: 'Yes, this is a regular apparition. The knight always passes by here between twelve and one o'clock and has being doing so for a very long time [for centuries, Jung gathered], and everyone knows about it.'[6]

This mysterious and impressive encounter with the medieval knight in the midst of the bustle of a modern city reminds one of the old Celtic feeling about the Otherworld as 'the Land of the Living' (not of the dead), a world within the everyday world, concealed by a magic haze, but which could become visible under special conditions and to particular people. The knight in the dream comes indeed from another world in the psyche. He embodies a fragment of ancestral soul which is not dead and buried in the past, but constitutes a living presence; he brings with himself the breath of the centuries and prepares the ground for Jung's future transformations. For the appearance of the knight denotes, psychologically, an activation of the archetypal, myth-creating psyche.

'Even in the dream,' says Jung in his memories, 'I knew that the knight belonged to the twelfth century. That was the period when alchemy was beginning, and the quest for the Holy Grail.' And he adds: 'The stories of the Holy Grail had been of great importance for me ever since I read them, at the age of fifteen, for the first time. I had an inkling that a great secret lay hidden behind these stories. Therefore it seemed quite natural to me that the dream should conjure up the world of the knights of the Grail and their question—*for that was, in the deepest sense, my own world*, which had scarcely anything to do with Freud's. My whole being was seeking for something still unknown which might confer meaning upon the banality of life.'[7]

The next period in Jung's life was one of relative disorientation, loneliness and inner search. He called it 'Confrontation with the Unconscious'.[8] The image of the knight illuminates the darkness of this period as an intimation of a hidden meaning behind the prevailing feelings of uncertainty and confusion. What would otherwise appear to be a hopeless and aimless meandering through the labyrinths of his inner world acquired, under the aegis of the knight, the dignity of the Quest and linked Jung with the spiritual tradition of his own ancestry. It is as if he had found a companion on the journey he was about to start, perhaps his own inner equivalent to Perceval who, so legends tell, also groped his lonely way, step by uncertain step, towards the achievement of the highest value, the Holy Grail.[9]

One must ask oneself in what sense Jung's search—his search for 'something still unknown' which would bring a sense of higher meaning to life—is connected with the knight's quest for the Holy Grail. Could Jung be in the search for something analogous to the mysterious substance of the Grail? The answer to this question is important for two reasons: first, because it will help us to understand Jung's psychology in historical perspective, as part of a spiritual tradition in the West which is centuries old; second, because it will help us bring the mystery of the Grail in connection with the inner realm of psychological experience, as an expression of the life of the psyche, and not merely a desiccated relic of the past. The very fact that the legend catches one's imagination, that it fascinates one, speaks to one, reaching deep into one's soul through the bridge of the emotions, is already a proof that the Holy Grail is a living myth.

Jung's inner search, which led him to his decision to abandon his academic career, as well as to his separation from Freud's psychoanalysis, represented in reality a movement away from any theoretical framework about the psyche available at that time, in favour of a more direct *experience* of the psyche. He felt such theoretical viewpoints to be unendurably narrow, failing to encompass the complexity of the human psyche as a whole. It was his intention, instead of speaking about the psyche, to let the psyche *itself* speak. Thus in his work with his patients he limited himself to help them to understand the dream-images by themselves, without application of any rules or theories. His working hypothesis was to regard the spontaneous autonomous manifestations of the unconscious as self-representations of objective psychic processes which the conscious personality should confront directly in an intentionally unprogrammed and unprejudiced approach.

In order to be able to lead his patients into this adventure of inner discovery—which, like the quest for the Grail, is not without its dangers—Jung had first to go through this journey himself, in order to get to know his fantasy material from his own direct experience. He had then consciously to submit himself to the impulses of the unconscious. This step took courage, for he had no model to follow. 'The knowledge I was concerned with or was seeking,' he says, could not be found in the science of those days. I myself had to undergo the original experience ...'[10]

It was only gradually that a pattern of order emerged from Jung's experience of the unconscious. After he went through this experience, the study of this pattern of order and meaning which emerges from the confrontation of the conscious personality with the unconscious psyche (i.e., the individuation process) became Jung's life task. In an attitude of feeling akin to the *Minnedienst* and to spirit of chivalry, Jung called this life task 'the service of the psyche': 'It was then,' he says, 'that I dedicated myself to the service of the psyche. I loved it and hated it, but it was my greatest wealth. My delivering myself over to it, as it were, was the only way by which I could endure my existence and live it as fully as possible.'[11]

Marie-Louise von Franz, Jung's closest collaborator during the last 28 years of his life, emphasizes that the primordial experience of the unconscious was the basis and substance of Jung's entire life and work. The essence of this experience is 'the encounter of the single individual with his own god or daimon, his struggle with the overpowering emotions, affects, fantasies and creative inspirations and obstacles which come to light from within.'[12]

This careful observation of the autonomous powers within was Jung's true *religio*, which then led to his discovery of a centre of order and meaning in the psyche, from which healing influences emanate. He called this centre the Self. This discovery is equivalent to the religious experience of 'God within' which one finds in all cultures. The vision of the Holy Grail, which culminates the toils of the knight's quest and brings healing to the king, restoring life to his kingdom, is one example of such experience.

From the historical point of view it is precisely his quest for the original experience of the creative spirit in the unconscious psyche that brings Jung close to the spiritual movements which stirred the West in the twelfth and thirteenth centuries, particularly alchemy, but also the Holy Ghost movement of Joachim of Flora. For these movements had an important common element, in that they followed the promptings of the inner man and sought for a direct, inner experience of the divine, rather than the mere belief in the outer dogma as officially formulated by the Church. The Grail Legend, a phenomenon of the same age, has a spiritual affinity with these movements. Thus, for example, one of the versions of the legend tells us that whenever Joseph of Arimathea listens to the counsel of the Grail he will hear the voice of the Holy Spirit speaking to him *in his heart*.[13] The Grail is therefore a mediator to the voice of God *personally and directly*. Consequently, when Perceval sets out on his quest for the wondrous vessel, he is also seeking for a knowledge achieved through an inner, individual experience of the Holy Spirit. One sees here the germ of an idea which was subsequently further developed by alchemy in the concept of *lumen naturae*, the light of nature, which is a kind of intuitive knowledge enkindled by the Holy Spirit in the heart of man.[14] For the alchemist the *lumen naturae* was a source of knowledge equal to revelation.

Looked at from the psychological standpoint, such emphasis on a direct experience of the divine stands in a compensatory relationship to a tendency in the development of Christianity which gradually led to the repression of individual symbol formation. During the first millennium of the Christian era the image of Christ, as Marie-Louise von Franz points out, 'was kept alive in and by its participation in the inner psychic life of men and women—through dreams and visions of the faithful and of the martyrs (one thinks of Paul on the road to Damascus), which were regarded as living witnesses to the reality of the Redeemer. With the institutionalization of belief, however, the repression of individual symbol formation ... began to set in.'[15] In other words, dreams and visions began to be censored and the Christian had to believe in the external tenets of the doctrine, rather than to follow his own inner experience. As the figure of Christ became more clearly defined and more spiritualized in the dogma, a rift slowly began to appear between the outer image of God and the empirical experience of the Redeemer in the soul, mediated through dreams and visions. A place was thus left vacant in the human heart, as Jung says in his essay 'The Visions of Zosimos': 'Men felt the absence of the "inner" Christ who also belonged to every man. Christ's spiritualness was too high and man's naturalness too low.'[16]

This tragic situation in which the King of Kings, that is, the conscious and collective image of the Redeemer, begins to lose its effectiveness, its power to grip, to touch the individual human being in the very depths of his soul and actually awaken the inner man or the greater personality slumbering therein, is portrayed in the Grail legend by the figure of the ailing King, the wounded Amfortas. In the alchemical texts the same situation is expressed in the image of the ageing King, whose renewal is the aim of the alchemical procedure, as one can see for example in Ripley's *Cantilena*[17] and in the *Visio Arislei*.[18]

For Jung the spiritual suffering of his father, a parson who wanted so much to 'believe' but was no longer able to, was an image of the Amfortas fate: 'My memory of my father,' he says, 'is of a sufferer stricken with an Amfortas wound, a "fisher" king whose wound would not heal—that Christian suffering for which the alchemists sought the panacea. I as a "dumb" Parsifal was the witness of this sickness during the years of my boyhood, and, like Parsifal, speech failed me. I had only inklings.' [19]

The eternal melody of the myth, however, demands that a situation of sterility and suspension of life like the one in the realm of the Grail King does not last indefinitely; the summons of the Grail soon started to make themselves felt, the *Merveilles de Bretagne* began to be told, announcing the 'dark stirrings of growth' in the myth, as Jung would say. Poets and common people began to weave fantasies around the tomb of Christ and the idea of the vessel containing the blood, the living soul of Christ, the mysterious essence of his being which he left on earth after he left us.[20] These fantasies are the expression of a deep longing for a more tangible experience of the Redeemer, whose image had perhaps became too distant, too abstract in the dogma.

In alchemy one finds the same need to search for an experience of the divine which was closer to man. The most important symbol for the divinity became the stone, the *lapis*. Described as something very cheap which could be found everywhere, the stone was a the same time a symbol of the eternal in man. The *lapis* was invested by the alchemist with all the attributes of the Trinity, becoming nothing less than an image of God within, hinting at a process of incarnation of the Son of Man in the heart of the imperfect (cheap), earthly human being.[21] Thus Alchemy gives us, in the *lapis*, a concrete idea of what Christ means *in the realm of the subjective experience*, being concerned not with belief but with actual experience of the divine.

As is well known, in Wolfram von Eschbenbach's *Parzifal*, the Grail is a *stone*, pointing to this development in the Christian myth in the course of which the God-image leaves the state of projection onto a purely 'metaphysical' realm and penetrates more and more deeply in the human realm.[22]

This transformation of the God image in the soul of man is beautifully illustrated in the symbol of the Grail as the vessel containing Christ's blood, i.e. his soul substance. The vessel is essentially a feminine symbol, a 'maternal comb in which the image of the God-man is transformed and reborn in a new form'.[23]

For the mystical man of the Middle Ages, the vessel is a symbol of the soul. In his quest for the Grail vessel Perceval is therefore concerned with the problem of finding the new form in which the essential life of the Redeemer continues to exist in the soul of man, once the dogmatic image begins to lose its effectivness. The great secret which Jung felt to be hidden behind the stories of the Grail, as well as the seemingly abstruse preoccupations of the alchemist, is, as we can see, the mystery of transformation of God in the soul of man.

In these symbolic creations of the medieval mind Jung saw an anticipation of the major spiritual crisis which affects the West in our days. According to him the present is a time of God's death and disappearance. God as the highest value, which gives life and meaning, has become lost. '(God) has put off our image,' he says in Psychology and Religion. 'Where shall we find him again?'[24] This is the question which the poetic myth of the Grail tries to answer in the years which followed the dream of the medieval knight. In fact, as Marie-Louise von Franz points out, 'one could understand Jung's whole life as a struggle to free the "new King" (Perceval!) from the depths of the collective unconscious'.[25]

In his book Mysterium Coniunctionis Jung explains why the 'old king' of the alchemist became senile: he lacked contact with the dark, chthonic aspects of nature. And this was not only the darkness of the animal sphere, which the Christian view of the world tried to overcome, but also the nature spirit, the antique, pagan feeling for nature which in the Middle Ages was considered a false track and an aberration.[26]

In a similar way, the wounding of the Grail King was inflicted by the lance of a heathen adversary. Psychologically, one would say that he was struck by an impulse coming from the unchristian layer of the soul.[27] As the King represents the Christian view of the world in the Middle Ages, what cripples him is the activation of the 'pagan' aspects of the human nature which either were negatively evaluated or had no room in that view of the world: the relation with nature, with the earthly aspects of the feminine and, last but not least, with evil.

It is in this context of profound conflict that the figure of Merlin emerges as the great healer and bringer of wholeness in the stories of the Grail. As the son of the devil and of a pure virgin, he is a creature of opposite origins, with divine and demonic qualities, and therefore embodies the union of the opposite forces which had been split in the Christian view of the world. From the psychological point of view Merlin would therefore be a symbol of wholeness and at the same time that impulse in the soul which strives towards wholeness, that is to say, for a more comprehensive experience of man as he really is. He compensates and heals the somewhat one-sided striving of the Christian for perfection, for an ideal image of man as he should be, purified from the dark side of nature. In this sense, Merlin is a *natural* symbol of wholeness, in contrast to the Christ-image developed in the dogma of the Church.

In his memories Jung says the following about Merlin:

> Merlin represents an attempt by the medieval unconscious to create a parallel figure to Parsifal. Parsifal is a Christian hero and Merlin, son of the devil and a pure virgin, is his dark brother. In the twelfth century, when the legend arose, there were as yet no premises by which his intrinsic meaning could be understood. Hence he ended in exile, and hence 'le cri de Merlin' which still sounded from the forest after his death. This cry that no one could understand implied that he lives on in unredeemed form. His story is not yet finished and he still walks abroad. It might be said that the secret of Merlin was carried on by alchemy, primarily in the figure of Mercurius. *Then Merlin was taken up again in my psychology of the unconscious* and—remains uncomprehended to this day! That is because most people find it quite beyond them to live on close terms with the unconscious. Again and again I have had to learn how hard this is for people.[28]

One must ask oneself in what sense the experience of the unconscious is connected with the figures of Merlin and Mercurius.

The unconscious, in the sense of the collective human psyche, 'is a piece of nature, an objective something that is not "made" by our subjective ego, but which confronts us as an objective other'.[29] In the autonomous manifestations of the unconscious

Jung discovered a creative activity, 'a principle of spontaneous psychic motion which produces and orders symbolic images freely and in accordance to its own laws'.[30] For him the idea of 'spirit' refers precisely to this principle of spontaneous motion in the psyche, whose activity is nowhere clearer than in the dream. In this sense spirit, according to Jung, 'is in the first instance the *composer of dreams*'.[31]

In the shaping of the dream one finds therefore the workings of a natural spirit, and this is the source of that individual symbol formation which the institutionalized Church tried to repress. But this spirit lived on in alchemy, in the figure of Mercurius. Merlin is also a personification of this spirit in its unspoiled, original condition, close to nature. About this spirit Jung says the following: 'We need to find our way back to the original living spirit which, because of its ambivalence, is also the mediator and uniter of opposites.'[32] One could say that the living experience of the mysterious workings of this spirit in the vessel of one's soul is the secret Jung sensed behind the stories of the Holy Grail.

To conclude, I would like to tell a dream Jung had in India when he was well over 60, which illustrates better than anything his profound connection with the myth of the Grail. In his own words, the dream runs as follows:

I found myself, with a large number of my Zurich friends and acquaintances, on an unknown island, presumably situated not far off the coast of southern England. It was small and almost uninhabited. The island was narrow, a strip of land about twenty miles long, running in a north-south direction. On the rocky coast at the southern end of the island was a medieval castle. We stood in its courtyard, a group of sight-seeing tourists. Before us rose an imposing *belfroi*, through whose gate a wide stone staircase was visible. We could just manage to see that it terminated above in a columned hall. This hall was dimly illuminated by candlelight. I understood that this was the castle of the Grail, and that this evening there would be a 'celebration of the Grail' here. This information seemed to me of a secret character, for a German professor among us, who strikingly resembled old Mommsen, knew nothing of it. I talked most animatedly with him, and was impressed by his learning and sparkling intelligence. Only one thing disturbed me: he spoke constantly about a dead past and lectured very learnedly on the relationship of the British to the French sources of the Grail story. Apparently he was not conscious of the meaning of the legend, nor of its living presentness, whereas I was intensely aware of both. Also, he did not seem to perceive our immediate, actual surroundings, for he behaved as though he were in a classroom, lecturing to his students. In vain I tried to call his attention to the peculiarity of the situation. He did not see the stairs or the festive glow in the hall.

I looked around somewhat helplessly, and discovered that I was standing by the wall of a tall castle; the lower portion of the wall was covered by a kind of trellis, not made of the usual wood, but of black iron artfully formed into a grapevine complete with leaves, twining tendrils, and grapes. At intervals of six feet on the horizontal branches were tiny houses, likewise of iron, like birdhouses. Suddenly I saw a movement in the foliage; at first it seemed to be that of a mouse, but then I saw distinctly a tiny, iron, hooded gnome, a *cucullatus*, scurrying from one little house to the next. 'Well,' I exclaimed in astonishment to the professor, 'now look at that, will you ...'

At that moment a hiatus occurred, and the dream changed. We—the same company as before, but without the professor—were outside the castle, in a treeless, rocky landscape. I knew that something had to happen, for the Grail was not yet in the castle and still had to be celebrated that same evening. It was said to be in the northern part of the island, hidden in a small, uninhabited house, the only house there. There were about six of us who set out and tramped northwards.

After several hours of strenuous hiking, we reached the narrowest part of the island, and I discovered that the island was actually divided into two halves by an arm of the sea. At the smallest part of this strait the width of the water was about a hundred yards. The sun had set, and night descended. Wearily, we camped on the ground. The region was unpopulated and desolate; far and wide there was not a tree or shrub, nothing but grass and rocks. There was no bridge, no boat. It was very cold; my companions fell asleep, one after the other. I considered what could be done, and came to the conclusion that I alone must swim across the channel and fetch the Grail. I took off my clothes. At that point I awoke.'[33]

Notes and References

1   See the Foreword to the Fourth Edition of *Symbols of Transformation*, vol. 5 of the Collected Works of C.G. Jung (hereafter abbr. as CW) (London: Routledge & Kegan Paul,

1981), p. xxvi.

2   C.G. Jung, 'The Stages of Life', CW10, §785.

3   Published in 1912. Extensively revised, it was published in 1952 with the title *Symbols of Transformation*.

4   *Symbols of Transformation*, CW5 p. xxiv.

5   Ibid., pp. xxivff.

6   C.G. Jung, *Memories, Dreams and Reflections*, ed. A. Jaffé (London: 1989), pp. 188ff.

7   Ibid., p. 189. (My italics.)

8   Ibid., pp. 194ff.

9   E. Jung and M.-L. von Franz, *The Grail Legend* (New York: 1970), p. 215.

10 C.G. Jung, *Memories, Dreams and Reflections*, p. 217.

11 Ibid.

12 M.-L. von Franz, C.G. *Jung: His Myth in Our Time* (Boston: 1975), pp. 13f.

13 *The Grail Legend*, pp. 336f (My italics.)

14 C.G. Jung, 'Paracelsus as a Spiritual Phenomenon', CW13, §148.

15 M.-L. von Franz, C.G. *Jung: His Myth in Our Time*, p. 271.

16 C.G. Jung, 'The Visions of Zosimos', CW13, §127.

17 _____ *Mysterium Coniunctionis*, CW14, §§368ff.

18 Discussed by Jung in his *Psychology and Alchemy*, CW12, §§234ff.

19 See C.G. Jung, *Memories Dreams and Reflections*, p. 241 and M.-L. von Franz, C.G. *Jung: His Myth in Our Time*, p. 274.

20 M.-L. von Franz, op.cit., p. 271.

21 C.G. Jung, 'The Visions of Zosimos', CW13, §§126ff.

22 E. Jung and M.-L. von Franz, *The Grail Legend*, p. 158.

23 M.-L. von Franz, C.G. *Jung*, p. 271.

24 CW11, §144.

25 See her C.G. *Jung*, p. 11.

26 CW14, §427.

27 E. Jung and M.-L. von Franz *The Grail Legend*, p. 91.

28 C.G. Jung, *Memories, Dreams and Reflections*, p. 255 (My italics.)

29 M.-L. von Franz, C.G. *Jung*, p. 33.

30 Ibid., p. 82.

31 Ibid.

32 C.G. Jung, *Memories, Dreams and Reflections*, pp. 310ff.

33 Ibid.

12
JOSEPH CAMPBELL AND THE GRAIL MYTH

by
Jules Cashford

Joseph Campbell is arguably the greatest mythographer of our age. In seminal works such as *Hero With a Thousand Faces*, *Masks of God* and most recently the best-selling *Power of Myth*, based on the hugely successful TV series of the same name, which had audiences in the USA glued to their TV sets over the six weeks of its screening in 1987, Campbell reawoke a latent fascination with the subject which has been present in mankind from the earliest times. Throughout his life he 'followed the bliss' of his innermost dreams much as the Grail knights followed their obsession. He brought fresh and illuminating insights to the myth which have opened it up for a fresh generation of students. His influence has reached far, even into Hollywood, where the director of the *Star Wars* trilogy drew heavily on the *Hero With a Thousand Faces* for the overall shape of his epic. No better contender could be found to end this collection, for if any man could be called one of the Household of the Grail, Joseph Campbell is he.

For Joseph Campbell, the Grail myth was the beginning of Europe. The unprecedented sense of yearning and striving towards an unknown end, not knowing what to look for or how to look for it, while at the same time believing that whatever is to be discovered must be found inside the seeker's own heart—this inaugurated the characteristically Western living of life which we inherit. The age-old theme of the quest had now turned irrevocably inwards; the inspiration, motive, direction and guide are for the first time wholly individual and utterly unique. There is no authorized way or teacher to be followed, for all ways already found, known and proven, are wrong ways, since they are not the person's own.

In the thirteenth-century legend *La Queste del Saint Graal*, when the vision of the veiled Grail appears to the knights in Arthur's banquet hall to summon them each to their quest of unveiling it, the knights decide to ride forth singly, for to go in a group would have been shameful. This is the point which Campbell—the greatest mythologist of this century—holds up as testimony to a new moral initiative that is of the essence of European spirituality. When all the knights had put on their arms, attended Mass and expressed their gratitude to their king, they 'entered into the forest, at one point and another, there where they saw it to be thickest, *all in those places where they found no way or path* ...' (his italics) (CM, 540). So they start their journey as individuals, each trusting to their own authority and to the mysterious power of their calling. As it transpired, though, in this story written by a Cistercian monk, there was finally only one way to be followed, the 'straight path to Paradise', and so the orthodox Christian opposition of the spiritual and the physical worlds—the world of God distinct from the world of nature—remained unchallenged. The Grail is revealed as a symbol of a supernatural grace dispensed by way of sacraments, not a blessing upon the choice and persistence in the dark and lonely path.

Wolfram von Eschenbach's *Parzival* was the book which inspired Campbell beyond all the other stories of the Grail. For him it was not only the greatest book of the Middle Ages, beyond even Dante, but also 'the first sheerly individualistic mythology of the human race'. (CM, 553) It is Wolfram's achievement to have taken a Christian symbol—with all the customary associations of an historical and literal interpretation—and to have opened it out to its universal and psychological meaning, so becoming the first example in world literature of a consciously developed secular Christian myth. (CM, 476)

The crowning moment is Parzival's failure. He honours the code and he dishonours his heart, and thus a new ethic is disclosed. As Campbell tells the tale in his book *Creative Mythology* (the last of four volumes of his monumental work *The Masks of God*), Parzival is the one figure through whom this crucial distinction between individual and collective can be worked out. Like the meaning of his name 'right through the middle', he is destined to get to the centre of things. For he has been brought up in the country by a mother, disillusioned of the court, who wanted her son to know nothing of its elaborate rules and codes of conduct. His life is lived in terms of the dynamic of his own natural impulses, and when he first sees three knights riding by on their prancing horses he falls to the ground on his knees imagining they are Gurnemanz—never to lose the sense of shame, to be compassionate to the needy, not to ask too many questions, and so on—and when he has mastered these the prince then offers him his daughter in marriage. But Parzival says, 'No, I must earn a wife, not be given a wife,' passing the first spiritual test of both Wolfram and Campbell.

Having later earned his true bride, whom he loves, he rides to the next test a married man, and is eventually conducted to the Castle of the Grail. There he sees the Grail resting on its deep green cloth of gold-threaded silk and he shares the cup of its infinite sweetness with his suffering and melancholy host who, resting on a litter unable to sit or stand or lie, tells him God has maimed him. And Parzival thought, remembering Gurnemanz: 'He counselled me, in sincerity and truth, not to ask too many questions.'

'For that I pity him,' Wolfram comments, 'and I pity too his sweet host, whom divine displeasure does not spare, when a mere question would have set him free.' (CM, 446)

Parzival's fault was not to act on his impulse of compassion. He was moved to ask, 'What ails you, Uncle?' But he quells his spontaneous moment of sympathy, the natural opening of the human heart to another human being, believing it to be more important to obey the rule of courteous restraint given to him by his teacher who had helped him come this far. Yet his question was an expression of compassion, and as a truly individual human feeling could not fall under any general notion of society. It was not curiosity—'another' question—not one of 'too many'; it was *the* Question, his question.

Parzival does not fully understand what he has done wrong until, poised for the glory of acceptance at the Round Table of King Arthur, the summit and consummation of knightly virtue, he is shamed before the meal begins by the dog-nosed, boar-tusked Cundrie, who curses him for his empty heart. She shames him because, Campbell explains, she is the messenger of a deeper sphere of values and possibilities than was yet sensed or understood by his socially conscious mind, but which, in the dreamlike, visionary image of the Castle of the Grail, had appeared to him as the first sign of a kingdom still to be earned, beyond the sphere of the world's flattery, proper to his own unfolding life. (CM, 454) It was his own inward knowledge, but he did not yet know it. Parzival takes up Cundrie's challenge: 'I am resolved to know no joy until I have seen again the Grail,' he declares, in defiance now of the rule that proclaims there are no second chances. Then, in answer to Gawain's gentle wish that God would give him good fortune in battle, he makes this momentous reply:

> Alas, what is God? Were He great, He would not have heaped undeserved disgrace on us both. I was in his service, expecting His grace. But I now renounce Him and His service. If He hates me, I shall bear that. Good friend, when your own time comes for battle, let a woman be your shield. (CM, 452)

Parzival's denunciation of God, or of what he takes to be God—the god-image 'up there' reported by his mother and the knightly code—marks, Campbell says, 'a deep break in the spiritual life not only of this Christian hero, as a necessary prelude to his healing of the Maimed King and assumption of the role without inheriting the wound, but also of the Gothic age itself and thereby Western man.' (CM. 452) For Parzival has now to confront directly the void without and within, where, as Nietzsche tells, the dragon of 'Thou Shalt' is to be slain. By saying No to the social, collective morality, and No to the image he takes to be God, he casts himself into the wilderness where he wanders desolate for five years, but in so doing he frees his own authentic experience, since that has become the only thing and everything he has.

Only the Grail can redeem the Wasteland, yet what is the Wasteland but the absence of the Grail? Before this, Parzival lived in the Wasteland, but did not suffer it; now he experiences the anguish of that life and so takes on symbolically the wound of the Grail king whose maiming is the expression of the Wasteland. For only when Parzival has healed himself will he be able to heal Anfortas and take upon himself the role of king. But what is the Wasteland? For Campbell it is simply the inauthentic life, a state of being which is barren of the truth of who you are.

Wolfram could see it all around him in the twelfth century, but it belongs to any age or person who lives a life handed down by society and does not take up the challenge of his or her own destiny. In practice, this means that you put what (you think) is expected or required of you (the social 'ought') before the impulse of your own heart, wherever it may lead. This is exactly parallel to Jung's radical distinction between the individual and the collective life, which is the life you inherit—the ideals, beliefs, perspectives—you have not yet made your own. The appeal of the collective sensibility is clear with Parzival: why should he be blamed, he protests, when he only behaved courteously, as any true knight would? And in Wolfram's ironic aside, he had indeed been 'true to the dictates of good breeding'. But the often beguilingly reasonable claims of the society are never valid, Campbell insists. To be persuaded that they are is the third temptation of the Buddha—'Perform your Duty to Society'. Your duty to society is no good, he persists, unless it is you. First, you have to be an individual, and it takes a hero to be one.

In 1949, Campbell wrote a book called *The Hero with a Thousand Faces*, which is a book not just to learn from but one which lives and grows as the reader's own understanding of its meaning and implications deepens. There, the world of myth comes brilliantly alive:

> Throughout the inhabited world, in all times and under every circumstance, the myths of man have flourished; and they have been the living inspiration of whatever else may have appeared out of the activities of the human body and mind. It would not be too much to say that myth is the secret opening through which the inexhaustible energies of the cosmos pour into human cultural manifestation. (H, 3)

The images and symbols of mythology are not, therefore, manufactured; they are natural phenomena, born out of and rooted in the human imagination.

> They cannot be ordered, invented, or permanently suppressed. They are spontaneous productions of the psyche, and each bears within it, undamaged, the germ power of its source. (H, 4).

How, then, are the images of myth different from the images of a dream?

Dream is the personalized myth, myth the depersonalized dream; both myth and dream are symbolic in the same general way of the dynamics of the psyche. But in the dream the forms are quirked by the peculiar troubles of the dreamer, whereas in myth the problems and solutions shown are directly valid for all mankind. (H, 19)

The essential drama of mythology is the visionary quest which is the myth of the hero. The particular function of the hero myth is to carry the human spirit forward, offering the model and guide by means of which people may be assisted across 'those difficult thresholds of transformation that demand a change in the patterns not only of conscious but also of unconscious life.' (H, 10) For while the passage of the mythological hero may be overground, incidentally:

Fundamentally it is inward—into depths where obscure resistances are overcome, and long lost forgotten powers are revivified, to be made available for the transfiguration of the world. (H, 29)

All heroes follow a characteristic path. Whether Prometheus, Jason, Theseus, Odysseus, Aeneas, the Buddha, Jesus or Parzival, they all fall into the same pattern of *Separation-Initiation-Return*. The first task of the hero is to turn away from his society—the false, restrictive consciousness entranced with the infinitely various and bewildering spectacle of phenomena. So, dying to the world, he must venture bravely forth into the lonely realm of night—the belly of the whale, the underworld, the descent to hell—a region, typically, of supernatural wonder where fabulous forces are encountered. Suffering first the trials and then the victories of initiation, often with the unsuspected assistance that comes to one who has undertaken his proper adventure, the hero is reborn into his own true nature, and thereby into the nature of the wonder of being. Finally, he returns once again to the society he had originally to leave behind, bearing now his gift of a vision transformed.

Campbell calls Parzival the Grail Hero, and here his immense range of study into the mythologies of the world allows him to discern the universal dimension within the specific cultural ideas of medieval Europe. It was essential, he taught, to distinguish the 'ethnic' or 'folk ideas' of a particular time and place from the 'elementary ideas', (in Bastian's term), or the 'archetypes of the collective unconscious', (in Jung's term), which are the mythic motifs common to all human beings. For a recognition of the two aspects, a universal and a local, in the constitution of sacred stories everywhere—whether called myths, religion, literature, or even history—prevents the fruitless debate on which one is 'right'. Mythology, he declares, 'is psychology, misread as biology, history, cosmology.' (H, 256)

Parzival's separation from Arthur's Court and his refusal of the courtly God marks, then, the first stage of the hero's solitary journey to fulfilment, that lonely dangerous quest, which is the only way to an individual life. As a boy, he was first 'called' away from his childhood by the knightly messengers—'angels', as he thought. Later, a knight himself, after his loving marriage to Condwiramurs and his unwitting visit to the Castle of the Grail, he was ritually conducted to Arthur's Table by the gentlest knight of all, Gawain, the only one who understands his gazing at the drops of blood upon the ground to be the trance of love. The second messenger who summons him, this time away from the rewards of his worldly goal, and sets him irrevocably on the inward, visionary quest, is no angel of light but the dark apparition of the Loathly Damsel, Cundrie, richly arrayed and ugly as a hog.

The Loathly Damsel or Ugly Bride is a familiar figure in Celtic legend and fairy-tale, a maiden who is seen as ugly by the wicked and as fair by the good, and whom a loving kiss can transform from ugly to beautiful in an instant. (Compare the Russian tale of the Toad Bride, *Beauty and the Beast*, and also the play on this motif by Papagena in Mozart's *The Magic Flute*.) In the Celtic folk-tale, this mythic figure appears as the daughter of the King of the Land of Youth, who was cursed with the head of a pig, but, when boldly kissed, became beautiful and granted her saviour the kingship of her timeless realm. Here, buried in the image of Cundrie's boar tusks, is a vital clue to the nature of the Kingdom of the Grail, and one, furthermore, that would most likely be overlooked without the kind of mythic reach that Campbell offers. For, he argues, the Kingdom of the Grail is such a land as is suggested by this image: 'To be achieved only by one capable of transcending the painted wall of space-time with its foul and fair, good and evil, true and false display of the names and forms of merely phenomenal pairs of opposites.' (CM, 455) Consequently, the image prepares us for a passage beyond the known bounds and forms of space, time and causality to a domain of vision, where time and eternity are at one: in Parzival's case, the Grail Castle, and in Gawain's—summoned at the same time, as though they were soul brothers—the enchanted Château Merveil.

Entering, then, the Wasteland of their own disoriented lives, the next stage of trial begins in the enchanted underworld, and here the story passes to Gawain who, having lifted the spell on the enchanted castle, then meets the Lady Orgeluse, sitting by a spring. Seeing in her the reflection of the moving principle of his life, his lifelong service to love in general is irreversibly transformed into a service to that particular love. His spiritual test is now to hold to that *one* experience in loyalty and love beyond both fear and desire for distraction, the model already established in the Buddha's holding to the 'immovable point' beneath the Bodhi Tree, which neither fear nor desire could move. Again, the mythic resonance is necessary to transform our perception of the image: 'The sense of such a female by a spring is of an apparition of the abyss: psychologically, the unconscious; mythologically, the Land below Waves, Hell, Purgatory or Heaven. She is a portion of onself, one's destiny.' (CM, 489) The larger point being made here, and one which is essential to an understanding of the meaning of the Grail, is that 'initiations transpire through the revelations of chance, according to the readiness of the psyche.' (CM 484) Campbell frequently refers to James Joyce's *Ulysses* as a parallel contemporary myth, comparing Stephen Dedalus and Parzival as the solitary introverts moved by a sense of purpose, and Bloom and Gawain as love-questing extroverts. So similarly, Joyce writes of Dedalus: 'He found in the world without as actual what was in his world within as possible.' (CM 197) Since, in the case of both Gawain and Parzival, their trials were proper to their own lives, they were consequently their match. And so the second heroic stage of Initiation was achieved.

What then, finally, is the Holy Grail? Campbell did not leave the symbol vague and general, in the bafflingly opaque terms of the cup of transformation which would grant eternal life. In all the Grail stories, the Grail is the supreme spiritual value, but which one? Since, also, 'it is a law of symbolic life that the god beheld is a function of the state of consciousness of the beholder',

(CM 566) it is a matter of some consequence which author is
doing the beholding. In the monastic version of the Grail story
(*La Queste del Saint Graal*), the Grail is exclusively associated
with Christ's passion, as it is in Wagner's opera *Parzival* and
Tennyson's *Idylls of the King*: The Grail is the chalice of the Last
Supper and the chalice that received Christ's blood when he was
taken down from the cross. Thus the reference of the symbol
remains enclosed within the Christian orthodox tradition,
dependent on the dualistic opposition of spirit and nature, and
on belief in the sacraments as administered by the Church. Here
the source of the Grail's gift is imagined as coming from outside
nature, so nature is still inherently fallen, or cursed, not itself,
even potentially, divine. So the reawakening to nature that was
springing up everywhere in the twelfth and thirteenth centuries
was, in this work, reversed, and the supernatural reimposed as
the proper authority, leaving, as Campbell characteristically
puts it, 'nature, man, history, and all womankind except
baptized nuns, to the Devil'. (CM, 566)

It is hardly surprising that one who was not just a comparative
mythologist but who practically 'invented' comparative
mythology as an independent study should place the claims of
psychology beyond those of any particular theology. Campbell's
criterion for evaluating the different Grail myths was always
their relation to the archetypal order. Does the local, specific
image become translucent to a universal truth? Is it a statement
about the nature of humanity, valid for the whole human race?
For the ultimate reference of mythology is to the human being as
human. So it was to Wolfram's *Parzival* that he again turned for
an understanding of the Grail as a symbol of a metaphysical
truth. Wolfram tells a story of the origins of the Grail in which
it was once carried from heaven to earth by the angels who had
remained neutral when Satan opposed God and there was war in
heaven. These were the angels in the middle, between the
warring factions, and so the Grail here stands for that spiritual
path that is between pairs of opposites, between fear and desire,
black and white, good and evil (hence the meaning of Parzival's
name). As he says at the beginning of his tale: 'Every act has both
good and evil results.' Between these opposites, where the Grail
is to be found, is the spontaneous *natural* impulse of a noble
heart.

The Grail, as Campbell describes it, drawing on the meaning

of Wolfram's image, is then the inexhaustible vessel, the centre of life continuously coming into being, energy pouring into creation, energy as creation, out of which civilizations arise, mountains are formed—the unquenchable fountain of the source. If we relate that image to ourselves, it is the place in us where life comes into being inside us—'the still point of the turning world', as T.S. Eliot calls it in *The Four Quartets*—which is a place before or beyond desiring and fearing, just pure becoming. This is an image which emerges in very different cultures separated by time and space, and so must be a reflection of certain powers or spiritual potentialities in the psyche of every one of us. Furthermore, by contemplating this and other mythic images, we evoke their powers in our own lives.

In Celtic mythology, for instance—the immediate origins of all Arthurian Romance—there was not a chalice but a cauldron of plenty in the mansion of the god of the sea, Manannan Mac Lir, himself the Northern Celtic counterpart of the Roman Neptune and the Greek Poseidon, who in turn was the Occidental counterpart of the Oriental Shiva. Beneath the waves, Manannan served the flesh of pigs that, killed today, were alive tomorrow, and an ambrosial ale which bestowed immortality on all his guests, enacting, in the ceaseless ebb and flow of the tides of the sea, the continual filling and emptying of the celestial cup of the moon above. These are the images that point, in turn, to the distant roots of the mythology of the Celts in the most ancient native European mythological tradition: that of the old Megalithic, Bronze Age Goddess of many names, mother of all creation—gods and humans—and the immanent power of all nature: the earth, not as dust (as it became in the Judeo-Christian tradition), but as the source, the living body which was herself, out of whom all things proceed and to whom they return at peace.

Nearer to Celtic myth, in place and time, was Germanic myth. And there, similarly, the life-giving vessel is central. Odin (Wotan) gave an eye for a sip from the Well of Wisdom at the foot of the World Ash, Yggdrasil, where it was guarded by the dwarf, Mimir; while high above in Valhalla, the warrior dead drank a mead, served by the Valkyries, which restored them to life and joy. The late Classical Orphic sects (themselves rooted in the earlier Bronze Age Mother Goddess cultures of Mesopotamia, Crete, Egypt and Old Europe), also conducted their mystery rites through the drinking of liquid from sacramental bowls, though the symbols there were read in the inward anagogical way that is proper to symbols, not reduced to a literal sense and referred outward to supposed, actual or possible historical events. These cults were carried by the Roman armies as they advanced into northern Europe in the Gallo-Roman period, when at the same time the native Celto-Germanic gods which they encountered in the lands they occupied were identified with their Greco-Roman counterparts, allying, thereby, the classical mystery tradition with local Celtic myth and ritual.

Wolfram linked his central symbol to both these traditions—the Celtic and the Classical—and their ancient sources, as well as extending its reference to include Islam. For in his work, while the Grail acts *like* a vessel—in its presence whatever anyone stretched out their hands for it was waiting for, food and drink alike—it was actually a stone, the 'Wish of Paradise', called 'lapsit exillis', the name of the Philosophers' Stone of the alchemists, but also suggesting the Ka'aba of Islam. The Grail, which 'was the very fruit of bliss, a cornucopia of the sweets of this world and such that it scarcely fell short of what they tell us of the Heavenly Kingdom', (P, 127) was a symbol which unified the different, even warring, traditions in a new image of the human being released from any one ecclesiastical authority, serving the world through individual love.

In his television conversations with Bill Moyers, entitled *The Power of Myth*, and in the book of the same name in which many of these conversations are recorded, Campbell interprets these myths of the vessel, bowl and cauldron, or the Grail stone as cornucopia, as meaning that it is out of the depths of the unconscious that the energies of life come to us, the bubbling spring from which all life proceeds. And not only the unconscious of the race—the collective unconscious, as Jung calls it—but also the vale of the world. It is not just the psyche and it is not just the world; it is from the depths of both that life comes irrepressibly forth, since one is the reflection of the other. There had been other images of the inexhaustible source of creation, but no myth before this had linked that image to the spontaneous outpouring of an individual heart, rendering the outward Grail consubstantial with the inward point of becoming life in the human being.

Then how is the Grail attained? Wolfram's answer, conveyed

first through Parzival's failure and then through the terms on which he and Gawain finally succeed, is that it is won through the act of compassion that comes spontaneously out of an individual who lives his or her own authentic life. The Maimed Grail King, Anfortas, had not earned his castle or his throne; they had come to him as a gift, and for this reason he could not withstand the lance of the pagan, the Muslim knight, who rode at him in the woods. The Grail King's lance kills the pagan, but the pagan's lance castrates the Grail King. What this means, Campbell explains, is that 'the Christian separation of matter and spirit, of the dynamism of life and the realm of the spirit, of natural grace and supernatural grace, has really castrated nature ... The true spirituality, which would have come from the union of matter and spirit, has been killed.' (PM, 197) For the pagan represents the natural man, and yet, astonishingly, the word 'Grail' was written on the head of his lance: 'That is to say,' he continues, 'nature intends the Grail. Spiritual life is the bouquet, the perfume, the flowering and fulfilment of a human life, not a supernatural virtue imposed upon it.' (PM, 197).

This battle is in a sense re-enacted between Parzival and the pagan knight, his half-brother Feirfiz, whose nobility (and compassion) in fighting (throwing away his sword when Parzival's had broken) allows a recognition to take place between them, after which Cundrie appears to summon Parzival to heal the King and receive the Grail along with his wife and son. When the moment arrives, Feirfiz cannot see the Grail but only the eyes of her who carried it, the Queen Repanse de Schoye, and he was urged to be baptized and to renounce his gods if he would marry her (Parzival's aunt, as it turned out). In a lecture that he gave on the Grail myth which was taped, Campbell, telling the story to a room already resounding with laughter, expostulates at this point: 'Good God, I thought, is Wolfram going to let me down here at the end of the story?' But it was all right; Wolfram played with the idea of baptism and the one true god. Feirfiz asks: 'Is your god her god?' 'Yes,' says Parzival. 'Then for the sake of your aunt's god, let me be baptized,' says Feirfiz with much enthusiasm. (CM, 563)

Courtly love, Campbell explains, is exemplified in this idea of putting the loved person before any other authority in utmost particularity. For it is not the two impersonal relations of *Eros* and *Agape*—earthly and spiritual love, neither of which require a personal relationship between two unique people—but *Amor*, the specific, discriminating love that both Parzival and Gawain achieve for the one person who could be no other, and who is loved for who she is. One of Parzival's tests was at the marriage of Gawain when he chose to leave the scene of festivities because of his love for Condiramors—she who leads him to love. His pagan brother simply loves the god in his lady, whoever it is.

Now when the newly baptized heathen sees the Grail with his own eyes, he sees written upon the Grail a hitherto unprecedented statement of compassion extended to the political world: 'If any member of the Grail Company should, by the grace of God, be given mastery over a foreign folk, he must not speak to them of his race or of his name, and must see to it that they gain their rights.' (FG, 221)

In the lecture, and in many places in his books, Campbell turns to Schopenhauer for an understanding of the power and meaning of compassion. In *The Foundation of Morality*, Schopenhauer asks the question: How is it that a human being can so participate in the pain and danger of another that, forgetting his own self-protection, he moves spontaneously to the other's rescue? How is it that what we think of as the first law of nature—self-protection—is suddenly dissolved and another law asserts itself spontaneously? Schopenhauer answers: this is the breakthrough of a metaphysical truth—that you and the other are one, and that separateness is a secondary effect of the way our minds experience the world in the frame of time and space. At the metaphysical level, we are all manifestations of that consciousness and energy which is the consciousness and energy of life. This is Schopenhauer:

> The experience that dissolves the distinction between the I and the Not I ... underlies the mystery of compassion, and stands, in fact, for the reality of which compassion is the prime expression. That experience, therefore, must be the metaphysical ground of ethics and consist simply in this: that one individual should recognize in another, himself in his own true being ... Which is the recognition for which the basic formula is the standard Sanskrit expression, 'Thou are that', *tat tvam asi*. (CM, 75)

When Parzival can ask 'what ails you?' he has experienced the other in himself. If this is the impulse which wins the Grail, then the Grail, in its widest implication, is an image of the unity of creation—the reality of which compassion is in humanity the prime expression.

Campbell's own life could itself be seen as an enactment of the Grail myth. His whole life is marked with the passion of the hero on his visionary quest, and, retrospectively at least, the events of his life would seem to fall into the imaginative pattern of the hero's journey of transfiguration and return for the enlightenment of the human tribe. He lived his own description of the hero as 'the one who, while still alive, knows and represents the claims of the superconsciousness which throughout creation is more or less unconscious'. (H, 259)

Mythology was the way that was most truly his own. It was not simply a lifelong study of a subject which he also taught; it was a profound religious position, one that refused the doctrine of a divinity transcendent to nature: 'The great realization of mythology,' he said, 'is the immanence of the divine.' (OL, 32) He often quoted the saying of Jesus from the Gnostic *Gospel of Thomas*: 'See the Kingdom of Heaven is spread out upon the earth, and men do not see it.' By contrast, religion, in the orthodox sense of unilateral belief, was best defined as 'a misinterpretation of mythology', where 'the misinterpretation consists precisely in attributing historical references to symbols which properly are spiritual in their reference'. (OL, 79) The mythic image is here, now, and always; myths are great poems which render insights into the wonder and miracle of life. Though they are deeply meaningful, they do not offer meaning or answers so much as delight and the longing to participate in the mystery of this finally inscrutable universe. As a union of psyche and metaphysics, myths put you in touch with your hearts.

Later in his life, in conversations on TV and taped dialogues, Campbell was often asked how to live the authentic life of an individual, how even to begin to try. To this he had one answer which remained constant throughout his life: 'Follow your Bliss.'

I feel that if one follows what I call one's bliss—the thing that really gets you deep in the gut and that you feel is your life—doors will open up. They do! They have in my life and they have in many lives that I know of. (OL, 24)

If you follow your bliss you put yourself on a kind of track that has been there all the while, waiting for you, and the life that you ought to be living is the one you are living. When you can see that, you begin to meet people who are in the field of your bliss, and they open the doors to you. I say, follow your bliss and don't be afraid ... (PM, 120)

He came to this idea of bliss, he explains, because of three terms in Sanskrit, which is the great spiritual language of the world: *Sat, Chit, Ananda. Sat* means being; *Chit* means consciousness; *Ananda* means bliss or rapture, and these terms represent the brink, the jumping-off place to the ocean of transcendence. 'I thought,' he said, 'I don't know whether what I know of my being is my proper being or not; but I do know where my rapture is. So let me hang on to my rapture, and that will bring me both my consciousness and my being.' (PM, 120)

Yet it is not always easy to hang on to your rapture, and here the hero myth, and specifically the Grail myth, offers a guide. If the Call comes—the feeling that there is an adventure there for you—the risk must be taken. In *An Open Life*, a compilation of taped interviews with Michael Toms from 1975–85, Campbell speaks from the experience of an idea he has personally tested: 'When I wrote about the Call forty years ago (in *The Hero with a Thousand Faces*), I was writing out of what I had read. Now that I've lived it, I know it's correct ... These mythic clues work.' (OL, 26) Elsewhere, he adds: 'I always tell my students, go where your body and soul want to go. When you have the feeling, then stay with it, and don't let anyone throw you off.' (PM, 118) When you follow your bliss, you come to bliss. But how to find your bliss, if it has not called you? 'We are having experiences all the time which may on occasion render some sense of this, a little intuition of where your bliss is. Grab it. No one can tell you what it is going to be. You have to learn to recognize your own depth.' (PM, 118)

When still at an early age, Campbell had to take on the challenge of seeing things differently from those around him. While he was brought up in the Roman Catholic faith, which he took very seriously, he was at the same time going with his father to see the Museum of Natural History with its rooms of totem poles, learning about the American Indians. So he was comparing virgin births, deaths and resurrections in both mythological systems at an early age. When he was a kid, he said, he never let anyone push him off course, and in this his family always supported him.

In his university years, he studied the literature of the Middle Ages and classical mythology, finding the same images which occurred in the Christian tradition, but inflected towards the more universal point of view. Graduate work in medieval literature took him first to Paris, in 1927, where he discovered James Joyce, and also modern art—particularly, Picasso and Klee. Then, in 1928-9, he went to Germany, to the University of Munich to study philology—the history of language—which brought him to Sanskrit, and introduced him to the whole world of the Orient. He had met Krishnamurti by chance (or synchronicity) on a boat to Europe in 1924, and had been given a book on the life of the Buddha, which prepared him for his later translating and editing of the *Upanishads* and *The Gospel of Sri Ramakrishna* with Swami Nikhilananda.

In Germany he discovered Thomas Mann, and also Freud and Jung who opened up for him a new psychological dimension in the field of mythology. When he wrote *The Hero with a Thousand Faces*, the two men were equal in his thinking, Freud relating to (what Jung calls) the personal unconscious and Jung to the collective unconscious. But in the years following, Jung became more and more eloquent for him: 'Freud tells us what myths mean to neurotics. On the other hand, Jung gives us clues as to how to let the myth talk to us in its own terms, without putting a formula on it.' (OL, 121) Jung's *Symbols of Transformation* was 'one of those things that sends all the lights up in all directions.' (OL, 50) Campbell and Jung both saw mythology as the expression of the collective unconscious (though Campbell was more interested in diffusion and relationships historically than Jung was), and when they met, years later, it was as co-editors of the work of Heinrich Zimmer, the great Indologist and interpretor of symbols, whom he regarded as 'supplementary to Jung'. (OL, 120) It was Zimmer who, beyond anyone, gave him the courage to interpret myths out of what he knew to be their common symbols. There's always a risk in such an interpretation, he added, pointing us to the operation of the hero myth at any moment of our lives, whatever we are doing.

When Cundrie appears to Parzival at Arthur's Table, she disrupts the vision he had of how his life would be, and he got up and left it all behind. Campbell describes an experience in the little garden of Cluny in Paris, in which he was similarly struck by an impulse to change the course of his life, one that he, like Parzival, immediately followed. He was sitting in the garden, having put some years of study into his Ph.D., when:

It suddenly struck me: What in heaven's name am I doing? I don't even know how to eat a decent nourishing meal, and here I'm learning what happened to vulgar Latin when it passed into Portugese and Spanish and French. So I dropped work on my Ph.D. On my return I found a place in upstate New York and read the classics for 12 hours a day. I was enjoying myself enormously, and realized I would never finish my degree because it would have required me to do things I had already outgrown. In Europe, the world had opened up: Joyce, Sanskrit, the Orient, and the relationship of all these to Psychology. I couldn't go back and finish up that Ph.D. thesis; besides, I didn't have the money. And that free-wheeling maverick life gave me a sense of the deep joy in doing something meaningful to me. (OL, 125-6)

Like Parzival, he spent five years without a job! He came back from Europe in 1929, just three weeks before the Wall Street crash, which meant there were no jobs to be had, so he found a retreat up in Woodstock, New York, in 'a little chicken coop place', with no running water, and here he did most of his basic reading and work: 'It was great. I was following my bliss.' (PM, 120) When, after five years, he was invited to teach at Sarah Lawrence College, it was on his own terms: 'I would not have taken a job otherwise, just as I wouldn't take the Ph.D.' (OL, 126)

He was to stay at Sarah Lawrence College from 1934 until he retired as Professor Emeritus in 1972, pursuing his own vision, and offering it back to the many students and friends who have found his life an inspiration. He makes it sound easy, but he once shared with a friend something of what it had asked of him. They were in front of some statue, and Campbell was bringing the mythic resonances of the image to life by comparing it with similar images in other cultures, and— to temper somewhat his friend's appreciative enthusiasm— Campbell said: 'Yes, but think of all the hundreds of hours spent reading, all the days, all the parties missed ...'

The image of courtly love also played through his relationship to his wife, Jean Erdman, the dancer and choreographer, to whom he was married for 49 years. Marriage, he said, was a sacrament in which you give up your personal simplicity to participate in a relationship, but you give not so much to the other person as to the relationship. In 1984, towards the end of his life, he was perhaps speaking of his own experience of *Amor*: 'What a beautiful thing is a life together as growing personalities, each helping the other to flower, rather than just moving into the standard archetype.'

Jean Erdman writes of his work: 'Throughout his long career, Joseph Campbell endeavoured to communicate his under-standing of myth—his passion. And he tirelessly pursued the task he had set himself. Besides his books and lectures, there were workshops and interviews, which he eagerly welcomed because he believed scholarship should not mean isolation.' (OL, Foreward)

Before *The Hero with a Thousand Faces* was published in 1949, which took four years to write, he had already edited the posthumous works of Heinrich Zimmer—*Philosophies of India* and *The Art of Indian Asia*—as well as six volumes of the papers from the Eranos conferences set up by Jung to explore the issues around analytical psychology, called the *Eranos Notebooks*. Next came *The Flight of the Wild Gander* (1951), which, as he wrote in his introduction, 'occupied, or rather punctuated, a period of twenty-four years, during the whole of which I was circling, and from many quarters striving to interpret, the mystery of mythology.' (FG, 3) There followed his unique discussion of the world's archetypal images of divinity in their historical contexts, called *The Masks of God*, which was published over a period of 12 years as four separate but related books: *Primative Mythology*; *Oriental Mythology*; *Occidental Mythology*; and *Creative Mythology* (1959-1968). He also wrote *A Skeleton Key to Finnegan's Wake*, and edited *The Portable Jung* and *The Portable Arabian Knights*. *Myths To Live By* (1971) was a selection of talks on mythology delivered in New York City between 1958 and 1971. In 1975, *The Mythic Image* was published by Princeton University Press after 10 years in preparation, a book which, incidentally, sets a standard for the right relation of text to image that has never subsequently been met. In 1983, *The Way of the Animal Powers* was published as the first volume of the *Historical Atlas of World Mythology*, followed in 1988 by the second volume, *The Way of the Seeded Earth*. In 1986, a record of various lectures in San Francisco, given between 1981 and 1984, was published under the title of *The Inner Reaches of Outer Space: Metaphor as Myth and as Religion*. Since then, in 1988, his conversations with Bill Moyers on TV (collected in *The Power of Myth*) and with Michael Toms on the 'New Dimension' tapes (compiled in *An Open Life*) have shown how profoundly he lived his own myth. His great gifts of story-telling and scholarship were offered to his students and readers that they also might engage in the call of the age:

> The adventure of the Grail—the quest within for those creative values by which the Waste Land is redeemed—has become today for each the unavoidable task; for, as there is no more any fixed horizon, there is no more any fixed center, any Mecca, Rome, or Jerusalem. Our circle today is that announced, c. 1450, by Nicolas Cusanus (1401-64): whose circumference is nowhere and whose center is everywhere; the circle of infinite radius, which is also a straight line. (OC, 522)

The study of mythology was for Campbell a truly sacred task because it allowed a move out of the dogma of formal religion and into the spontaneous nature of one's own inward drama and vitality of being. It is inevitable, then, that his life might seem to us to be the mythic image that he taught us how to understand, for mythology and the way of his life were one. If the Grail represents, as he said, 'the fulfilment of the highest spiritual possibilities of the human consciousness', (PM, 197) then his lifelong quest of the Holy Grail may indeed have been rewarded.

Abbreviations

H — *The Hero with a Thousand Faces*, Joseph Campbell.
FG — *The Flight of the Wild Gander*, Joseph Campbell.
OC — *Occidental Mythology*, Joseph Campbell.
CM — *Creative Mythology*, Joseph Campbell.
PM — *The Power of Myth*, Joseph Campbell.
OL — *An Open Life*, Joseph Campbell.
P — *Parzival*, Wolfram von Eschenbach. trans. A.T. Hatto (Harmondsworth: Penguin Classics, 1980).

Bibliography

The Hero with a Thousand Faces, Bollingen Series XVII (Princeton Univ. Press, 1949).

The Flight of the Wild Gander: Explorations in the Mythological Dimensions (Gateway Edition, 1951).

The Masks of God: Primitive Mythology (New York: Viking Press, 1959).

The Masks of God: Oriental Mythology (New York: Viking Press, 1962).

The Masks of God: Occidental Mythology (New York: Viking Press, 1964).

The Masks of God: Creative Mythology (New York: Viking Press, 1968).

Myths To Live By (London: Bantam, 1972).

The Mythic Image, Bollingen Series C (Princeton Univ. Press, 1974).

The Inner Reaches of Outer Space: Metaphor as Myth and as Religion (London: St James Press, 1986).

Historical Atlas of World Mythology:
   Vol. 1, *The Way of the Animal Powers* (London: Times Books, 1984).
   Vol. 2, *The Way of the Seeded Earth* (New York: Harper & Row, 1988).

The Power of Myth, with Bill Moyers, from transcripts of the TV series (New York: Doubleday, 1988).

An Open Life In Conversation with Michael Toms. (Compilations of Interviews from 1975-85) (Larsons Publications, 1988).

The Grail Tapes of lecture given in 1982 (Living Dharma Tapes).

Completed and edited the papers of Heinrich Zimmer: *Myths and Symbols in Indian Art and Civilization, The King and the Corpse, Philosophies of India*, and *The Art of Indian Asia*.

Translated and edited, with Swami Nikhilananda, *The Upanishads* and *The Gospel of Sri Ramakrishna*.

Edited *Papers from the Eranos Yearbooks* (6 vols.), *Myths, Dreams and Religion, The Portable Jung*, and *The Portable Arabian Nights*.

Co-authored, with Henry Morton Robinson, *A Skeleton Key to Finnegans Wake*.

NOTES ON CONTRIBUTORS

Jules Cashford studied Philosophy at St Andrews, and Literature at Cambridge, where she was a Supervisor in English for some years. She now teaches Mythology and works as a Jungian analyst. She has published translations of *The Homeric Hymns*, and written a book, with Anne Baring, *The Myth of the Goddess* (Viking Penguin, 1991).

Prudence Jones came across the Old Religion of Europe, in its form of the Greek Mysteries, while still doing undergraduate work into the foundations of logic and mathematics. Her investigations led her to the modern world of esoteric Paganism, and eventually to the mystical symbol of the Holy Grail. Her publications include articles on ancient callendration, two booklets, *The Path to the Centre: The Grail Initiation in Wicca* (1988) and *Europe's Forgotten Heritage: the Pagan Mysticism of Courtly Love* (1989), and two books, *Voices from the Circle: the Heritage of Western Paganism* co-edited with Caitlín Matthews (Aquarian Press, 1990) and *Creative Astrology* (Unwin Hyman, 1990). She contributed a translation of *The Childhood of Gawain* to John Matthews's *Gawain: Knight of the Goddess* (Aquarian Press, 1990).

Gareth Knight has been a dedicated student of magic for 30 years. He was trained initially in the occult school founded by Dion Fortune and is well known for a series of major books on the subject which combine academic erudition with practical experience. These include *A Practical Guide to Qabalistic*

Symbolism (Helios, 1965), *The Secret Tradition in Arthurian Legend* (Aquarian Press, 1983) and *The Rose Cross and the Goddess* (Aquarian Press, 1985). He is at present at work on a study of the magical symbolism of the Inklings, to be published by Element Books in 1990.

Pedro de Salles P. Kujawski Brazilian-born Jungian analyst, practising in London. Member of the International Association for Analytical Psychology, extraordinary member of the Swiss Society for Analytical Psychology. His diploma thesis for the C.G. Jung Institute, Zurich, *The Nago Religion in Brazil*, studies the healing impact on the psyche of a (non-African) Brazilian. The thesis has been translated into German and will be published in Zurich in 1989.

Charles Lawrie was born in Edinburgh and grew up on Ynys Mon. He edits *Shoreline* journal and has published four books of poems. He encountered the work of W.J. Stein in 1968 and was impressed with the warm directness in the latter's written word. He soon met friends of Stein such as the late Helen Salter who, with T. Ramachandra, pioneered the Rudolf Steiner Education Movement and Anthroposophical Society in India. Charles lives and works with his family in Gwynedd. Do contact him on 0766-513747 (if your message is polite!)

Caitlín Matthews is perhaps best known for her work in the field of Celtic Studies, especially for her two-volume study of *The Mabinogion*, entitled *Mabon and the Mysteries of Britain* and *Arthur and the Sovereignty of Britain* (Arkana, 1987, 1989). She has also written extensively on the Goddess. She works widely in the Western Mysteries as a priestess and shamanka, giving courses in Britain, Europe and America. Her other books include *The Elements of the Goddess* (Element Books, 1989), *Hallowquest: Tarot Magic and the Arthurian Mysteries* (with John Matthews) and *The Elements of Celtic Tradition* (Element Books, 1989). She edited *Voices of the Goddess* (Aquarian Press, 1990) and co-edited *Tarot Tales* with Rachel Pollack (Century, 1989) and *Voices from the Circle* with Prudence Jones (Aquarian Press, 1990). Her long-awaited study of wisdom, *Sophia, Goddess of Wisdom*, is to be published by Unwin Hyman in the autumn of 1990.

John Matthews has been writing about and studying the Grail stories for over 20 years. He has so far written five books on the subject, as well as numerous titles on the Arthurian legends, esoterica, and the British Mysteries. His much acclaimed volume *Gawain: Knight of the Goddess* was published by Aquarian Press in 1990, and among forthcoming titles are *Taliesin: Shamanic Mysteries in Britain and Ireland* (Unwin Hyman), *Elements of the Grail Tradition* (Element Books, 1990) and *The Arthurian Book of Days* (with Caitlín Matthews). He is at present at work on a quartet of Celtic novels, drawing heavily on his studies in the field.

Diana L. Paxson received her B.A. in English Literature from Mills College in 1961, and her M.A. in Comparative Literature (English and French with a medieval emphasis) from the University of California at Berkeley in 1966. It was during her graduate work at the university that she first began to study the Grail legend, which has fascinated her ever since. In 1981 her first novel, *Lady of Light*, was published in the USA. Since then she has produced a dozen more, and over two dozen short stories. Her first British publications were *White Mare, Red Stallion*, set in the 'anti-Roman' period in Scotland, and *The White Raven*, a treatment of the legend of Tristan and Iseult (both published by New English Library). In addition to her work as a writer of faction, Ms Paxson is a consecrated priestess of the Old Religion and founder of the Fellowship of the Spiral Path. She has also served as First Officer of the Covenant of the Goddess, an international federation of Wiccan organizations. Ms Paxson recently contributed to the collection *Voices of the Goddess* (ed. Caitlín Matthews) and is currently working on a contemporary novel about the quest for the Grail.

Greg Stafford has been 'arthuring' since he was five years old. He has been practising shamanism for almost 10 years, and is president of the Cross Cultural Shamanism Network, the publisher of *Shaman's Drum* magazine. He is also president of Chaosium Inc., and author of the experiential role-playing games *King Arthur Pendragon* and *Prince Valiant*. He teaches in workshops on Experiential Arthurianism, mythology and shamanism, and is a sweat lodge leader and vision quest leader. He is a single parent, and lives in California.

Robin Waterfield spent his early years in the Sudan and France. After rejecting a medical career in favour of publishing, he studied Jung and became a member of the Jung Institute, as well as running a home for maladjusted children with his wife. He spent 16 years in Iran working with the Persian Episcopal Church and now lives in Oxford. He is the author of *René Guénon and the Future of the West* (Crucible, 1987).

GAWAIN: KNIGHT OF THE GODDESS
Restoring an Archetype

John Matthews

Gawain was once the most important knight at Arthur's court, a shining example of all that was best in the chivalry of the time. However, as the popularity of the Arthurian romances grew the character of Gawain diminished, leaving him represented as a villain rather than as a Champion of the Goddess. How this transformation came about, and the reasons why, are explored here by John Matthews.

In this fully researched volume he examines all the known texts relating to Gawain, beginning with early Celtic references, working through the Latin romances and the vivid stories of the Middle Ages, including the famous *Morte d'Arthur* of Sir Thomas Malory. From these texts the author has rediscovered the original Gawain — a figure of great mythical, magical and historical importance.

Gawain's many adventures and several identities are studied in detail, providing a completely fresh and exciting appraisal of the texts in question, and this work adds considerably to our understanding of the Arthurian cycle and Gawain's part in it.

Gawain: Knight of the Goddess is the result of more than 20 years' research into Arthurian and Celtic texts and it presents a unique view of the mythology of Britain and its connections with the historical changes which took place over a period of many hundreds of years in the religious and mystical traditions of the country. It also contains a thorough investigation of the actual site of the famous 'Green Chapel' and the first English translation of the fragmentary medieval text *The Childhood of Gawain*.

THE AQUARIAN GUIDE TO LEGENDARY LONDON

Edited by John Matthews and Chesca Potter

An unusual collection of diverse works on the many legends of London, together offering intriguing insights into the well known buildings and streets of the world's most legendary capital. Among topics discussed are the mythic foundation of the city, the goddesses associated with it, the talismanic internment of the head of the Celtic god Bran beneath the present-day Tower of London, the practice of witchcraft and magic and Blake's vision of the city.

From the esoteric significance of the buildings — including Westminster Abbey and St Paul's cathedral — to the location of the London leys, from the Arthurian legends to the folklore rituals and observances that continue to this day, *The Aquarian Guide to Legendary London* introduces a completely new view of the city — perhaps the first since William Blake's visionary poetry.

As well as 11 essays by contemporary experts, the book contains key essays by earlier writers and a wealth of illustrations. Contributors include Gareth Knight, Caitlín Matthews, Bernard Nesfield-Cookson, Ross Nichols, Nigel Pennick, Lewis Spence and R.J. Stewart.

For those wishing to uncover a different aspect of the capital, maps, charts and a gazetteer of sites are also included, providing a ground-plan for discovering London's legendary sites — the winding ways and mysterious mounds, the crypts and spires, the very stuff of myth and legend upon which foundation our cities are built.

THE ARTHURIAN TAROT

Caitlín and John Matthews
Illustrated by Miranda Gray

The Arthurian Tarot represents the ultimate in Tarot design. Steeped in the sheer unequalled magic of the legends, history and traditions of Arthurian Britain, these exceptional cards capture in 78 frames all the wonder and beauty of King Arthur's realm. Conceived and designed by Caitlín and John Matthews and beautifully executed by Miranda Gray, this original pack reveals the ancient traditions of the Arthurian Mysteries as a living mythos for creative visualization and personal transformation.

This exclusive pack comes complete with *The Arthurian Tarot: A Hallowquest Handbook*, a fully-illustrated guide to the divinatory and archetypal meanings of the cards — the 22 Greater Powers and the 56 Lesser Powers. The suits of Sword, Spear, Grail and Stone, corresponding to the four elements of Western esoteric tradition as well as to the four seasons, empower the reader through the sacred quest for the Hallows. The book also gives original methods for reading and using the Tarot, including the Merlin's Mirror and Excalibur spreads, with sample readings to show their practical significance.

Hallowquest: Tarot Magic and the Arthurian Mysteries by Caitlín and John Matthews is also available from the Aquarian Press.